W9-BWN-626

Contents

List of Maps

ABOUT THE AUTHOR

A freelance writer based in Italy, **John Moretti** has written for *The International Herald Tribune, The Independent on Sunday, Italy Daily, The Associated Press,* and www.ft.com (*Financial Times* online). He is the author of *Living Abroad in Italy,* co-editor of *Rome in Detail,* and a contributor to *Time Out Milan* and *Time Out Naples* city guides.

AN INVITATION TO THE READER

In researching this book, we discovered many wonderful places—hotels, restaurants, shops, and more. We're sure you'll find others. Please tell us about them, so we can share the information with your fellow travelers in upcoming editions. If you were disappointed with a recommendation, we'd love to know that, too. Please write to:

Frommer's Portable Florence, 4th Edition
Wiley Publishing, Inc. • 111 River St. • Hoboken, NJ 07030-5774

AN ADDITIONAL NOTE

Please be advised that travel information is subject to change at any time—and this is especially true of prices. We therefore suggest that you write or call ahead for confirmation when making your travel plans. The authors, editors, and publisher cannot be held responsible for the experiences of readers while traveling. Your safety is important to us, however, so we encourage you to stay alert and be aware of your surroundings. Keep a close eye on cameras, purses, and wallets, all favorite targets of thieves and pickpockets.

FROMMER'S STAR RATINGS, ICONS & ABBREVIATIONS

Every hotel, restaurant, and attraction listing in this guide has been ranked for quality, value, service, amenities, and special features using a **star-rating system.** In country, state, and regional guides, we also rate towns and regions to help you narrow down your choices and budget your time accordingly. Hotels and restaurants are rated on a scale of zero (recommended) to three stars (exceptional). Attractions, shopping, nightlife, towns, and regions are rated according to the following scale: zero stars (recommended), one star (highly recommended), two stars (very highly recommended), and three stars (must-see).

In addition to the star-rating system, we also use **seven feature icons** that point you to the great deals, in-the-know advice, and unique experiences that separate travelers from tourists. Throughout the book, look for:

Finds	Special finds—those places only insiders know about
Fun Fact	Fun facts—details that make travelers more informed and their trips more fun
Kids	Best bets for kids and advice for the whole family
Moments	Special moments—those experiences that memories are made of
Overrated	Places or experiences not worth your time or money
Tips	Insider tips—great ways to save time and money
Value	Great values—where to get the best deals

The following **abbreviations** are used for credit cards:

AE	American Express	DISC	Discover	V	Visa
DC	Diners Club	MC	MasterCard		

FROMMERS.COM

Now that you have this guidebook to help you plan a great trip, visit our website at **www.frommers.com** for additional travel information on more than 3,600 destinations. We update features regularly to give you instant access to the most current trip-planning information available. At Frommers.com, you'll find scoops on the best airfares, lodging rates, and car rental bargains. You can even book your travel online through our reliable travel booking partners. Other popular features include:

- Online updates of our most popular guidebooks
- Vacation sweepstakes and contest giveaways
- Newsletters highlighting the hottest travel trends
- Online travel message boards with featured travel discussions

Planning Your Trip to Florence

The capital of Tuscany is **Florence,** one of Italy's most famous cities. It was once the home of the colorful Medici dynasty, which actively encouraged the development of the Renaissance by sponsoring masters such as Donatello, Leonardo, and Michelangelo. Art treasures such as those found at the Accademia (Michelangelo's *David*), the Uffizi Galleries (Botticelli's *Birth of Venus*), and the Pitti Palace (Raphael's *La Velata*) draw millions of visitors every year. Throw into the mix fabulous architecture (the Duomo with Brunelleschi's dome, Giotto's campanile, Santa Croce), fine restaurants and earthy *trattorie,* and leading designer boutiques and bustling outdoor markets, and the city of the Renaissance becomes quite simply one of the world's must-see sights.

Planning a trip doesn't have to be hard work. This chapter will help you smooth out most of your preparations for a trip to Florence.

1 Visitor Information & Maps

TOURIST OFFICES

For general information in your home country, try your local branch of the **Italian Government Tourist Board (ENIT)** or **www.italian tourism.com**. Some Frommer's readers have reported that the office isn't really that helpful.

In the United States: 630 Fifth Ave., Suite 1565, New York, NY 10111 (© **212/245-4822** or 212/245-5618; fax 212/586-9249); 500 N. Michigan Ave., Suite 2240, Chicago, IL 60611 (© **312/644-0996** or 312/644-0990; fax 312/644-3019); and 12400 Wilshire Blvd., Suite 550, Los Angeles, CA 90025 (© **310/820-1898** or 310/820-9807; fax 310/820-6357).

In Canada: 175 Bloor St. E., Suite 907, South Tower, Toronto, Ontario M4W 3R8 (© **416/925-4882;** fax 416/925-4799; enit.canada@on.aibn.com).

In the United Kingdom: 1 Princes St., London W1B 2AY England (© **020/7399-3562;** italy@italiantouristboard.co.uk).

For more specific details on Tuscany, contact the regional tourist office in Florence: APT, Via Manzoni 16, 50121 Firenze (© **055-23-320;** fax 055-234-6286; www.firenzeturismo.it). For Umbria, contact the **Ufficio Promozione Turistica,** Corso Vannucci 30, 06100 Perugia (© **075-50-41;** fax 075-504-2483). To get even more details, put yourself in contact with the regional and city tourism offices, listed in each chapter section (or you can get a list from the ENIT).

Local tourist offices are the best places to pick up a free map of that city, and they are usually very good. For a map of Tuscany and/or Umbria, your best bet is to check out the wide selection at any downtown *edicola,* or news kiosk. This will be especially important if you are driving around the countryside, as maps from rental-car agencies are far from adequate. For basic navigation around Italy, I rely on country maps from Michelin, which are sometimes available at news kiosks, and almost always sold at Autogrill highway rest stops. They are not very useful, though, for backcountry roads.

USEFUL WEBSITES

Websites and e-mail addresses are included throughout this guide for everything from tourist offices, hotels, and restaurants to museums and festivals.

The official site for Tuscany is **www.turismo.toscana.it**, with links to every provincial tourist office site. The official Florence information site, **www.firenzeturismo.it**, contains a wealth of up-to-date information (events, museums, practical details) on Florence and its province. Included is a searchable "hotels" form that allows you to specify amenities, categories, and the like; it responds by spitting out a list of comparable hotels, and it lists contact info and current room rates. The official site for Umbria is **www.umbria-turismo.it**.

Firenze by Net (www.mega.it/florence), **Firenze.Net** (http://english.firenze.net), and **FlorenceOnLine** (www.fol.it) are all Italy-based websites with English translations and good general information on Florence. Also check out **The Heart of Tuscany** (http://nautilus-mp.com/tuscany), and **Chianti Doc Marketplace.** And of course there's **Frommer's** (www.frommers.com), where you'll find excerpts from this guide, occasional updated information, and links to travel packages.

Italy

2 Entry Requirements

U.S., Canadian, U.K., Irish, Australian, and New Zealand citizens
with a **valid passport** don't need a visa to enter Italy, if they don't
expect to stay more than 90 days and don't expect to work there. If,
after entering Italy, you find you want to stay more than 90 days, you
can apply for a permit for an extra 90 days, which, as a rule, is
granted immediately. Go to the nearest *questura* (police headquarters) or your home country's consulate.

Allow plenty of time before your trip to apply for a passport; processing normally takes 3 weeks but can take longer during busy peri-
ods (especially spring). And keep in mind that if you need a passport
in a hurry, you'll pay a higher processing fee.

For Residents of Australia: You can pick up an application from
your local post office or any branch of Passports Australia, but you
must schedule an interview at the passport office to present your
application materials. Call the **Australian Passport Information
Service** at ✆ **131-232,** or visit the government website at **www.
passports.gov.au**.

For Residents of Canada: Passport applications are available at
travel agencies throughout Canada or from the central **Passport
Office,** Department of Foreign Affairs and International Trade,
Ottawa, ON K1A 0G3 (✆ **800/567-6868;** www.ppt.gc.ca).

For Residents of Ireland: You can apply for a 10-year passport at
the **Passport Office,** Setanta Centre, Molesworth Street, Dublin 2
(✆ **01/671-1633;** www.irlgov.ie/iveagh). Those under age 18 and
over 65 must apply for a 3-year passport. You can also apply at 1A
South Mall, Cork (✆ **021/272-525**), or at most main post offices.

For Residents of New Zealand: You can pick up a passport application at any New Zealand Passports Office or download it from their
website. Contact the **Passports Office** at ✆ **0800/225-050** in New
Zealand, or 04/474-8100; or log on to **www.passports.govt.nz**.

For Residents of the United Kingdom: To pick up an application for a standard 10-year passport (5-year passport for children
under 16), visit your nearest passport office, major post office, or
travel agency; or contact the **United Kingdom Passport Service** at
✆ **0870/521-0410,** or search its website at **www.ukpa.gov.uk**.

For Residents of the United States: Whether you're applying in
person or by mail, you can download passport applications from the
U.S. Department of State website at **http://travel.state.gov**. To
find your regional passport office, either check the U.S. Department

of State website or call the **National Passport Information Center** toll-free number (© **877/487-2778**) for automated information.

CUSTOMS
WHAT YOU CAN BRING INTO ITALY

Foreign visitors can bring along most items for personal use duty-free, including fishing tackle; a sporting gun and 200 cartridges; a pair of skis; two tennis racquets; a baby carriage; two hand cameras with 10 rolls of film; and 200 cigarettes or 50 cigars or pipe tobacco not exceeding 250 grams. There are strict limits on importing alcoholic beverages. However, limits are much more liberal for alcohol bought tax-paid in other countries of the European Union. For more information regarding Customs, visit the Italian-language website **www.agenziadogane.it** and follow links to "carta doganale del viaggiatore," the travelers' custom charter.

WHAT YOU CAN TAKE HOME

FOR AUSTRALIAN CITIZENS   A helpful brochure available from Australian consulates or Customs offices is *Know Before You Go.* For more information, call the **Australian Customs Service** at © **1300/363-263,** or log on to **www.customs.gov.au**.

FOR CANADIAN CITIZENS   For a clear summary of Canadian rules, write for the booklet *I Declare,* issued by the **Canada Border Services Agency** (© **800/461-9999** in Canada, or 204/983-3500; www.cbsa-asfc.gc.ca).

FOR NEW ZEALAND CITIZENS   Most questions are answered in a free pamphlet available at New Zealand consulates and Customs offices: *New Zealand Customs Guide for Travellers, Notice no. 4.* For more information, contact **New Zealand Customs,** The Customhouse, 17–21 Whitmore St., Box 2218, Wellington (© **04/473-6099** or 0800/428-786; www.customs.govt.nz).

FOR U.K. CITIZENS   For information, contact **HM Customs & Excise** at © **0845/010-9000** (from outside the U.K., 020/8929-0152), or consult their website at **www.hmce.gov.uk**.

FOR U.S. CITIZENS   For specifics on what you can bring back and the corresponding fees, download the invaluable free pamphlet *Know Before You Go* online at **www.cbp.gov**. (Click on "Travel," and then click on "Know Before You Go! Online Brochure.") Or contact the **U.S. Customs & Border Protection (CBP)** by mail at 1300 Pennsylvania Ave., NW, Washington, DC 20229 (© **877/287-8667**) and request the pamphlet.

3 When to Go

The best times to visit Florence are in the spring and fall. Starting in late May, the **summer** tourist rush really picks up; and from July to mid-September, Italy is teeming with visitors. August is the worst month to visit. Not only does it get uncomfortably hot, muggy, and crowded (the lines for the Uffizi and the Accademia can stretch for blocks), but the entire country goes on vacation at least from August 15 until the end of the month, and many Italians take off the entire month. Many hotels, restaurants, and shops are closed—except at the spas, beaches, and islands, which are where 70% of the Italians are headed. In **winter** (late Oct to Easter), most sights go to shorter winter hours or are closed for restoration and rearrangement, many hotels and restaurants take a month or two off between November and February, spa and beach destinations become padlocked ghost towns, and it can get much colder than most people expect—it may even snow on occasion.

WEATHER

It can get uncomfortably hot at the height of August in Florence, a valley city. The long spring is temperate and very comfortable, with occasional showers. Fall is also fairly mild, with lots of rainfall being the only drawback. Winter, though mild for most months, can get quite cold in late December or January; it can drizzle a great deal, and snowfall isn't impossible.

HOLIDAYS

Official state holidays include January 1, January 6 (Epiphany), Easter Sunday and Monday, April 25 (Liberation Day), May 1 (Labor Day), August 15 (Ferragosto and Assumption Day), November 1 (All Saints' Day), December 8 (Day of the Immaculate Conception), December 25, and December 26 (Santo Stefano). Florence also shuts down to honor its patron, St. John the Baptist, on June 24.

Hot Tickets

For major events where tickets should be procured well before arriving on the spot, check out **Box Office** at ✆ **055-210-804** or **www.boxoffice.it**. They will only deliver tickets to an Italian address, but you can buy ahead of time and have tickets held for you.

---

4 Getting There

BY PLANE
FROM NORTH AMERICA

No carrier flies directly from the United States to Florence. Still, most airlines and their affiliates connect through a handful of European cities to the small international airports at Pisa or Florence. Aside from a new route on Delta, which flies nonstop from New York to Pisa (in Tuscany), usually the most convenient way to get here is to fly to Rome and connect by plane (a bit over 1 hr.) or by train (close to 3 hr.).

THE MAJOR AIRLINES Italy's national airline, **Alitalia** (© 800/223-5730; www.alitalia.it), offers more flights daily to Italy than any other airline. It flies direct to both Rome-Fiumicino (FCO) and Milan-Malpensa (MXP) from New York, Newark, Boston, Chicago, Los Angeles, and Miami. You can connect in Rome or Milan to any other Italian destination, including Florence (FLR). If you're flying from the New York City area and planning to connect directly to Florence, note that itineraries that route you through Milan often have a layover that's 3 hours shorter than one that routes you through Rome's airport.

Delta (© 800/241-4141; www.delta.com) now flies four times a week from New York JFK nonstop to Pisa—the only direct U.S.-to-Tuscany flight available. It also flies daily out of JFK to Rome and Milan, where it's possible to change to one of Delta's local partner airlines (Lufthansa, Iberia, and so on) for the last leg to Tuscany. From either city you can take a train to Tuscany, or from Rome you can connect to an Alitalia flight to Florence or Pisa.

British Airways (© 800/247-9297; www.ba.com) flies direct from dozens of U.S. and Canadian cities to London, where you can get connecting flights to Pisa, Rome, or Milan. **Air Canada** (© 888/247-2262 or 800/361-8071; www.aircanada.ca) flies daily from Toronto and Vancouver to Rome. **Continental** (© 800/231-0856; www.continental.com) doesn't fly to Italy itself, but it's partnered with Alitalia for the Newark-to-Rome and New York JFK-to-Milan flights, so if you're a Continental Frequent Flyer you can reserve through Continental and rack up the miles.

Possibly less convenient alternatives are **American Airlines** (© 800/433-7300; www.aa.com), whose flights from the United States to Milan and Rome usually go through Chicago, but they do offer seasonal daily nonstops between New York and Rome from April to October; **United** (© 800/528-2929; www.ual.com), which flies once daily to Milan out of New York, Newark, and Washington, D.C., Dulles; or **US Airways** (© 800/622-1015; www.usairways. com), which offers one flight daily to Rome out of Philadelphia. (You can connect through Philly from most major U.S. cities.) Discount carrier **Eurolfy** (© 800/459-0581; www.euroflyusa.com) offers nonstop, thrice-weekly seasonal (June–Sept) service between New York and Bologna.

FROM GREAT BRITAIN & IRELAND

British Airways (© 0845/773-3377; www.ba.com) flies twice daily from London's Gatwick to Pisa. **Alitalia (020/8745-8200;** www. alitalia.it) has four daily flights from London to both Rome and Milan and three daily from London Gatwick into Florence. **KLM UK** (formerly Air UK; © 08705/074-074; www.klm.com) flies several times per week from London Heathrow to Milan (both airports) and Rome. In each case, there's a layover in Amsterdam. No-frills **Ryanair** (© 0871/246-0000 in the U.K.; www.ryanair.com) has hubs in the U.K. and on the Continent; you can fly from London to Pisa (as well as to Rome, Milan, Bologna, Ancona, Turin, and other Italian destinations); its competitor **EasyJet** (© 0871/244-2386 in the U.K.; www.easyjet.com) flies from many locations in the U.K. (as well as from a few hubs on the Continent) to Italy, including London to Milan, Bologna, Turin, Venice, and Rome and Bristol to Pisa. Another U.K.-based, low-cost carrier, **BMI (© 0871/246-0000** in the U.K., or 800/788-0555 from the U.S.; www.flybmi. com), flies from London to Venice and Milan.

FROM AUSTRALIA & NEW ZEALAND

Alitalia (© 02-9922-1555; www.alitalia.it) has a flight from Sydney to Rome every Thursday and Saturday. **Qantas** (© 13-13-13 in Australia, or 0649/357-8900 in Auckland, NZ; www.qantas.com) flies three times daily to Rome via Bangkok, leaving Australia from Sydney, Melbourne, Brisbane, or Cairns. Qantas will also book you through one of these Australian cities from Auckland, Wellington, or Christchurch in New Zealand. You can also look into flying first into London and connecting to Italy from there. (There are more flights, and it may work out to be cheaper.)

GETTING TO TUSCANY OR UMBRIA FROM ROME'S AIRPORTS

Most international flights to Rome will arrive at **Fiumicino Airport** (officially named **Leonardo da Vinci International Airport,** but

> ## *Tips* The Milan Connection
>
> Note that if you find yourself **flying into Milan,** the domestic air-
> port (Linate) is separate from the international one (Malpensa),
> and transferring planes to a connecting flight to Florence or
> Pisa requires switching airports (a 9€/$12 bus connects the two
> airports), sometimes changing airlines, and an innate trust in
> the gods of luggage transfer. If you fly into Milan, a train to Tus-
> cany is probably your best bet. This isn't a problem for flights on
> Alitalia, however, which uses Milan's Malpensa airport for both
> international arrivals and domestic departures—a blatantly
> nationalistic protectionist scheme which has all other major air-
> lines, European and American, up in arms.

few, including the airlines themselves, call it that). Some inter-Euro-
pean and transatlantic charter flights may land at **Ciampino Airport,** which is closer to the center, but not connected by an express
train. You can connect to a plane at either to take you to Florence's
airport, but it's often simpler, almost as fast in the long run, and
cheaper to take the train.

Fiumicino (© **06-659-51;** www.adr.it) is 30km (19 miles) from
Rome's center. You can take the **express train** (9.50€/$13) from
Fiumicino to Rome's central train station, Termini. A taxi to the sta-
tion costs about 40€ ($52). From Termini, you can grab one of
many daily trains to Florence. If you happen to fly into **Ciampino
Airport** (© **06-7934-0297**), 15km (9 miles) south of the city, a
none-too-frequent COTRAL bus will take you to the Anagnina
Metro station, where you can take the Metro to Termini, the entire
trip costing around 3€ ($3.90). A taxi to Rome's center from
Ciampino is 30€ ($39).

GETTING TO FLORENCE FROM MILAN'S AIRPORT
Your flight may land at either **Linate Airport** (© **02-7485-2200;**
www.sea-aeroportimilano.it), about 8km (5 miles) southeast of the
city, or **Malpensa Airport** (© **02-2680-0613**), 45km (28 miles)
from downtown—closer to Como than to Milan itself.

From **Malpensa,** a 40-minute express train heads half-hourly to
Cadorna train station in western Milan rather than to the larger and
more central Stazione Centrale from which most trains onward to
Tuscany will leave (you'll have to take the Metro to get there). The
Malpensa Express train costs 11€ ($14). To grab a bus instead,

which will take you directly to the central downtown rail station, take the **Malpensa Shuttle** (© 02-5858-3185) for 5€ ($6.50), which leaves two or three times per hour for the 50-minute ride to the east side of Milan's Stazione Centrale. A taxi to the city center runs about 70€ ($91).

From **Linate, STAM buses** (© 02-717-100) make the 25-minute trip to Milan's Stazione Centrale, every 20 to 30 minutes daily from 7am to 11pm, and cost 2€ ($2.60; buy on bus). The slightly slower city bus no. 73 leaves hourly for the S. Babila Metro stop downtown (1€/$1.30 for a regular bus ticket bought from any newsagent inside the airport, but not onboard). From Milan's Stazione Centrale, you can get trains to Florence (see "Arriving," in chapter 2).

BY CAR

You'll get the **best rental rate** if you book your car from home instead of renting direct in Italy—in fact, if you decide to rent once you're over there, it's worth it to call home to have someone arrange it all from there. You must be older than 25 to rent from most agencies (although some accept ages 21 and up).

Though it once was smart shopping to see what rates Italian companies were offering, they're all now allied with the big agencies in the States: **Avis** (© **800/230-4898,** in Italy toll-free 199-100-133; www.avis.com), **Budget** (© **800/527-0700;** www.budget.com), **Hertz** (© **800/654-3131** or 800/654-3001; www.hertz.com), and **National** (© **800/227-7368;** www.nationalcar.com).

You can usually get a better rate by going through one of the rental companies specializing in Europe: **Auto Europe** (© **888/223-5555;** www.autoeurope.com), **Europe by Car** (© **800/223-1516** or 212/581-3040; www.europebycar.com), **Kemwell** (© **800/678-0678;** www.kemwell.com), and **Maiellano** (© **800/223-1616** or 718/727-0044). With constant price wars and special packages, it always pays to shop around among all of the above. Also, if you're planning to rent a car in Italy during high season, you really should book well in advance: It's not at all unusual to arrive at the airport in Milan or the train station in Rome in June and July to find that every last agent is all out of cars, perhaps for a week.

When offered the choice between a compact car and a larger one, always choose the smaller car (unless you have a large group)—you'll need it for maneuvering the winding, steeply graded Italian roads and the impossibly narrow alleyways of towns and cities. Likewise, if you can drive a stick shift, order one; it'll help you better navigate the hilly terrain. It's also a good idea to opt for the **Collision Damage Wavier (CDW),** which, for only $10 to $20 a day, gives you the peace of mind and nerves of steel that driving in Italy requires; you can pay only $7 per day for this service if you buy it through a third-party insurer such as **Travel Guard** (www.travelguard.com). Although the 19% IVA value-added tax is unavoidable, you can do away with the government airport pickup tax of 10% by picking up your car at an office in town.

BY TRAIN

Every day, up to 14 **Eurostar** trains (reservations in London ℂ **0875/186-186;** www.eurostar.com) zip from London to Paris's Gare du Nord via the **Chunnel** (Eurotunnel) in a bit over 4 hours. In Paris, you can transfer to the Paris Gare de Lyon station or Paris Bercy for one of three daily direct trains to **Milan** (from which you can transfer to Florence), two to **Pisa,** or two to **Florence.** Some of the Milan runs are high-speed TGV trains, a 6½-hour ride requiring a seat reservation. At least one will be an overnight Euronight (EN) train, with reservable sleeping couchettes; the Euronight leaves Paris around 10pm and gets into Milan around 8:45am. The two Euronight trains going directly from Paris to Pisa take about 10 hours; to Florence, it takes 12½ hours.

The definitive 500-page book listing all official European train routes and schedules is the ***Thomas Cook European Timetable,*** available in the United States for $28 (plus $4.50 shipping and handling) from Forsyth Travel Library, P.O. Box 2975, Shawnee Mission, KS 66201 (ℂ **800/367-7984**), or at travel specialty stores. You can also order the schedule online at **www.thomascooktimetables.com**.

5 Money & Costs

Euro coins are issued in denominations of .01€, .02€, .05€, .10€, .20€, and .50€ as well as 1€ and 2€; bills come in denominations of 5€, 10€, 20€, 50€, 100€, 200€, and 500€.

Exchange rates are established daily and listed in most international newspapers, and websites such as **www.xe.com**. To get a transaction as close to this rate as possible, pay for as much as possible with credit cards and get cash out of ATMs.

Traveler's checks, while still the safest way to carry money, are going the way of the dinosaur. The aggressive evolution of international computerized banking and consolidated ATM networks has led to the triumph of plastic throughout the Italian peninsula—even if cold cash is still the most trusted currency, especially in smaller

What Things Cost in Florence	US$	UK£
Taxi (from the train station to Ponte Vecchio)	7.80	3.90
Public bus (to any destination)	1.20	0.60
Local telephone call	0.15	0.07
Double room at Hotel Helvetia and Bristol (very expensive)	429.00– 611.00	215.00– 306.00
Double room at Il Guelfo Bianco (moderate)	156.00– 250.00	78.00– 125.00
Double room at Pensione Maria Luisade' Medici (inexpensive)	96.00– 114.00	52.00– 62.00
Continental breakfast (cappuccino and croissant, standing at a bar)	3.00	1.65
Lunch for one at Nerbone (inexpensive)	7.80	3.90
Dinner for one, with table wine, at La Giostra (expensive)	72.00	36.00
Dinner for one, with table wine, at Il Latini (moderate)	30.00– 36.00	15.00– 18.00
Dinner for one, with table wine, at Le1 Mossacce (inexpensive)	6.80	8.40
Glass of wine	1.30– 7.80	0.65– 3.90
Coca-Cola (standing/sitting in a bar)	2.60/ 3.90	1.30/ 1.95
Cup of espresso (standing/ sitting in a bar)	1.00/ 1.50	0.50/ 0.75
Admission to the Uffizi Galleries	7.20	3.90
Movie ticket	10.00	5.00

towns or cheaper mom-and-pop joints, where credit cards may not be accepted.

You'll get the best rate if you **exchange money** at a bank or one of its ATMs. The rates at "cambio/change/wechsel" exchange booths are invariably less favorable but still a good deal better than what you'd get exchanging money at a hotel or shop (a last-resort tactic only). The bill-to-bill changers you'll see in some touristy places exist solely to rip you off.

ATMs

The easiest and best way to get cash away from home is from an ATM (automated teller machine), referred to in Italy as a "Bancomat." The **Cirrus** (© **800/424-7787;** www.mastercard.com) and **PLUS** (© **800/843-7587;** www.visa.com) networks span the globe. Go to your bank card's website to find ATM locations at your destination. Be sure you know your daily withdrawal limit before you depart. *Note:* Many banks impose a fee every time you use a card at another bank's ATM, and that fee can be higher for international transactions (up to $5 or more) than for domestic ones (where they're rarely more than $2). In addition, the bank from which you withdraw cash may charge its own fee, although this is not common practice in Italy. For international withdrawal fees, ask your bank.

Note: Banks that are members of the **Global ATM Alliance** charge no transaction fees for cash withdrawals at other Alliance member ATMs; these include Bank of America, Scotiabank (Canada, Caribbean, and Mexico), Barclays (U.K. and parts of Africa), Deutsche Bank (Germany, Poland, Spain, and Italy), and BNP Paribas (France).

Be sure to check with your bank that your card is valid for international withdrawal and that you have a four-digit PIN. (Most ATMs in Italy will not accept any other number of digits.)

If at the ATM you get a message saying your card isn't valid for international transactions, don't panic: It's most likely the bank just can't make the phone connection to check it (occasionally this can be a citywide epidemic) or else simply doesn't have the cash. Try another ATM or another town.

CREDIT CARDS

Credit cards are another safe way to carry money. They also provide a convenient record of all your expenses, and they generally offer relatively good exchange rates. You can withdraw cash advances from your credit cards at banks or ATMs but high fees make credit-card cash advances a pricey way to get cash. Keep in mind that you'll pay interest from the moment of your withdrawal, even if you pay your monthly bills on time. Also, note that many banks now assess a 1% to 3% "transaction fee" on **all** charges you incur abroad (whether you're using the local currency or your native currency).

Visa and **MasterCard** are almost universally accepted at hotels, plus most restaurants and shops; the majority of them also accept

American Express. Diners Club is gaining some ground, especially in Florence and in more expensive establishments throughout the region. *Note:* It is an unfortunately common practice among many restaurants in Italy to claim that the credit card machine is down when, in fact, it is more often the case that the owner simply doesn't want to pay the merchant fees. On more than one occasion I've insisted that they try it just in case, as I had no cash, and—surprise—it's been instantly fixed! The best way to avoid this chicanery is to inform the waitstaff upfront that you intend to use a credit card. If they tell you it's broken, you have the option of finding a restaurant where the machine actually "works."

TRAVELER'S CHECKS

You can buy traveler's checks at most banks. They are offered in denominations of $20, $50, $100, $500, and sometimes $1,000. Generally, you'll pay a service charge ranging from 1% to 4%.

The most popular traveler's checks are offered by **American Express** (✆ 800/807-6233, or 800/221-7282 for card holders—this number accepts collect calls, offers service in several foreign languages, and exempts Amex gold and platinum cardholders from the 1% fee); **Visa** (✆ 800/732-1322)—AAA members can obtain Visa checks for a $9.95 fee (for checks up to $1,500) at most AAA offices or by calling ✆ 866/339-3378; and **MasterCard** (✆ 800/223-9920).

Be sure to keep a record of the traveler's checks serial numbers separate from your checks in the event that they are stolen or lost. You'll get a refund faster if you know the numbers.

American Express, Thomas Cook, Visa, and **MasterCard** offer **foreign currency traveler's checks,** useful if you're traveling to one country or to the euro zone; they're accepted at locations where dollar checks may not be.

Another option is the new prepaid traveler's check cards, reloadable cards that work much like debit cards but aren't linked to your checking account. The **American Express Travelers Cheque Card,** for example, requires a minimum deposit, sets a maximum balance, and has a one-time issuance fee of $15. You can withdraw money from an ATM (for a fee of $2.50 per transaction, not including bank fees), and the funds can be purchased in dollars, euros, or pounds. If you lose the card, your available funds will be refunded within 24 hours.

Frankly, however, the practice of using traveler's checks in Italy is so infrequent these days that most waiters and hotel staff will squint at one and have no idea what it is. In name, at least, some places do accept traveler's checks, but it is not advisable to depend on them in Italy.

6 Travel Insurance

The cost of travel insurance varies widely, depending on the destination, the cost and length of your trip, your age and health, and the type of trip you're taking, but expect to pay between 5% and 8% of the vacation itself. You can get estimates from various providers through **InsureMyTrip.com**. Enter your trip cost and dates, your age, and other information, for prices from more than a dozen companies.

U.K. citizens and their families who make more than one trip abroad per year may find an annual travel insurance policy works out cheaper. Check **www.moneysupermarket.com**, which compares prices across a wide range of providers for single- and multi-trip policies.

Most big travel agencies offer their own insurance and will probably try to sell you their package when you book a holiday. Think before you sign. **Britain's Consumers' Association** recommends that you insist on seeing the policy and reading the fine print before buying travel insurance. **The Association of British Insurers** (*©* **020/7600-3333;** www.abi.org.uk) gives advice by phone and publishes *Holiday Insurance,* a free guide to policy provisions and prices. You might also shop around for better deals: Try **Columbus Direct** (*©* **0870/033-9988;** www.columbusdirect.net).

TRIP-CANCELLATION INSURANCE   Trip-cancellation insurance will help retrieve your money if you have to back out of a trip or depart early, or if your travel supplier goes bankrupt. Trip cancellation traditionally covers such events as sickness, natural disasters, and Department of State advisories. The latest news in trip-cancellation insurance is the availability of **expanded hurricane coverage** and the **"any-reason"** cancellation coverage—which costs more but covers cancellations made for any reason. You won't get back 100% of your prepaid trip cost, but you'll be refunded a substantial portion. **TravelSafe** (*©* **888/885-7233;** www.travelsafe.com) offers both types of coverage. Expedia also offers any-reason cancellation coverage for its air-hotel packages.

For details, contact one of the following recommended insurers: **Access America** (*©* 866/807-3982; www.accessamerica.com); **Travel Guard International** (*©* 800/826-4919; www.travelguard.com);

Travel Insured International (© 800/243-3174; www.travelinsured. com); and **Travelex Insurance Services** (© 888/457-4602; www. travelex-insurance.com).

MEDICAL INSURANCE   For travel overseas, most U.S. health plans (including Medicare and Medicaid) do not provide coverage, and the ones that do often require you to pay for services upfront and reimburse you only after you return home.

As a safety net, you may want to buy travel medical insurance, particularly if you're traveling to a remote or high-risk area where emergency evacuation might be necessary. If you require additional medical insurance try **MEDEX Assistance** (© 410/453-6300; www. medexassist.com) or **Travel Assistance International** (© 800/821-2828; www.travelassistance.com; for general information on services, call the company's **Worldwide Assistance Services, Inc.,** at © 800/777-8710).

Canadians should check with their provincial health plan offices or call **Health Canada** (© 866/225-0709; www.hc-sc.gc.ca) to find out the extent of their coverage and what documentation and receipts they must take home in case they are treated overseas.

LOST-LUGGAGE INSURANCE   On international flights (including U.S. portions of international trips), baggage coverage is limited to approximately $9.07 per pound, up to approximately $635 per checked bag. If you plan to check items more valuable than what's covered by the standard liability, see if your homeowner's policy covers your valuables, get baggage insurance as part of your comprehensive travel-insurance package, or buy Travel Guard's "BagTrak" product.

If your luggage is lost, immediately file a lost-luggage claim at the airport, detailing the luggage contents. Most airlines require that you report delayed, damaged, or lost baggage within 4 hours of arrival. The airlines are required to deliver luggage, once found, directly to your house or destination free of charge.

7 Health

There are no special health risks you'll encounter in Italy. The tap water is safe—excellent, even—and medical resources are high quality.

GENERAL AVAILABILITY OF HEALTH CARE

With Italy's partially socialized medicine, you can usually stop by any hospital emergency room with an ailment, get swift and courteous service, receive a diagnosis and a prescription, and be sent on your way with a wave and a smile—without filling out a single sheet of paperwork.

Pharmacies offer essentially the same range of generic drugs available in the United States, plus a lot of them that haven't been approved yet by the Federal Drug Administration. Pharmacies are also the only place you'll find simple stuff such as aspirin and run-of-the-mill cold medicines: You won't find Tylenol at any old corner store (even if there were such a thing as a corner store).

Strangely, though, I have found it very hard to locate decongestants in Italy the way you can in other countries. If you regularly suffer from a stuffy nose, it is best to pack a good supply of Sudafed with you before you leave.

Travel Health Online (www.tripprep.com), sponsored by a consortium of travel medicine practitioners, may also offer helpful advice on traveling abroad. You can find listings of reliable medical clinics overseas at the **International Society of Travel Medicine** (www.istm.org).

8 Specialized Travel Resources

TRAVELERS WITH DISABILITIES

Most disabilities shouldn't stop anyone from traveling. There are more options and resources out there than ever before. In Italy, a few of the top museums and churches have installed ramps at the entrances, and a few hotels have converted first-floor rooms into accessible units by widening the doors and bathrooms.

Other than that, don't expect to find much of Tuscany and Umbria easy to tackle. Builders in the Middle Ages and the Renaissance didn't have wheelchairs or mobility impairments in mind when they built narrow doorways and spiral staircases, and preservation laws keep modern Italians from being able to do much about this. Buses and trains can cause problems as well, with high, narrow doors and steep steps at entrances. There are, however, seats reserved on public transportation for travelers with disabilities.

Luckily, there's an endless list of organizations to help you plan your trip and offer specific advice before you go. Many travel agencies offer customized tours and itineraries for travelers with disabilities. Among them are **Flying Wheels Travel** (© 507/451-5005; www.flyingwheelstravel.com); and **Accessible Journeys** (© 800/846-4537 or 610/521-0339; www.disabilitytravel.com).

Flying with Disability (www.flying-with-disability.org) is a comprehensive information source on airplane travel. **Avis Rent a Car**

(© **888/879-4273**) has an "Avis Access" program that offers services for customers with special travel needs. These include specially out-fitted vehicles with swivel seats, spinner knobs, and hand controls; mobility scooter rentals; and accessible bus service. Be sure to reserve well in advance.

Also check out the quarterly magazine *Emerging Horizons* (www.emerginghorizons.com), available by subscription ($16.95 year U.S.; $21.95 outside the U.S.).

The "Accessible Travel" link at **Mobility-Advisor.com** (www.mobility-advisor.com) offers a variety of travel resources to persons with disabilities.

British travelers should contact **Holiday Care** (© **0845-124-9971** in the U.K. only; www.holidaycare.org.uk) to access a wide range of travel information and resources for elderly people and those with disabilities.

GAY & LESBIAN TRAVELERS

Italy as a whole, and Northern and Central Italy in particular, are gay-friendly. Homosexuality is legal, and the age of consent is 16. Luck-ily, Italians are already more affectionate and physical than Americans in their general friendships, and even straight men occasionally walk down the street with their arms around each other—however, kissing anywhere other than on the cheeks at greetings and goodbyes will cer-tainly draw attention. As you might expect, smaller towns tend to be less permissive and accepting than cities. Florence has the largest and most visible homosexual population (not that that's saying much), though university cities such as Pisa also take gayness in stride. Elba's beaches are Tuscany's big gay-vacation destination.

Italy's national association and support network for gays and les-bians is **ARCI-Gay/ARCI-Lesbica.** The national website is **www.arcigay.it**, but they've recently launched a Tuscany-specific one at **www.gaytoscana.it**, and the new head regional office is in **Siena** at Via Massetana Romana 18, 53100 Siena (© **0577-288-977;** fax 0577-271-538; www.gaysiena.it). There are other offices in **Pisa (Arcigay Pride!),** Via San Lorenzo 38 (© **050-555-618;** fax 050-831-0605; www.gay.it/pride), **Pistoia** (© **333-667-6873;** www.gaypistoia.it), and **Grosseto,** Via Ravel 7 (© **339-440-9049** or 347-078-8972; www.grossetogay.it). Their cousin association in **Florence** is called **Ireos** (©/fax **055-216-907;** www.ireos.org), in the Oltrarno at Via dei Serragli 3, 50124 Firenze.

The International Gay and Lesbian Travel Association (IGLTA; © **800/448-8550** or 954/776-2626; www.iglta.org) is the trade association for the gay and lesbian travel industry, and offers an online directory of gay- and lesbian-friendly travel businesses and tour operators.

Many agencies offer specific tours and travel itineraries for gay and lesbian travelers. **Above and Beyond Tours** (𝄯 **800/397-2681;** www.abovebeyondtours.com) are Australian gay-tour specialists. San Francisco–based **Now, Voyager** (𝄯 **800/255-6951;** www.now voyager.com) offers worldwide trips and cruises, and **Olivia** (𝄯 **800/ 631-6277;** www.olivia.com) offers lesbian cruises and resort vacations.

Gay.com Travel (𝄯 **800/929-2268** or 415/644-8044; www.gay. com/travel or www.outandabout.com), is an excellent online successor to the popular *Out & About* print magazine. It provides regularly updated information about gay-owned, gay-oriented, and gay-friendly lodging, dining, sightseeing, nightlife, and shopping establishments in every important destination worldwide. British travelers should click on the "Travel" link at **www.uk.gay.com** for advice and gay-friendly trip ideas.

The Canadian website **GayTraveler** (gaytraveler.ca) offers ideas and advice for gay travel all over the world.

The following travel guides are available at many bookstores, or you can order them from any online bookseller: *Spartacus International Gay Guide, 35th Edition* (Bruno Gmünder Verlag; www. spartacusworld.com/gayguide); *Odysseus: The International Gay Travel Planner, 17th Edition* (www.odyusa.com); and the *Damron* guides (www.damron.com), with separate, annual books for gay men and lesbians.

SENIOR TRAVEL

Italy is a multigenerational culture that doesn't tend to marginalize its seniors, and older people are treated with a great deal of respect and deference throughout Italy. But there are few specific programs, associations, or concessions made for them. The one exception is on admission prices for museums and sights, where those ages 60 or 65 and older will often get in at a reduced rate or even free. There are also special train passes and reductions on bus tickets and the like in various towns. As a senior in Italy, you're *un anziano* (*una anziana* if you're a woman), or "ancient one"—consider it a term of respect, and let people know you're one if you think a discount may be in order.

Members of **AARP,** 601 E St. NW, Washington, DC 20049 (𝄯 **888/687-2277;** www.aarp.org), get discounts on hotels, airfares, and car rentals. AARP offers members a wide range of benefits, including *AARP: The Magazine* and a monthly newsletter. Anyone over age 50 can join.

Many reliable agencies and organizations target the 50-plus market. **Elderhostel** (© **800/454-5768;** www.elderhostel.org) arranges worldwide study programs for those ages 55 and over. **ElderTreks** (© **800/741-7956** or 416/558-5000 outside North America; www.eldertreks.com) offers small-group tours to off-the-beaten-path or adventure-travel locations, restricted to travelers 50 and older.

Recommended publications offering travel resources and discounts for seniors include the quarterly magazine *Travel 50 & Beyond* (www.travel50andbeyond.com) and the best-selling paperback *Unbelievably Good Deals and Great Adventures That You Absolutely Can't Get Unless You're Over 50 2005–2006, 16th Edition* (McGraw-Hill), by Joann Rattner Heilman.

FAMILY TRAVEL

Italy is still a family-oriented society, and kids have free rein just about anywhere they go. A crying baby at a dinner table is greeted with a knowing smile rather than with a stern look. Children under a certain age almost always receive discounts, and maybe a special treat from the waiter, but the availability of such North American accouterments as child seats for cars and dinner tables are more the exception to the rule than the norm.

To locate accommodations, restaurants, and attractions that are particularly kid-friendly, refer to the "Kids" icon throughout this guide.

WOMEN TRAVELERS

It is hard not to notice that, on the streets of Florence, young foreign women far outnumber any other category of people. Women feel remarkably welcome in Italy—sometimes a bit too welcome, actually. It seems every young Italian male is out to prove himself the most irresistible lover on the planet; remember, this is the land of Romeo and Casanova, so they have a lot to live up to. And with most every Italian woman playing the especially hard-to-get Juliet, well, you see what's coming next for attractive foreign women.

The more exotic you look—statuesque blondes, ebony-skinned beauties, or simply an American accent—the more irresistible you become to these suitors. And, as everyone around the world knows from watching Hollywood movies, American women are uninhibited and passionate sex kittens. That this isn't always true doesn't make much of a dent in Italian boys' fantasies.

Flirting back at these would-be Romeos, even mildly, only convinces them that you're ready to jump into bed. Heck, mere eye contact encourages them to redouble their efforts. Unless you want all this attention, take your cue from Italian women, who may wear tight skirts and fishnets but, you'll notice, usually ignore the men around them entirely unless it's someone they're already walking with.

Note that much of the attention is kept to verbal flirtation and that occasional inappropriate touching deserves a slap in the face. These men want to conquer you with their charm, not their muscles. Rape is much rarer in Italy than in the United States—but it does happen, mostly by non-Italian men, if you believe the newspapers. Though most foreign women report feeling far safer wandering the deserted streets of an Italian city to their hotels at 2am than they do in their own neighborhoods back home, use some common sense. You'll probably get tons of ride offers, mostly from would-be chivalrous knights atop their Vespa or Fiat steeds, but remind yourself that criminals do exist in this romantic part of the world, just as anywhere else.

Check out the award-winning website **Journeywoman** (www.journeywoman.com), a "real life" women's travel-information network where you can sign up for a free e-mail newsletter and get advice on everything from etiquette and dress to safety. The travel guide *Safety and Security for Women Who Travel* by Sheila Swan and Peter Laufer (Travelers' Tales Guides), offering common-sense tips on safe travel, was updated in 2004.

AFRICAN-AMERICAN TRAVELERS

Italy for centuries was and, to a large degree, still is a homogenous culture. Add to that the fact that issues of race here are discussed so frankly and openly—there's apparently no taboo to saying, in a loud voice, "That black guy over there . . ." Moreover, the reality is that most people of African descent in Italy are working as street vendors, not bankers. All this may make travelers with darker skin feel—correctly at times—as if they're being singled out.

Pockets of racism do exist in Italy (primarily in the Northeast) just like anywhere else in the world, but on the whole, it is an extremely warm and racially tolerant country. As one Pakistani friend of mine put it, "They're just curious, that's all."

Black Travel Online (www.blacktravelonline.com) posts news on upcoming events and includes links to articles and travel-booking sites. **Soul of America** (www.soulofamerica.com) is a comprehensive

Getting Your VAT Refund

Most purchases have a built-in **value added tax (IVA)** of 20%. Non-E.U. (European Union) citizens are entitled to a refund of this tax if they spend more than 154.94€ (before tax) at any one store. To claim your refund, request an invoice from the cashier at the store and take it to the Customs office *(dogana)* at the airport to have it stamped *before* you leave. *Note:* If you're going to another E.U. country before flying home, have it stamped at the airport Customs office of the last E.U. country you'll be visiting (so if flying home via Britain, have your Italian invoices stamped in London).

Once back home, mail the stamped invoice back to the store within 90 days of the purchase, and they'll send you a refund check. Many shops are now part of the "Tax Free for Tourists" network. (Look for the sticker in the window.) Stores participating in this network issue a check along with your invoice at the time of purchase. After you have the invoice stamped at Customs, you can redeem the check for cash directly at the tax-free booth in the airport, or mail it back in the envelope provided within 60 days. For more info, check out **www.globalrefund.com**.

website, with travel tips, event and family-reunion postings, and sections on historically black beach resorts and active vacations.

Agencies and organizations that provide resources for black travelers include **Rodgers Travel** (© **800/825-1775;** www.rodgerstravel.com); the **African American Association of Innkeepers International** (© **877/422-5777;** www.africanamericaninns.com); and **Henderson Travel & Tours** (© **800/327-2309** or 301/650-5700; www.hendersontravel.com), which has specialized in trips to Africa since 1957.

Go Girl: The Black Woman's Guide to Travel & Adventure (Eighth Mountain Press) is a compilation of travel essays by writers including Jill Nelson and Audre Lorde. *The African-American Travel Guide* by Wayne C. Robinson (Hunter Publishing; www.hunterpublishing.com) was published in 1997, so it may be somewhat dated. *Travel and Enjoy Magazine* (© **866/266-6211;** www.travelandenjoy.com) is a travel magazine and guide. The well-done

Pathfinders Magazine (℡ 877/977-PATH; www.pathfinders travel.com) includes articles on everything from Rio de Janeiro to Ghana to upcoming ski, diving, golf, and tennis trips.

STUDENT TRAVEL

The **International Student Travel Confederation (ISTC;** www.istc.org) was formed in 1949 to make travel around the world more affordable for students. Check out its website for comprehensive travel services information and details on how to get an **International Student Identity Card (ISIC),** which qualifies students for substantial savings on rail passes, plane tickets, entrance fees, and more. It also provides students with basic health and life insurance and a 24-hour help line. The card is valid for a maximum of 18 months. You can apply for the card online or in person at **STA Travel** (℡ 800/781-4040 in North America; www.statravel.com), the biggest student travel agency in the world; check out the website to locate STA Travel offices worldwide. If you're no longer a student but are still under 26, you can get an **International Youth Travel Card (IYTC)** from the same agency, which entitles you to some discounts. **Travel CUTS** (℡ 800/592-2887; www.travelcuts.com) offers similar services for both Canadians and U.S. residents. Irish students may prefer to turn to **USIT** (℡ 01/602-1904; www.usit. ie), an Ireland-based specialist in student, youth, and independent travel.

2

Getting to Know Florence

Mary McCarthy famously described Florence (Firenze) as a "City of Stone." This assessment digs deeper than merely the fact that the buildings, streets, doorjambs, sidewalks, windowsills, towers, and bridges are all cobbled together in shades of gray, stern rock hewn by generations of the stonecutters Michelangelo grew up with. Florence's stoniness is evident in both its countenance and its character. Florentines often seem more serious and slower to warm to strangers than other Italians. The city's fundamental rhythms are medieval, and it's fiendishly difficult to get beyond the touristy surface and see what really makes Florence tick. Although the historic center is compact, it takes time and effort to get to know it, get the hang of its alleys, and understand the deep history of its palace-lined streets.

This chapter will equip you with the basic tools (the hammer and chisel, so to speak) you'll need to get under the stony skin of Florence. It breaks down the city layout and neighborhoods and provides useful facts and service information.

1 Essentials

ARRIVING

BY PLANE For flights into Florence, see "Getting There," in chapter 1. Several European airlines are now servicing Florence's expanded **Amerigo Vespucci Airport** (© 055-30-615 for the switchboard, or 055-373-498 for flight updates; 055-306-1700 for national flight info, 055-306-1702 for international flight info; www.aeroporto.firenze.it), also called **Peretola,** just 5km (3 miles) northwest of town. There are no direct flights to or from the United States, but you can make easy connections through London, Paris, Amsterdam, Frankfurt, and other major European cities. The regularly scheduled **city bus no. 62** connects the airport with Piazza della Stazione downtown, taking about 30 minutes and costing 1€ ($1.30). Rather more expensive (4€/$5.20), but without the local stops, is the half-hourly **SITA bus** to and from downtown's bus station at Via Santa Caterina 15r (© **055-214-721,** 800-424-500, or

Florence Orientation

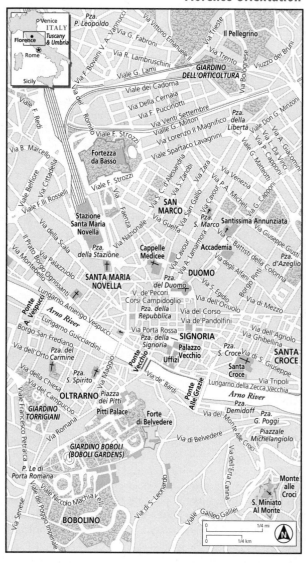

25

800-373-760), behind the train station. Metered **taxis** line up out-side the airport's arrival terminal and charge a flat, official rate of 15€ ($20) to the city center.

The closest major international airport is Pisa's **Galileo Galilei Airport** (© **050/500-707;** www.pisa-airport.com), 97km (60 miles) west of Florence. Two to three **trains** per hour leave the airport for Florence (70–100 min.; 5.40€/$7). If your flight leaves from this airport and you'll be going there by train from Florence, you can check in your baggage and receive your boarding pass at the Air Ter-minal on Track 5 in Florence's Stazione Santa Maria Novella; show up 30 minutes before your train departure. Early-morning flights might make train connections from Florence to the airport difficult; the solution is the regular train from Florence into downtown Pisa, with a 10-minute taxi ride 2.60€ ($3.40) from the Pisa train station to the nearby Pisa airport; the no. 7 bus makes the same hop in twice the time for .75€ ($1).

BY TRAIN   Florence is Tuscany's rail hub, with connections to all the region's major cities. To get here from Rome, you can take the Pendolino (four daily; 1¾ hr.; make sure it's going to Santa Maria Novella station, not Rifredi; you must reserve tickets ahead), an EC or IC train (24 daily; just under 2 hr.), or an *interregionale* (seven daily, around 3 hr.). There are also about 16 trains daily from Milan (3 hr.) through Bologna (1 hr.).

Most Florence-bound trains roll into the **Stazione Santa Maria Novella,** Piazza della Stazione (© **800-888-088** toll-free in Italy, or 055-288-765; www.trenitalia.it), which you'll often see abbreviated as **S.M.N.** The station is on the northwestern edge of the city's com-pact historic center, a 10-minute walk from the Duomo and a 15-minute walk from Piazza della Signoria and the Uffizi. There are loads of budget hotels immediately east of there around Via Faenza and Via Fiume.

With your back to the tracks, toward the station's left exit (across from track 16) and next to a 24-hour pharmacy, you'll find a tiny **tourist info office,** open daily from 8:30am to 9pm, with a hotel-booking service (charging 2.30€–8€/$3–$10). The **train informa-tion office** is near the opposite exit to your right, across from Track 5. The yellow posters on the wall inside the anteroom list all train times and routes for this and other major Italian stations. Another copy of the Florence poster is just inside the sliding glass doors of the second, main room. For personalized help, you have to take a number from the color-coded machine (pink is for train information) and wait your turn—often for more than an hour.

At the head of the tracks, the **ticketing room** (Salone Biglietti) is located through the central doors; at *sportelli* (windows) 9 to 18 you can buy ordinary, unreserved train tickets. The automatic ticket machines have taken some pressure off the ticket windows, but they still attract long lines (when they aren't out of order). Around the corner from this bank of ticket windows is a smaller room where you can buy **international tickets** (window 7), make **reservations** for high-speed and overnight trains (windows 1–4), or pay for a spot on the **Pendolino/ETR express** to Milan, Bologna, or Rome (window 5).

Back at the head of Track 16 is a 24-hour luggage depot where you can drop your bags (2.60€/$3.40 per piece for 12 hr.) while you search for a hotel.

Exit out to the left coming off the tracks and you'll find many bus lines as well as stairs down to the underground **pedestrian underpass** which leads directly to Piazza dell'Unità Italiana and saves you from the traffic of the station's piazza.

Note that some trains stop at the outlying **Stazione Campo di Marte** or **Stazione Rifredi,** both of which are worth avoiding. Although there's 24-hour bus service between these satellite stations and S.M.N., departures aren't always frequent and taxi service is erratic and expensive.

BY BUS   Because Florence is such a well-connected train hub, there's little reason to take the longer, less comfortable intercity coaches. Dozens of companies make dozens of runs here daily from all of Tuscany, much of Umbria, and the major cities in Italy (the express bus from Rome's Tiburtina Station takes 4½ hr.). Most bus stations are near the train station.

BY CAR   The **A1 autostrada** runs north from Rome past Arezzo to Florence and continues to Bologna. The **A11** connects Florence with Lucca, and **unnumbered superhighways** run to Siena and Pisa.

Driving to Florence is easy; the problems begin once you arrive. Almost all cars are banned from the historic center—only residents or merchants with special permits are allowed in. You'll likely be stopped at some point by the traffic police, who'll assume from your rental plates that you're a visitor heading to your hotel. Have the name and address of the hotel ready and they'll wave you through. You can drop off baggage there (the hotel will give you a sign for your car advising traffic police you're unloading), and then you must relocate to a parking lot. Ask your hotel which is most convenient: Special rates are available through most of the hotels and their nearest lot.

Standard rates for parking in private lots near the center are at least 3€ ($3.90) per hour; many lots offer a daily rate of 18€ to 30€ ($20–$39). However, it's difficult to find open spots, and private lots often keep weird hours, so your best bet is one of the city-run garages, which are also less pricey. Although the parking lot under Santa Maria Novella (1.55€/$2 per hour) is closer to the city center, the best deal if you're staying the night (better than most hotels' garage rates) is at the **Parterre parking lot** under Piazza Libertà, north of Fortezza del Basso. If you're staying at least 1 night at a hotel in Florence, you can park here, are welcome to a free bike, and (on presentation of your hotel receipt as you leave, or the hotel's stamp on your parking receipt) pay only 10€ ($13) per night.

Don't park your car overnight on the streets in Florence; if you're towed and ticketed, it will set you back substantially—and the headaches to retrieve your car are beyond description.

VISITOR INFORMATION

TOURIST OFFICES   The city's **largest tourist office** is at Via Cavour 1r (© **055-290-832;** fax 055-276-0383; www.firenze turismo.it), about 3 blocks north of the Duomo. Outrageously, they now charge for basic, useful info: .50€ (65¢) for a city map (though there's still a free one that differs only in lacking relatively inane brief descriptions of the museums and sights), 2€ ($2.60) for a little guide to museums, and 1€ ($1.30) each for pamphlets on the bridges and the *piazze* of Florence. The monthly *Informacittà* pamphlet on events, exhibits, and concerts is still free. The tourist office is open Monday through Saturday from 8:30am to 6:30pm and Sunday from 8:30am to 1:30pm.

At the head of the tracks in Stazione Santa Maria Novella is a **tiny info office** with some maps and a hotel-booking service (see chapter 3, "Where to Stay in Florence"), open Monday through Saturday from 9am to 9pm (to 8pm Nov–Mar), but the station's **main tourist office** (© **055-212-245**) is outside at Piazza della Stazione 4. With your back to the tracks, take the left exit, cross onto the concrete median, and turn right; it's about 30m (100 ft.) ahead. The office is usually open Monday through Saturday from 8:30am to 7pm (often to 1:30pm in winter) and Sunday 8:30am to 1:30pm.

Another office sits on an obscure side street south of Piazza Santa Croce, Borgo Santa Croce 29r (© **055-234-0444**), open Monday through Saturday from 9am to 7pm and Sunday 9am to 2pm.

PUBLICATIONS   At the tourist offices, pick up the free monthly *Informacittà*. The bilingual *Concierge Information* (www.florence-concierge.it) magazine, free from the front desks of top hotels, contains a monthly calendar of events and details on attractions. *Firenze Spettacolo,* a 1.55€ ($2) Italian-language monthly sold at most newsstands, is the most detailed and up-to-date listing of nightlife, arts, and entertainment. As for English-language publications, *The Florentine* has sort of picked up where the now-defunct *Italy Daily* left off.

WEBSITES   The official Florence information website, **www.firenzeturismo.it**, contains a wealth of up-to-date information on Florence and its province, including a searchable hotels form that allows you to specify amenities, categories, and the like.

Firenze By Net (www.mega.it/florence), **Firenze.Net** (http://english.firenze.net), and **FlorenceOnLine** (www.fol.it) are all Italy-based websites with English translations and good general information on Florence. The site for **Concierge Information** (www.florence-concierge.it) is an excellent little guide to the current month's events, exhibits, concerts, and theater.

CITY LAYOUT

Florence is a smallish city, sitting on the Arno River and petering out to olive-planted hills rather quickly to the north and south but extending farther west and, to a lesser extent, east along the Arno valley with suburbs and light industry. It is a compact city best negotiated on foot. No two sights are more than a 20- or 25-minute walk apart, and all the hotels and restaurants in this chapter are in the relatively small *centro storico* (**historic center**), a compact tangle of medieval streets and *piazze* (squares) where visitors spend most of their time. The bulk of Florence, including most of the tourist sights, lies north of the river, with the Oltrarno, an old artisans' working-class neighborhood, hemmed in between the Arno and the hills on the south side.

MAIN STREETS & *PIAZZE*   The center is encircled by a traffic ring of wide boulevards, the Viale, that were created in the late 1800s by tearing down the city's medieval defensive walls. The descriptions below all refer to the *centro storico* as the visitor's city. From Piazza Santa Maria Novella, south of the train station, Via de' Panzani

The Red & the Black

The address system in Florence has a split personality. Private homes, some offices, and hotels are numbered in black (or blue), while businesses, shops, and restaurants are numbered independently in red. This means that 1, 2, 3 (black) addresses march up the block, numerically oblivious to their 1r, 2r, 3r (red) neighbors. You might find the doorways on one side of a street numbered: 1r, 2r, 3r, 1, 4r, 2, 3, 5r . . .

The color codes occur only in the *centro storico* and other older sections of town; outlying districts didn't bother with the codes and use the international standard system common in the United States.

angles into Via de' Cerretani to Piazza del Duomo and the connected Piazza San Giovanni, the city's religious heart around the cathedral. From Piazza del Duomo, Via dei Calzaiuoli, the wide road popular during the *passeggiata* (evening stroll), leads south to Piazza della Signoria, Florence's civic heart near the river, home to the Palazzo Vecchio and the Uffizi Galleries. Traffic winds its way from the back of the Duomo to behind the Uffizi along Via del Proconsolo.

Another route south from the Duomo takes you down Via Roma, through cafe-lined Piazza della Repubblica, and continues down Via Calimala and Via Por Santa Maria to the Ponte Vecchio, the most popular and oldest bridge over the Arno, lined with overhanging jewelry shops. Via degli Strozzi leads east of Piazza della Repubblica to intersect Florence's main shopping drag, Via de' Tornabuoni, running north toward Piazza Santa Maria Novella and south to Piazza Santa Trínita on the river. Borgo de' Greci connects Piazza della Signoria with Piazza Santa Croce on the city center's western edge.

North from the Duomo, Via dei Servi leads to Florence's prettiest square, Piazza Santissima Annunziata. Via Riscasoli leads from the Duomo past the Accademia Gallery (containing Michelangelo's *David*) to Piazza San Marco, where many city buses stop. Via de' Martelli/Via Cavour is a wide traffic-laden road also connecting the Duomo and Piazza San Marco. From the Duomo, Borgo San Lorenzo leads to Piazza San Lorenzo, the old neighborhood of the Medici that's these days filled with the stalls of the outdoor leather market.

On the Oltrarno side of the river, shop-lined Via Guicciardini runs toward Piazza dei Pitti and its museum-filled Pitti Palace. From here, Via Mazzetta/Via Sant'Agostino takes you past Piazza Santo Spirito to Piazza della Carmine; these two squares are the Oltrarno's main centers.

STREET MAPS   The tourist offices hand out two versions of a Florence *pianta* (city plan) free: Ask for the one *con un stradario* (with a street index), which shows all the roads and is better for navigation. The white pamphlet-size version they offer you first is okay for basic orientation and Uffizi-finding, but it leaves out many streets and has giant icons of major sights that cover up Florence's complicated back-alley systems.

If you want to buy a more complete city plan, your best bets are at the newsstand in the ticketing area of the train station and at **Feltrinelli International** and **Libreria Il Viaggio** bookstores (see chapter 6, "Shopping," for more information). Falk puts out a good pocket-size version, but my favorite is the palm-size 1:9,000 **Litografica Artistica Cartografia** map with the yellow and blue cover. It covers the city in three overlapping indexed sections that fold out like a pop-up book. If you need to find a tiny street not on your map, ask your hotel concierge to glance at his or her *TuttoCittà,* a very complete magazine of fully indexed streets that you can't buy but residents (and hotels and bars) receive along with their phone books.

THE NEIGHBORHOODS IN BRIEF

I've used the designations below to group hotels, restaurants, and (in chapter 5) sights in Florence. Although the city does contain six "neighborhoods" centered on the major churches (Santa Maria Novella, Il Duomo, Santa Croce, San Lorenzo, and Santo Spirito and San Frediano in the Oltrarno), these are a bit too broad to be useful here. I've divided the city up into more visitor-oriented sections (none much more than a dozen square blocks) focused around major sights and points of reference. The designations and descriptions are drawn to give you a flavor of each area and to help you choose a zone in which to base yourself.

The Duomo   The area surrounding Florence's gargantuan cathedral is about as central as you can get. The Duomo is halfway between the two great churches of Santa Maria Novella and Santa Croce as well as at the midpoint between the Uffizi Galleries and the Ponte Vecchio to the south and San Marco and the Accademia Gallery with Michelangelo's *David* to the north. The streets north of the Duomo are long and often traffic-ridden, but those to the south make up a wonderful medieval tangle of alleys and tiny squares heading toward Piazza della Signoria.

This is one of the most historic parts of town, and the streets still vaguely follow the grid laid down when the city began as a Roman colony. Via degli Strozzi/Via dei Speziali/Via del Corso was the *decumanus maximus,* the main east-west axis; Via Roma/Via Calimala was the key north-south *cardo maximus.* The site of the Roman city's forum is today's Piazza della Repubblica. The current incarnation of this square, lined with glitzy cafes, was laid out by demolishing the Jewish ghetto in a rash of nationalism during Italian unification in the late 19th century, and (until the majority of neon signs were removed in the early 1990s), by and large, it was the ugliest piazza in town. The area surrounding it, though, is one of Florence's main shopping zones. The Duomo neighborhood is, understandably, one of the most hotel-heavy parts of town, offering a range from luxury inns to student dives and everything in between.

Piazza Della Signoria This is the city's civic heart and perhaps the best base for museum hounds—the Uffizi Galleries, Bargello sculpture collection, and Ponte Vecchio leading toward the Pitti Palace are all nearby. It's a well-polished part of the tourist zone but still retains the narrow medieval streets where Dante grew up—back alleys where tour-bus crowds running from the Uffizi to the Accademia rarely set foot. The few blocks just north of the Ponte Vecchio have good shopping, but unappealing modern buildings were planted here to replace the district destroyed during World War II. (A Nazi commander with a romantic soul couldn't bring himself to blow up the Ponte Vecchio during the German army's retreat, as they had every other bridge over the Arno, so he blew up the buildings at either end of it to impede the progress of Allied tanks pushing north.) The entire neighborhood can be stiflingly crowded in summer, but in those moments when you catch it off-guard and empty of tour groups, it remains the most romantic heart of pre-Renaissance Florence.

San Lorenzo and the Mercato Centrale This small wedge of streets between the train station and the Duomo, centered on the Medici's old church of San Lorenzo and its Michelangelo-designed tombs, is market territory. The vast indoor food market is here, and most of the streets are filled daily with hundreds of stalls hawking leather jackets and other wares. It's a colorful neighborhood, if not the quietest.

Piazza Santa Trinita This piazza sits just off the river at the end of Florence's shopping mecca, Via de' Tornabuoni, home to

Florence Neighborhoods

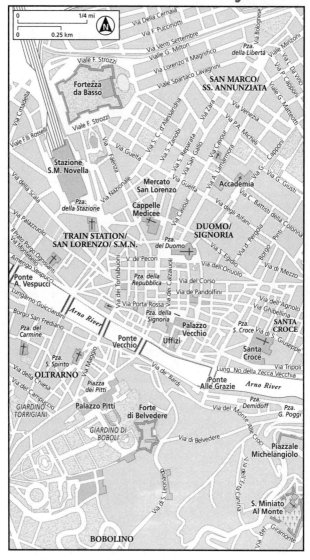

Gucci, Armani, Ferragamo, Versace, and more. Even the ancient narrow streets running out either side of the square are lined with the biggest names in high fashion. It's a very pleasant, well-to-do (but still medieval) neighborhood in which to stay, even if you don't care about haute couture. But if you're a shopping fiend, there's no better place to be.

Santa Maria Novella   This neighborhood, bounding the western edge of the *centro storico,* really has two characters: the rundown unpleasant zone around Santa Maria Novella train station and the much nicer area south of it between the church of Santa Maria Novella and the river.

In general, the train-station area is the least attractive part of town to be based. The streets, most of which lie outside the pedestrian zone, are heavily trafficked, noisy, and dirty, and you're removed from the major sights and the action. This area, however, does have more budget options than any other quarter. Some streets, such as Via Faenza and its tributaries, contain a glut of budget joints, with dozens of choices every block and often two, three, or even six bottom-scraping dives crammed into a single building. It's the best place to go if you can't seem to find a room anywhere else; just walk up the street and try each place you pass. And while many hotels simply pander without inspiration to tourists, a few (those recommended later) seem to try twice as hard as central inns to cater to their guests and are among the friendliest hotels in town. *Tip:* Just avoid anything on traffic-clogged Via Nazionale.

The situation improves dramatically as you move into the San Lorenzo area and pass Santa Maria Novella church and head toward the river. Piazza Santa Maria Novella and its tributary streets are attracting something of a bohemian nightlife scene (but parts of it can be seedy). One of Florence's premier inns, the Grand, is on the Arno at Piazza Ognissanti—just a bit south of the station but miles away in atmosphere.

San Marco and Santissima Annunziata   These two churches are fronted by *piazze*—Piazza San Marco, now a busy traffic center, and Piazza Santissima Annunziata, the most beautiful in the city—that together define the northern limits of the *centro storico.* The neighborhood is home to the university, Michelangelo's *David* at the Accademia, the San Marco monastery, and long, quiet streets with some real hotel gems. The daily walk back from the heart of town up here may tire some, but others welcome being removed from the worst of the high-season tourist crush.

Santa Croce This eastern edge of the *centro storico* runs along the Arno. The bulky Santa Croce church is full of famous Florentine art and famous dead Florentines. The church is also the focal point of one of the most genuine neighborhoods left in the old center. While the area's western edge abuts the medieval district around Piazza della Signoria—Via Bentacordi/Via Torta actually trace the outline of the old Roman amphitheater—much of the district was rebuilt after World War II in long blocks of creamy yellow plaster buildings with residential shops and homes. Few tourists roam off Piazza Santa Croce, so if you want to feel like a city resident, stay here. This neighborhood also boasts some of the best restaurants in the city.

The Oltrarno "Across the Arno" is the artisans' neighborhood, still packed with workshops where craftspeople hand-carve furniture and hand-stitch leather gloves. It began as a working-class neighborhood to catch the overflow from the expanding medieval city on the Arno's opposite bank, but it also became a rather chic area for aristocrats to build palaces on the edge of the countryside. The largest of these, the Pitti Palace, later became the home of the grand dukes and today houses a set of museums second only to the Uffizi. Behind it spreads the landscaped baroque fantasies of the Boboli Gardens, Florence's best park. Masaccio's frescoes in Santa Maria della Carmine here were some of the most influential of the early Renaissance.

Florence tacitly accepted the Oltrarno when the 14th-century circuit of walls was built to include it, but the alleys and squares across the river continued to retain that edge of distinctness. It has always attracted a slightly bohemian crowd—the Brownings lived here from just after their secret marriage in 1847 until Elizabeth died in 1861. The Oltrarno's lively tree-shaded center, Piazza Santo Spirito, is a world unto itself, lined with bars and trendy salad-oriented restaurants (good nightlife, though young druggies have recently been encroaching on it); and its Brunelleschi-designed church faces pointedly away from the river and the rest of Florence.

In the Hills From just about any vantage point in the center of Florence, you can see that the city ends abruptly to the north and south, replaced by green hills spotted with villas, small farms, and the expensive modern homes of the upper-middle class. To the north rises Monte Ceceri, mined for the soft gray *pietra serena* that accented so much of Renaissance architecture and home to the hamlet of Settignango, where Michelangelo was wet-nursed by a stonecutter's wife. The high reaches harbor the Etruscan village of

Fiesole, which was here long before the Romans built Florence in the valley below.

Across the Arno, the hills hemming in the Oltrarno—with such names as Bellosguardo (Beautiful Glimpse) and Monte Uliveto (Olive Grove Hill)—are blanketed in farmland. With panoramic lookouts such as Piazzale Michelangiolo and the Romanesque church of San Miniato al Monte, these hills offer some of the best walks around the city, as Elizabeth Browning, Henry James, and Florence Nightingale could tell you. They're crisscrossed by snaking country roads and bordered by high walls over which wave the silvery-green leaves of olive trees.

Owing to the lack of public transportation, first-time visitors who plan a strenuous sightseeing agenda probably will not want to choose accommodations in the hills. But for those who don't need to be in town every day and want a cooler, calmer, and altogether more relaxing vacation, the hills can be heaven.

2 Getting Around

Florence is a walking city. You can leisurely stroll between the two top sights, the Duomo and the Uffizi, in less than 5 minutes. The hike from the most northerly sights, San Marco with its Fra' Angelico frescoes and the Accademia with Michelangelo's *David*, to the most southerly, the Pitti Palace across the Arno, should take no more than 30 minutes. From Santa Maria Novella across town to Santa Croce is an easy 20- to 30-minute walk.

Most of the streets, however, were designed to handle the moderate pedestrian traffic and occasional horse-drawn cart of a medieval city. Sidewalks, where they exist, are narrow—often less than .5m (2 ft.) wide. Though much of the *centro storico* is closed to traffic, this doesn't include taxis, residents with parking permits, people without permits who drive there anyway, and the endless swarm of noisy Vespas and *motorini* (scooters).

In high season, especially July and August, the cars and their pollution (catalytic converters aren't yet standard), massive pedestrian and tourist traffic, maniac moped drivers, and stifling heat can wear you down. On some days, Florence can feel like a minor circle of Dante's Inferno. Evenings tend to be cool year-round, bringing residents and visitors alike out for the traditional before-dinner *passeggiata* (stroll) up and down Via Calzaiuoli and down Via Roma and its continuations across the Ponte Vecchio.

> ## *Tips* A Walking Warning
>
> Florentine streets are mainly cobbled or flagstone, as are the sidewalks, and thus they can be rough on soles, feet, and joints after a while. Florence may be one of the world's greatest shoe-shopping cities, but a sensible pair of quality walking shoes or sneakers is highly recommended over loafers or pumps. In dress shoes or heels, forget it—unless you are an experienced stone walker.

BY BUS   You'll rarely need to use Florence's efficient **ATAF bus system** (© 055-565-0222; www.ataf.net) since the city is so wonderfully compact. Many visitors accustomed to such big cities as Rome step off their arriving train and onto a city bus out of habit, thinking to reach the center; within 5 minutes they find themselves in the suburbs. The cathedral is a mere 5- to 7-minute walk from the train station.

Bus tickets cost 1€ ($1.30) and are good for an hour. A four-pack *(biglietto multiplo)* is 3.90€ ($5.10), a 24-hour pass 4.50€ ($5.85), a 2-day pass 7.60€ ($9.90), a 3-day pass 9.60€ ($12), and a 7-day pass 16€ ($21). Tickets are sold at *tabacchi* (tobacconists), bars, and most newsstands. Once on board, validate your ticket in the box near the rear door to avoid a steep fine. If you intend to use the bus system, you should pick up a bus map at a tourist office. Since traffic is limited in most of the historic center, buses make runs on principal streets only, save four tiny electric buses that trundle about the *centro storico.*

BY TAXI   Taxis aren't cheap, and with the city so small and the one-way system forcing drivers to take convoluted routes, they aren't an economical way to get about town. Taxis are most useful to get you and your bags between the train station and your hotel in the virtually bus-free *centro storico.* The standard rate is .80€ ($1.05) per kilometer (slightly more than a half-mile), with a whopping minimum fare of 2.40€ ($3.10) to start the meter (that rises to 4.05€/$5.25 on Sun; 5.15€/$6.70 10pm–6am), plus .60€ (80¢) per bag. There's a taxi stand outside the train station; otherwise, you have to call **Radio Taxi** at © **055-4242,** 055-4798, 055-4390, or 055-4499.

BY BICYCLE & SCOOTER   In an effort to provide an alternative to driving in the city center, the city offers free bikes (well, in past years, there has been a nominal .50€/65¢ fee). **Firenze Parcheggi,**

the public garage authority (© **055-500-0453;** www.firenze parcheggi.it), has set up temporary sites about town (look for stands at the train station, Piazza Strozzi, Via della Nina along the south side of Palazzo Vecchio, and in the large public parking lots), where bikes are furnished free from 8am to 7:30pm; you return the bike to any of the sites.

If no bikes are left, you'll have to pay for them at a shop such as **Alinari,** Via Guelfa 85r (© **055-280-500;** www.alinarirental.com), which rents bikes (2.50€/$3.25 per hour; 12€/$16 per day) and mountain bikes (3€/$3.90 per hour; 18€/$23 per day). It also rents 50cc scooters (8€/$10 per hour; 28€/$36 per day) and 100cc mopeds (10€/$13 per hour; 47€/$61 per day). Another renter with the same basic prices is **Florence by Bike,** Via San Zanobi 120–122r (© **055-488-992;** www.florencebybike.it).

Illegally parked bicycles have become such an issue in Florence that authorities have begun "towing" them—that is, breaking the locks and impounding them. Make sure you park your bike at a rack or where it won't interfere with pedestrian traffic, which is heavy in the tourist season.

BY CAR   Trying to drive in the *centro storico* is a frustrating, useless exercise. Florence is a maze of one-way streets and pedestrian zones, and it takes an old hand to know which laws to break in order to get where you need to go—plus you need a permit to do anything beyond dropping off and picking up bags at your hotel. Park your vehicle in one of the huge underground lots on the center's periphery and pound the pavement.

BY GUIDED TOUR   **American Express** (see "Fast Facts: Florence," below) teams with venerable **CAF Tours,** Via Roma 4 (© **055-283-200;** www.caftours.com), to offer two half-day bus tours of town (39€/$51), including visits to the Uffizi, the Medici Chapels, and Piazzale Michelangiolo. They also offer several walking tours for 23€ to 26€ ($30–$34); day trips to Pisa, Siena/San Gimignano, the Chianti, Lucca, or Medici villas for 35€ to 69€ ($46–$90); and farther afield to Venice, Rome, or Perugia/Assisi for 82€ to 105€ ($107–$137). You can book similar tours through most other travel agencies around town.

Walking Tours of Florence (© **055-264-5033;** www.artviva. com) offers a basic 3-hour tour daily at 9:45am for 25€ ($33) adults, 20€ ($26) students under 26, or 10€ ($13) children aged 6 to 12. Meet at their office on the mezzanine level of Piazza Santa Stefano 2, a pocket-size piazza hidden off Via Por Santa Maria, between

Via Lambertesca and the Ponte Vecchio. They provide many other thematic tours as well as private guides.

Call **I Bike Italy** (© **055-234-237,** or 772/321-0267 in the U.S.; www.ibikeitaly.com) to sign up for 1-day rides in Fiesole for 65€ ($90), or 2 days to Siena for 203€ ($280). (This is a Florida-based company, and prearranged trips can be paid by checks made out in U.S. dollars.) A shuttle bus picks you up at 9am at the Ponte delle Grazie and drives you to the outskirts of town, and an enjoyable lunch in a local trattoria is included. You're back in town by 5pm. It might stretch your budget, but you should get out of this tourist-trodden stone city for a glimpse of the incomparable Tuscan countryside. They also offer summertime, 2-day trips (Tues–Wed) to Siena for 203€ ($280).

FAST FACTS: Florence

American Express AmEx, Piazza Cimatori/Via Dante Alighieri 22r, 50122 Firenze (© 055-50-981), will act as a travel agent (for a commission), accept mail on your behalf (see "Mail," below), and cash traveler's checks at no commission. (They don't have to be AmEx checks.) The office is open Monday through Friday from 9am to 5:30pm and Saturday from 9am to 12:30pm (no travel services on Sat).

Business Hours General open hours for **stores, offices,** and **churches** are from 9:30am to noon or 1pm and again from 3 or 3:30pm to 7:30pm. That early-afternoon shutdown is the *riposo,* the Italian *siesta.* In Florence, however, many of the larger and more central shops stay open through the midday *riposo* (note the sign ORARIO NO-STOP). Most stores close all day Sunday and many also on Monday (morning only or all day). Traditionally, **museums** are closed Mondays, and though some of the biggest stay open all day long, many close for *riposo* or are only open in the morning (9am–2pm is popular). Some churches open earlier in the morning, but the largest often stay open all day. **Banks** tend to be open Monday through Friday from 8:30am to 1:30pm and 2:30 to 3:30pm or 3 to 4pm.

Doctors & Dentists A **walk-in clinic** (© **055-483-363** or 0330-774-731) is run by Dr. Giorgio Scappini; Tuesday and Thursday office hours are brief, 5:30 to 6:30pm or by appointment at Via Bonifacio Lupi 32 (just south of the Tourist Medical Service; see "Hospitals," below); Monday, Wednesday, and Friday, go to Via Guasti 2 from 3 to 4pm (north of the Fortezza del Basso). **Dr. Stephen Kerr** keeps an office at Via Porta Rossa 1 (© 0335-836-1682 or 055-288-055 at home), with office hours Monday through Friday from 3 to 5pm without an appointment (home visits or clinic appointments available 24 hr.).

For general dentistry, try **Dr. Camis de Fonseca,** Via Nino Bixio 9, northeast of the city center off Viale dei Mille (© 055-587-632), open Monday through Friday from 3 to 7pm; he's also available for emergency weekend calls. The U.S. consulate can provide a list of other English-speaking doctors, dentists, and specialists. See also "Hospitals," below, for medical translator service.

Embassies & Consulates The U.S. Embassy is in Rome at Via Vittorio Veneto 119a (© 06-46-741; fax 06-488-2672 or 06-4674-2217; www.usembassy.it). The U.S. consulate in Florence—for passport and consular services but *not* for visas—is at Lungarno Amerigo Vespucci 38 (© 055-266-951; fax 055-284-088), open to drop-ins Monday through Friday from 9am to 12:30pm. Afternoons, from 2 to 4:30pm, the consulate is open by appointment only; call ahead. The U.K. Embassy is in Rome at Via XX Settembre 80a (© 06-4220-0001; fax 06-4220-2334; www.britain.it), open Monday through Friday from 9:15am to 1:30pm. The U.K. consulate in Florence is at Lungarno Corsini 2 (© 055-284-133; fax 055-219-112). It's open Monday to Friday 9:30am to 12:30pm and 2:30 to 4:30pm.

Of English-speaking countries, only the United States and Great Britain have consulates in Florence. Citizens of other countries must go to their consulates in Rome for help: The **Canadian** consulate in Rome is at Via Zara 30, on the fifth floor (© 06-445-981 or 06-44598-2905; www.canada.it), open Monday through Friday from 8:30am to 12:30pm and 1:30 to 4pm. **Australia**'s consulate in Rome is at Via Alessandria 215 (© 06-852-721; fax 06-8527-2300; www.australian-embassy.it). The consular section is open Monday through Thursday from 8:30am to noon and 1:30 to 4pm. The immigration and visa office is open Monday to Thursday 10am to noon; telephone hours are from 10 to 11:30am. **New Zealand**'s Rome consulate is at Via Zara 28 (© 06-441-7171; fax 06-440-2984), open Monday through Friday from 8:30am to 12:45pm and 1:45 to 5pm.

Emergencies Dial © 113 for an emergency of any kind. You can also call the **Carabinieri** (the national police force; more

useful than local branches) at ⓒ **112**. Dial an **ambulance** at
ⓒ **118,** and report a **fire** at ⓒ **115**. All these calls are free from
any phone. For **car breakdowns,** call ACI (Automobile Club of
Italy) at ⓒ **116.**

Hospitals The **ambulance number** is ⓒ **118.** There's a special
Tourist Medical Service, Via Lorenzo il Magnifico 59, north of
the city center between the Fortezza del Basso and Piazza
della Libertà (ⓒ **055-475-411**), open 24 hours; take bus no. 8
or 80 to Viale Lavagnini, or bus no. 12 or night bus no. 91 to
Via Poliziano.

Thanks to socialized medicine, you can walk into most any
Italian hospital when ill and get taken care of speedily with no
insurance questions asked, no forms to fill out, and no fee
charged. They'll just give you a prescription and send you on
your way. The most central hospitals are the **Arcispedale di
Santa Maria Nuova,** a block northeast of the Duomo on
Piazza Santa Maria Nuova (ⓒ **055-27-581**), and the **Misericordia Ambulance Service,** on Piazza del Duomo across from
Giotto's bell tower (ⓒ **055-212-222** for ambulance).

For a **free translator** to help you describe your symptoms,
explain the doctor's instructions, and aid in medical issues in
general, call the volunteers at the **Associazione Volontari
Ospedalieri (AVO;** ⓒ **055-425-0126** or 055-234-4567) Monday,
Wednesday, and Friday from 4 to 6pm and Tuesday and Thursday from 10am to noon.

Internet Access Most hotels in the city center now offer
either wireless connections or an Internet point to their customers. Otherwise, head to the now-massive **Internet Train**
(www.internettrain.it), with 15 locations in Florence, including their very first shop at Via dell'Oriuolo 25r, 3 blocks from
the Duomo (ⓒ **055-263-8968**); Via Guelfa 24a, near the train
station (ⓒ **055-214-794**); Borgo San Jacopo 30r, in the Oltrarno
(ⓒ **055-265-7935**); and in the underground tunnel from the
train station toward town (ⓒ **055-239-9720**). Actually, there
are now 126 offices across Italy (36 in Tuscany, 4 in Umbria—
in Perugia and Orvieto), and the magnetic access card you buy
is good at all of them, making plugging in throughout your
journey that much easier. Access is 4€ ($5.20) per hour, or 1€
($1.30) for 10 minutes; they also provide printing, scanning,
webcam, and fax services, plus others (bike rental, international shipping, 24-hr. film developing) at some offices. Open

hours vary, but run at least daily from 9am to 8:30pm, often later.

The **Netgate,** Via Sant'Egidio 10–20r (© **055-658-0207;** www. thenetgate.it), has similar rates but also offers a Saturday "happy hour" of free access from 10:30 to 11am and from 2 to 2:30pm. It's open daily from 10am to 10:30pm (until 8:30pm in winter).

Laundry & Dry Cleaning Though there are several coin-op shops (mostly of the OndaBlu chain), you can get your wash done for you even more cheaply at a pay-by-weight *lavanderia*—and you don't have to waste a morning sitting there watching it go in circles. The cheapest are around the university (east of San Marco), and one of the best is a nameless joint at **Via Alfani 44r** (© **055-247-9313**), where they'll do an entire load for 6€ ($7.80), have it ready by afternoon, and even deliver it free to your hotel. It's closed Saturday afternoon. At other, non-self-service shops, check the price *before* leaving your clothes—some places charge by the item. Dry cleaning *(lavasecco)* is much more costly and is available at *lavanderie* throughout the city (ask your hotel for the closest).

Mail You can buy *francobolli* (stamps) from any *tabacchi* or from the central post office. Florence's **main post office** (© **160** for general info, or 055-211-147) is on Via Pellicceria 3, 50103, Firenze, off the southwest corner of Piazza della Repubblica. You can pick up letters sent *Fermo Posta* (Italian for *poste restante,* or held mail) by showing ID; see below. The post office is open Monday through Friday from 8:15am to 7pm and Saturday 8:15am to 12:30pm. All packages heavier than 2 kilograms (4½ lb.) must be properly wrapped and brought around to the parcel office at the back of the building (enter at Via dei Sassetti 4, also known as Piazza Davanzati).

Drop postcards and letters into the boxes outside. To mail larger packages, drop them at *sportello* (window) 9/10, but first head across the room to window 21/22 for stamps. If that window is closed, as it often is, you buy your stamps at the next window, 23/24, which is also the pickup for *Fermo Posta.* You can also send packages via **DHL,** Via della Cupola 243 (© **055-308-877** or 800-345-345 for free pickup), or **UPS,** Via Pratignone 56a in Calenzano (© **055-882-5501**).

To receive mail at the central post office, have it sent to [your name], Fermo Posta Centrale, 50103 Firenze, Italia/ITALY.

They'll charge you .25€ (30¢) per letter when you come to pick it up at window 23/24; bring your passport for ID. For people without an AmEx card, this is a much better deal than American Express's similar service, which charges 1.50€ ($1.95) to receive and hold non-cardholders' mail. For AmEx members, however, this service is free, so you can have your mail sent to [your name], Client Mail, American Express, Via Dante Alighieri 22r, 50123 Firenze, Italia/ITALY.

Newspapers & Magazines You can pick up the *International Herald Tribune* and *USA Today* from almost any newsstand, and you'll find the *Wall Street Journal Europe* and the *London Times*, along with *Time* and *Newsweek* magazines, at most larger kiosks. There's a 24-hour newsstand in the train station. For upcoming events, theater, and shows, see "Visitor Information," earlier in this chapter.

Pharmacies For pharmacy information, dial ☎ 110. There are 24-hour pharmacies (also open Sun and state holidays) in **Stazione Santa Maria Novella** (☎ 055-216-761; ring the bell between 1 and 4am); at **Piazza San Giovanni 20r,** just behind the baptistery at the corner of Borgo San Lorenzo (☎ 055-211-343); and at **Via Cazzaiuoli 7r,** just off Piazza della Signoria (☎ 055-289-490). On holidays and at night, look for the sign in any pharmacy windows telling you which ones are open.

Police For emergencies, dial ☎ 112 for the Carabinieri. To report lost property or passport problems, call the *questura* (urban police headquarters) at ☎ 055-49-771.

Post Offices See "Mail," above.

Safety Central Italy is an exceedingly safe area with practically no random violent crime. As in any city, plenty of pickpockets are out to ruin your vacation, and in Florence you'll find light-fingered children (especially around the train station), but otherwise you're safe. Do steer clear of the Cascine Park after dark, when it becomes somewhat seedy and you may run the risk of being mugged; and you probably won't want to hang out with the late-night heroin addicts shooting up on the Arno mud flats below the Lungarno embankments on the edges of town.

3

Where to Stay in Florence

Throughout the 1990s, past the turn of the millennium, and especially at the introduction of the euro in 2002, inflation ran rampant in Italy. Hotel prices more than tripled in such cities as Florence in that period. Since 2006, thanks to growing competition and the high euro-dollar exchange rate, prices have begun to level off a bit, but it is still nearly impossible to find a double you'd want to stay in for less than 100€ ($130). Because hotel prices had outpaced inflation, the hoteliers stockpiled some surplus cash, and over the last decade they've been reinvesting in their properties. In many hotels, the amenity levels are now at or above what Americans expect to find at home, and the days of the bathroom-down-the-hall cheap *pensioni* are fading—or at least those properties are now mostly student dives. Almost everyone seems to have put in new bathrooms and some sort of Internet access. Extras such as heated towel racks, whirlpool tubs, satellite TVs with CNN and the BBC, and direct-dial phones, which once only the top few inns boasted, are now in four-fifths of the properties listed here. In the past few years, the trend has been to trade quantity of rooms for quality, eliminating small doubles to create larger suites and attract a higher-rolling clientele. I've tried to balance the selections to suit all tastes and budgets.

For help finding a room, visit the Santa Maria Novella train station for the **Consorzio Informazioni Turistiche Alberghiere (ITA)** office, near Track 9 (© **055-282-893**), and the tiny tourist office, near Track 16, both of which will find you a room in your price range (for a small commission). Or go to the official tourist office's website subsection on accommodations at **www.toscanaeturismo. net/dovedormire**.

Many budget hotels are concentrated in the area around the Stazione Santa Maria Novella. You'll find most of the hotels in this convenient and relatively safe (if charmless) area on noisy Via Nazionale and its first two side streets, Via Fiume and Via Faenza; an adjunct is the area surrounding the Mercato San Lorenzo. The area between the Duomo and Piazza della Signoria, particularly along and near Via dei Calzaiuoli, is a good, though invariably more expensive, place to look.

Peak season is mid-March through mid-July, September through early November, and December 23 through January 6. May and September are particularly popular in the city as well as in the outlying Tuscan hills.

To help you decide in which area you'd like to base yourself for exploring the city, consult "The Neighborhoods in Brief" section, in chapter 2. Note that I've included parking information only for those hotels or *pensioni* that offer it.

1 Near the Duomo

VERY EXPENSIVE

Hotel Savoy 🏛🏛   This 1893 hotel underwent a complete transformation in 2000 by Sir Rocco Forte and his sister, who designed the warm, stylishly minimalist modern interiors. Rooms are standardized, with walk-in closets, dark brown marble bathrooms, and mosaics over the tubs. The different room "styles"—classic, executive, and deluxe—really just refer to size. Four suites (two rooms, two TVs, leather easy chairs, white marble bathrooms) are on the back, four on the piazza. Two of them include a Turkish bath. Rooms on the fifth floor, added in 1958, just peep over the surrounding buildings for spectacular views, especially those on the Duomo (back) side. You're just a few steps in any direction from all the sights and the best shopping. The building actually belongs to Ferragamo, as do many of the other buildings in this square.

Piazza della Repubblica 7, 50123 Firenze. ℂ **800/223-6800** in the U.S., or 055-27-351 in Italy. Fax 055-273-5888. www.roccofortehotels.com. 102 units. 495€–627€ ($644–$815) double; 820€ ($1,066) studio; 1,089€–1,375€ ($1,416–$1,788) suite. Breakfast 25€ ($33). AE, DC, MC, V. Parking 29€ ($38). Bus: A, 22, 6, 11, 36, or 37. **Amenities:** Restaurant; bar; small gym w/view; concierge; tour desk; car-rental desk; courtesy car; secretarial services; 24-hr. room service; in-room massage; babysitting; laundry service; same-day dry cleaning; nonsmoking rooms; Wi-Fi in public spaces. *In room:* A/C, TV w/pay movies, VCR on request, fax on request, Wi-Fi, dataport, minibar, hair dryer, safe.

EXPENSIVE

Hotel Brunelleschi 🏛   The mishmash of historical structures making up this hotel—including a Roman *calidarium* in the foundations—was so confusing that they installed a small museum in the basement to explain it all. The property rambles through the remains of various medieval houses, a deconsecrated church, and a 6th-century Byzantine tower. Most of the interiors mix curving modern

Where to Stay in Florence

Albergo Azzi **1**
Albergo Merlini **2**
Burchianti **7**
Campeggio Michelangelo **41**
Grand Hotel Cavour **19**
Hotel Abaco **9**
Hotel Alessandra **13**
Hotel Aprile **6**
Hotel Bellettini **8**
Hotel Brunelleschi **22**
Hotel California **35**
Hotel Calzaiuoli **21**
Hotel Casci **34**
Hotel Chiari Bigallo **24**
Hotel de' Lanzi **23**
Hotel Firenze **20**
Hotel Helvetia & Bristol **10**
Hotel Hermitage **37**
Hotel La Scaletta **14**
Hotel Le Due Fontane **32**
Hotel Loggiato dei Serviti **31**
Hotel Mario's **3**
Hotel Medici **25**
Hotel Monna Lisa **36**
Hotel Nuova Italia **4**
Hotel Pensione Pendini **27**
Hotel Regency **29**
Hotel Ritz **39**
Hotel Savoy **26**
Hotel Tornabuoni Beacci **11**
Hotel Torre Guelfa **12**
Il Guelfo Bianco **33**
Instituto Gould **15**
Mia Cara/Archi Rossi Hostel **1**
Morandi alla Crocetta **30**
Palazzo Antellesi **38**

Pensione Benecistà **28**
Pensione Maria Luisade' Medici **18**
Pensione Sorelle Bandini **16**
Silla **40**
Torre di Bellosguardo **17**
Villa Azalee **5**
Villa Camerata (Ostello
   della Gioventù) **28**
Villa San Michele **28**

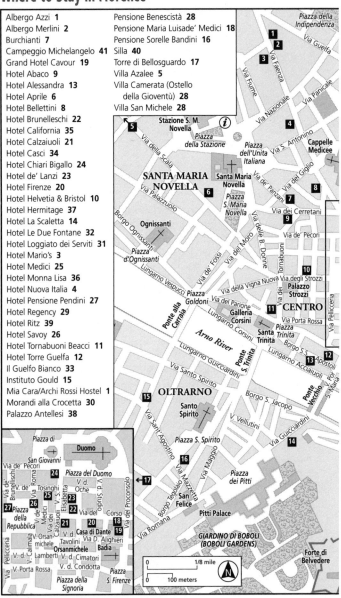

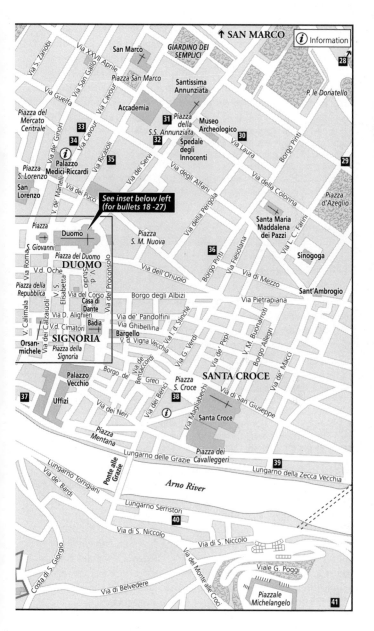

lines with the salvaged vestiges of the medieval buildings. The rooms are spacious and very comfortable, with large bathrooms, but they are disappointingly modern. A few, especially on the upper floors, share a view of the Duomo with the panoramic roof terrace. The location is prime but the price a bit steep for those who don't get a thrill from sleeping near the fossilized remnants of the Middle Ages.

Piazza Sant'Elisabetta 3 (off Via de' Calzioli), 50122 Firenze. © 055-27-370. Fax 055-219-653. www.hotelbrunelleschi.it. 96 units. 380€ ($494) double; 520€ ($676) junior suite. Rates include breakfast. AE, DC, MC, V. Valet parking in garage 30€ ($39). Bus: B, 14, 23, or 71. **Amenities:** Intimate restaurant; bar (in the tower); concierge; tour desk; car-rental desk; courtesy car; business center and secretarial services; limited room service; in-room massage; babysitting; laundry service; same-day dry cleaning; nonsmoking rooms. *In room:* A/C, TV, Wi-Fi, minibar, hair dryer, safe.

MODERATE

Burchianti *★★* *(Finds)*   In 2002, rising rents forced the kindly owner of this venerable inn (established in the 19th c.) to move up the block into the *piano nobile* of a neighboring 15th-century *palazzo.* She definitely traded up. Incredible frescoes dating from 17th century and later decorate every ceiling but one tiny single, and many of the walls—actually, virtually all the walls—are painted, but the yahoos of a previous age whitewashed over them and the hotel could afford to uncover only a few of them for the time being. The select few have now been completely refurbished. This is one of the most sought-after little hotels in Florence.

Via del Giglio 8 (off Via Panzani), 50123 Firenze. © 055-212-796. Fax 055-272-9727. www.hotelburchianti.com. 10 units. 130€–170€ ($169–$224) double; 160€–230€ ($208–$299) suite. Ask for a Frommer's discount of 5%. Rates include continental breakfast. AE, DC, MC, V. Parking in garage next door about 25€ ($33). Bus: A, 1, 6, 14, 17, 22, 23, 36, or 37. **Amenities:** Concierge; tour desk; car-rental desk; limited room service (breakfast); babysitting; laundry service; dry cleaning. *In room:* A/C, TV on request, high-speed Internet, minibar in suites, hair dryer, safe.

Grand Hotel Cavour *★*   The Cavour is an address of some refinement in Dante's old neighborhood, and about as central as you can get. The plush chairs in the large vaulted lobby are focused around an antique stone pillar, and the roof terrace has a positively spectacular view of the Duomo, the Palazzo Vecchio, and other Florentine landmarks. The rooms, carpeted and furnished with contemporary good taste, tend to be on the small side, though a few enjoy brick arches and other 10th-century holdovers. The bathrooms are new, and the firm beds are spread with patterned quilts. Accommodations along the front and side get a view of the towers sprouting from the Bargello and the Badia, but be warned: The double-glazed windows are no match for the clamorous buses that grumble down the busy street in front.

Via del Proconsolo 3 (next to the Badia), 50122 Firenze. © **055-266-271**. Fax 055-218-955. www.hotelcavour.com. 103 units. 245€–500€ ($328–$650) double (3 types). Rates include breakfast. AE, DC, MC, V. Valet parking in garage 28€ ($36). Bus: 14, 23, or 71. **Amenities:** Bike rental; concierge; tour desk; car-rental desk; salon; limited room service; babysitting; laundry service; same-day dry cleaning; nonsmoking rooms; Wi-Fi in lobby. *In room:* A/C, TV, dataport, minibar, hair dryer, safe.

Hotel Calzaiuoli ✦

As central as you can get, the Calzaiuoli offers comfortable, well-appointed rooms on the main strolling drag halfway between the Uffizi and the Duomo. The halls' rich runners lead up a *pietra serena* staircase to the midsize and largish rooms decorated with painted friezes and framed etchings. Rooms include stylish wood furnishings and mirrored armoires. The firm beds rest on patterned carpets, in the older rooms surrounded by functional furniture beginning to show some wear. The bathrooms range from huge to cramped, but all have fluffy towels (and a few have Jacuzzis). The rooms overlook the street, with its pedestrian carnival and some of the associated noise, or out the back—either over the rooftops to the Bargello and Badia towers or up to the Duomo's cupola.

Via Calzaiuoli 6 (near Orsanmichele), 50122 Firenze. © **055-212-456**. Fax 055-268-310. www.calzaiuoli.it. 45 units. 100€–200€ ($130–$260) double. Rates include breakfast. AE, DC, MC, V. Valet parking 23€–26€ ($30–$34) in garage. Bus: 22, 36, or 37. **Amenities:** Bar; concierge; tour desk; car-rental desk; limited room service; babysitting; laundry service; dry cleaning; Internet access at the bar. *In room:* A/C, TV, Wi-Fi, minibar, hair dryer, safe.

Hotel Chiari Bigallo ✦ *Finds*

Once upon a time, this was a super-cheap standby, but the owners decided to trade for *the* single best location (across from the Duomo)—and more than double the prices. Its rooms are modular modern now, but in the location competition, it still wins for being above the Loggia del Bigallo on the corner of Piazza del Duomo. If you get one of the few rooms facing the Duomo, you'll have a view like no other, within poking distance of Giotto's bell tower. The traffic-free zone doesn't mean you won't have significant pedestrian noise that drifts up from the cobbled street below, as this is the city's most tourist-trammeled intersection.

The owners renovated this place to bring it in line with their other three hotels, including, a few blocks away on Via delle Oche and with side views of this living postcard, the quieter de' Lanzi (see below).

Vicolo degli Adimari 2 (off the Via Calzaiuoli near the Piazza Duomo), 50122 Firenze. ©/fax **055-216-086**. www.hotelbigallo.it. 17 units. 186€ ($242) double; 251€

($326) triple. Rates include continental breakfast. AE, DC, MC, V. Valet parking in garage 21€ ($27). Bus: A, 1, 6, 11, 14, 17, 22, 23, 36, or 37. **Amenities:** Concierge; tour desk; car-rental desk; limited room service; laundry service; dry cleaning; non-smoking rooms. *In room:* A/C, TV, minibar, hair dryer, safe.

Hotel de' Lanzi ☆

A much quieter alternative to the Hotel Chiari Bigallo, its sister hotel around the corner (see above), the Lanzi is just as centrally located and more comfortable; it just doesn't have those drop-dead views of the Duomo and bell tower, and the entrance is not particularly photogenic. Still, the beds have firm mattresses and spreads embroidered in an antique Florentine pattern. The accommodations, in fact, are all done very tastefully for a hotel of this price. The rooms come with shiny new bathrooms sporting heated towel racks (in most). Many rooms on the front get a magnificent window-filling side view of the Duomo, but even if you don't get the vista, you can be assured of cozy, relaxing accommodations just steps from the city's major sights and shopping. Breakfast is a full buffet, with fruit and ham.

Via delle Oche 11 (off Via Calzaiuoli around the corner from the Duomo), 50122 Firenze. ✆/fax **055-288-043.** www.hoteldelanziflorence.com. 44 units. 186€ ($242) double; 251€ ($326) triple. Prices can drop as much as 40% in low season; also ask for Frommer's discounts. Rates include breakfast. AE, DC, MC, V. Valet parking 18€ ($23). Bus: 22, 36, or 37. **Amenities:** Concierge; tour desk; car-rental desk; limited room service; laundry service; dry cleaning; nonsmoking rooms. *In room:* A/C, TV, hair dryer, safe.

Hotel Pensione Pendini ☆

Built during the heyday of the 1880s, when Florence was briefly the capital of the newly unified Italy, the Pendini rises above the storefronts of Piazza della Repubblica. The Abolaffio brothers, Emmanuele and David, took over this former *pensione* in 1994 and since have installed double-glazing on all windows so that street noise has virtually disappeared. All bathrooms are also being redone in green tile with large tubs. Many rooms boast an airy country style, with original and reproduction antiques and brass-framed beds. The rather large accommodations on the piazza are best, with views over the bustle of the cafe-lined square. The lounge, offering 24-hour bar service, contains a comfortable mélange of 19th-century furnishings with scattered rugs, plus a computer with free Internet access. The location and price make this hotel a good choice for shoppers who'd rather give their money to Armani and Ferragamo.

Via Strozzi 2 (Piazza della Repubblica), 50123 Firenze. ✆ **055-211-170.** Fax 055-281-807. www.florenceitaly.net. 42 units, all with bathroom. 110€–150€ ($143–$195) double; 150€–210€ ($195–$273) triple; 170€–250€ ($221–$325) quad; 170€–330€ ($221–$429) family suite. Rates include continental breakfast.

AE, DC, MC, V. Valet parking in garage 21€–31€ ($27–$40). Bus: A, 6, 11, 22, 36, or 37. **Amenities:** Concierge; tour desk; car-rental desk; 24-hr. room service (breakfast and bar); Internet terminal. *In room:* A/C, TV, dataport, hair dryer on request.

INEXPENSIVE

Hotel Abaco ✦✦ (*Value*)   Bruno is a bit of a Calabrian dynamo, running his clean, efficient little hotel in a prime location with gusto, and he's one of the more helpful, advice-proffering hoteliers in town. The Abaco has inherited a few nice touches from its 15th-century *palazzo*, including high wood ceilings, stone floors (some are parquet), and, in tiny no. 5, a carved *pietra serena* fireplace. And each room is themed after a Renaissance artist, with framed reproductions of the painter's works and a color scheme derived from them. Bruno has replaced the mismatched furnishings with quirky antique-style pieces such as gilded frame mirrors and rich half-testers over the beds. The hotel is at a busy intersection, but the double-paned windows help. Bruno will even do a load of laundry for you for just 7€ ($9.10), wash and dry.

Via dei Banchi 1 (halfway between the station and the Duomo, off Via de' Panzani), 50123 Firenze. ☏ **055-238-1919.** Fax 055-282-2289. www.abaco-hotel.it. 7 units, 3 with shower and sink, 4 with full bathroom. 82€ ($96) double with shower only; 95€ ($124) double with bathroom. Breakfast 5€ ($6.50), free if you pay for the room with cash. AE, MC, V (they prefer cash). Valet parking 25€ ($33) in garage. Bus: 1, 6, 11, 14, 17, 22, 23, 36, or 37. **Amenities:** Bike rental; concierge; tour desk; car-rental desk; coin-op laundry; Internet terminal. *In room:* A/C (costs an extra 5€/$6.50 to turn on), TV, dataport, hair dryer.

Hotel Firenze   This former student hangout and now board-rated two-star hotel is still partly used as a study-abroad dorm, although its clientele ranges from college juniors to young adults to retirees, all attracted by the excellent price-to-location ratio: It is tucked away on its own little piazza at the heart of the *centro storico*'s pedestrian zone. The rooms are brightly tiled but bland. This is a large operation without any of the warmth or ambience of a small, family-run hotel, and the concierge and management are efficient but generally uninvolved.

Piazza Donati 4 (on Via del Corso, off Via dei Calzaiuoli), 50122 Firenze. ☏ **055-268-301** or 055-214-203. Fax 055-212-370. 57 units. 103€ ($134) double; 138€ ($180) triple. Breakfast 8€ ($10). MC, V. Parking 26€ ($34) in nearby garage. Bus: A, 14, or 23. **Amenities:** Tour desk; Internet point in lobby. *In room:* TV, hair dryer.

Hotel Medici ✦ (*Value*)   In the heart of town, with killer views, this place is more than worth it for budgeters who can secure a room on the fifth or (better yet) sixth floor. All rooms are a good size but plain, with functional furniture, tile floors, tiny bathrooms, and firm beds. But who looks at the room when your window is filled with a vista of Florence's Duomo—facade, campanile, dome, and all? Only the top two levels of rooms get the full effect, but the sixth floor has a wraparound terrace everyone can enjoy. If you're lucky, you might happen in at a moment when one of the many regulars hasn't booked one of the sixth-floor rooms with French windows opening directly onto the terrace. The price is excellent for this kind of location and panorama.

Via de' Medici 6 (between Piazza della Repubblica and Via de' Calzaiuoli), 50123 Firenze. ℂ **055-284-818.** Fax 055-216-202. www.hotelmedici.it. 39 units, 26 with bathroom (shower only). 110€ ($143) double with bathroom; 100€ ($130) double without bathroom. Rates include breakfast. MC, V. Valet parking 22€ ($29) in nearby garage. Bus: A, 22, 36, or 37. **Amenities:** Concierge; tour desk; car-rental desk; limited room service (breakfast). *In room:* Hair dryer.

Pensione Maria Luisa de' Medici 🅰🅰🅰 *(Kids)* *(Finds)*   In the 1970s and 1980s, the owner, Angido Sordi, was fascinated with baroque art, so the halls of this 17th-century are hung with canvases by the likes of Van Dyck, Vignale, and Sustermans, which contrast with the modernist furniture. While Dr. Sordi convalesces in a back room, his Welsh partner Evelyn Morris runs the place, cooking hearty breakfasts served to you in your room. Most rooms are large enough to accommodate four to five people comfortably. The firm beds are set on carpeted or tiled floors scattered with thick rugs. There are four shared bathrooms, so you usually don't have to wait in the morning. Two drawbacks: You have to walk up three flights, and there is a curfew, which varies with the season. However, if elevators and late nights are obligatory, the owners offer a *pensione* across the street, **Hotel Ferdinando II de' Medici** (Via del Presto 2; ℂ **055-210-947;** www.ferdinandode medici.com), that will suit your tastes, and possibly your budget as well. Doubles there are priced at 95€ ($123) per night.

Via del Corso 1 (2nd floor; between Via dei Calzaiuoli and Via del Proconsolo), 50122 Firenze. ℂ **055-280-048.** 9 units, 2 with private bathroom. 80€ ($104) double without bathroom; 95€ ($124) double with bathroom; 110€ ($143) triple without bathroom; 125€ ($152) triple with bathroom; 130€ ($169) quad without bathroom; 145€ ($191) quad with bathroom. Rates include breakfast. No credit cards. Nearby parking about 24€–28€ ($31–$36). Bus: A, 14, or 23. **Amenities:** Concierge; tour desk. *In room:* Hair dryer, no phone.

2 Near Piazza Della Signoria
EXPENSIVE
Hotel Hermitage 🅰   This ever-popular hotel right at the foot of the Ponte Vecchio was renovated in 1998 to give each room wood floors or thick rugs, shiny new bathrooms (most with Jacuzzis), and fresh wallpaper. The rooms are of moderate size, occasionally a bit

(Kids) Family-Friendly Hotels

Hotel Casci (p. 55)   This inexpensive family favorite near the Palazzo Medici-Ricciardi has a series of extra-large rooms set aside especially for families. The hotel is housed in a 15th-century *palazzo*, and the family that runs it is very friendly and helpful. A great family value!

Hotel Nuova Italia (p. 59)   The Italian-American couple that runs this hotel near the station are just about the most helpful hoteliers I've ever run across. The rooms aren't overly large but are immaculate. And here's an added perk: With this Frommer's guidebook in hand, you and your brood can get a discount off the already reasonable prices.

Instituto Gould (p. 68)   The best bet for families on a tight budget is like a hotel masquerading as a hostel. It draws more families than students to its institutionally clean and large accommodations. Almost all rooms have a private bathroom, and you can get a family of four into your own quad with a private bathroom for around 60€ ($69).

Pensione Maria Luisa de' Medici (p. 52)   An amicable pair of proprietors runs this very central hotel just a few blocks from the Duomo. Most rooms are enormous, with multiple beds and dressers and tabletops on which to spread your family's stuff. The home-cooked Welsh breakfast served in your room is included in the low prices. Just be sure to admonish the more curious youngsters from touching the genuine—and valuable—baroque paintings in the hall.

dark, but they're full of 17th- to 19th-century antiques and boast double-glazed windows to cut down on noise. Those that don't face the Ponte Vecchio are on side alleys and quieter. Their famous roof terrace is covered in bright flowers that frame postcard views of the Arno, Duomo, and Palazzo Vecchio. The charming breakfast room full of picture windows gets the full effect of the morning sun. The owners and staff excel in doing the little things that help make your vacation go smoothly—but prices are a bit inflated.

Vicolo Marzio 1/Piazza del Pesce (to the left of the Ponte Vecchio as you're facing it), 50122 Firenze. © 055-287-216. Fax 055-212-208. www.hermitagehotel.com.

28 units. 245€ ($319) double. Rates up to 20% lower in winter. Rates include break-fast. MC, V. Parking 21€–34€ ($27–$44) in nearby garage. Bus: 23 or 71. **Amenities:** Concierge; tour desk; limited room service; babysitting; laundry service; dry cleaning. *In room:* A/C, TV, hair dryer, safe.

3 Near San Lorenzo & the Mercato Centrale

MODERATE

Hotel Bellettini *⟨R⟩ ⟨Value⟩*   A hotel has existed in this Renaissance *palazzo* since the 1600s. Gina and Marzia, sisters and third-generation hoteliers, run this gem of terra-cotta tiles, wrought-iron or carved wood beds, antiques, and stained-glass windows. Room no. 44 offers a tiny balcony that, blooming with jasmine and geraniums by late spring, makes it second best only to room no. 45 with its view of the Medici chapels and the Duomo's dome. In 2000, they added a lovely six-room annex with frescoes, marble bathrooms, minibars, and coffeemakers.

Via dei Conti 7 (off Via dei Cerretani), 50123 Firenze. **⟨C⟩ 055-213-561.** Fax 055-283-551. www.hotelbellettini.com. 28 units. 105€ ($137) double without bathroom; 140€ ($182) double with bathroom; 180€ ($234) triple with bathroom. Rates include buffet breakfast. AE, DC, MC, V. Parking nearby 24€ ($31). Bus: A, 1, 6, 14, 17, 22, 23, 36, or 37. **Amenities:** Concierge; tour desk; limited room service; laundry service; dry cleaning; Internet terminal. *In room:* A/C, TV, hair dryer, safe.

Il Guelfo Bianco *⟨R⟩⟨R⟩*   Once you enter this refined hotel you'll forget it's on busy Via Cavour. Its windows are triple-paned, blocking out nearly all traffic noise, and many rooms overlook quiet courtyards and gardens out back. Once upon a time it was a great value, for providing excellent service and luxury rooms at low prices for a board-rated three-star hotel, but lately the rates have risen toward the level of their surroundings. (Though prices for a triple are still a bargain.) Decor is pretty, featuring marble-topped desks, antique-style furnishings, modern art, and painted tile work in the large new bathrooms. The ceilings faithfully reproduce the beam and terra-cotta look this 15th-century *palazzo* once had. Some rooms have retained such 17th-century features as frescoed or painted wood ceilings, carved wooden doorways, and the occasional parquet floor. Superior rooms are larger than executive ones (and can be made easily into triples), while "de luxe" rooms are larger still with a semiseparate sitting area—think junior suite. The friendly staff is full of advice, and they've installed a new bar and reading room on the ground floor.

Via Cavour 29 (near the corner of Via Guelfa), 50129 Firenze. **⟨C⟩ 055-288-330.** Fax 055-295-203. www.ilguelfobianco.it. 40 units. 120€–195€ ($156–$250) executive double; 150€–270€ ($185–$351) "de luxe" double; 135€–220€ ($175–$286) superior double; 150€–250€ ($195–$325) superior triple. Rates include breakfast.

AE, MC, V. Valet parking 24€–30€ ($31–$36) in garage. Bus: 1, 6, 7, 11, 17, 33, 67, or 68. **Amenities:** Bar, concierge; tour desk; car-rental desk; 24-hr. room service; in-room massage; babysitting; laundry service; same-day dry cleaning; Internet terminal and Wi-Fi in lobby. *In room:* A/C, satellite TV, VCR in some units, minibar, hair dryer, safe.

INEXPENSIVE

Hotel California ⓕ *Value*   The California is a good budget option on a lightly trafficked street near the Duomo. Rooms were completely overhauled in 2000–01 with stylish modern furnishings, richly colored bedspreads, and spanking new bathrooms—a few with Jacuzzi tubs, and almost all with spacious marble sink counters. There are 18th-century fresco fragments and stuccoes on many of the ceilings, and breakfast is served on a flower-covered terrace in nice weather. A few of the rooms have balconies and views of the Duomo's cupola, and they offer good deals for families.

Via Ricasoli 30 (1½ blocks north of the Duomo), 50122 Firenze. ⓒ **055-282-753.** Fax 055-216-268. www.californiaflorence.it. 22 units. 90€–180€ ($117–$234) double; 120€–240€ ($156–$312) triple; 140€–306€ ($182–$399) quad. Ask about special promotions that can lower rates up to 40%. Rates include breakfast. AE, DC, MC, V. Valet parking around 25€ ($33). Bus: 1, 6, 7, 10, 11, 17, 20, 25, 31, 32, 33, 67, 68, or 91. **Amenities:** Concierge; tour desk; limited room service. *In room:* A/C, TV, minibar in 10 units, hair dryer, safe.

Hotel Casci ⓕ *Kids*   This clean hotel in a 15th-century *palazzo* is run by the Lombardis, one of Florence's most accommodating and energetic families. It's patronized by a host of regulars who know a good value when they find it. The Lombardis even offer a free museum ticket to everyone who stays at least 3 nights (and with admissions running nearly 7.70€/$10 for most major museums, that's saying something). The frescoed bar room was, from 1851 to 1855, part of an apartment inhabited by Gioacchino Rossini, legendary composer of *The Barber of Seville* and *The William Tell Overture.* The rooms ramble on toward the back forever, overlooking the gardens and Florentine rooftops, and are mouse-quiet except for the birdsong. A few large family suites in back sleep four to five. The central location means some rooms (with double-paned windows) overlook busy Via Cavour, so for more quiet ask for a room facing the inner courtyard's magnolia tree. The hotel serves an ample breakfast buffet in a frescoed dining room.

Via Cavour 13 (between Via dei Ginori and Via Guelfa), 50129 Firenze. ⓒ **055-211-686.** Fax 055-239-6461. www.hotelcasci.com. 25 units. 90€–150€ ($117–$195) double; 120€–190€ ($156–$247) triple; 180€–220€ ($234–$286) quad. Rates include buffet breakfast. Off-season rates 20%–30% less; check website for special offers, especially Nov–Feb. AE, DC, MC, V. Valet parking 23€–25€

($30–$33), or in nearby garage (no valet) for 15€ ($20). Bus: 1, 6, 11, or 17. **Amenities:** Bar; concierge; tour desk; babysitting; laundry service; dry cleaning; nonsmoking rooms; free Internet access. *In room:* A/C, flatscreen TV, Wi-Fi, fridge, hair dryer, safe.

4 Near Piazza Santa Trinita

VERY EXPENSIVE

Hotel Helvetia & Bristol 🏵🏵   This Belle Epoque hotel is the most central of the top luxury properties in town, host in the past to the Tuscan Macchaioli painters as well as De Chirico, playwright Pirandello, and atom-splitting Enrico Fermi. The attentive staff oversees the rather cushy accommodations outfitted with marble bathrooms, large, firm beds, and heavy curtains. Most rooms have at least one antique work of art on the fabric-covered walls, and all are well insulated from the sounds of the outside world. The large 17th-century canvases add an air of dignity to the plush sofas of the lounge, while the Winter Garden bar/breakfast room is tricked out with trailing ivy and a splashing fountain. Prices, though, are starting to get a little exaggerated. In 2005, the hotel added a restaurant with outdoor seating.

Via dei Pescioni 2 (near the Palazzo Strozzi), 50123 Firenze. 📞 **888/770-0447** in the U.S., 800-505-050 toll-free in Italy, or 055-287-814. Fax 055-288-353. 67 units. 330€–470€ ($429–$611) double; 500€–650€ ($650–$845) suite. Breakfast 30€ ($39). AE, DC, MC, V. Valet parking in garage 35€ ($46). Bus: 6, 11, 36, 37, or 68. **Amenities:** Intimate restaurant; bike rental; concierge; tour desk; car-rental desk; 24-hr. room service; in-room massage; babysitting; laundry service; same-day dry cleaning; Wi-Fi. *In room:* A/C, TV, VCR in deluxe rooms, minibar.

EXPENSIVE

Hotel Tornabuoni Beacci 🏵🏵   From the Renaissance until the 19th century this was the sumptuous guesthouse of the Strozzi family. It later became a sort of luxury *pensione,* and then a grand hotel, taking its present name in 1978. The staff greets return guests and new friends alike with genuine warmth. Everything is a bit worn, but there's a concerted effort to furnish the rooms with period pieces. The dining room is sunny, and the lunches and dinners are well prepared. In summer, you can take breakfast on a terrace bursting with flowers and a view of the Bellosguardo hills. Off the terrace is a recently renovated bar, and there's an atmospheric reading room with a 17th-century tapestry and a large fireplace that roars to life in winter. They're currently expanding into the floor below with a small conference room and 12 more guest rooms, including a suite overlooking Piazza Santa Trínita and a honeymoon suite covered with beautiful 17th-century frescoes.

Via Tornabuoni 3 (off the north corner of Piazza Santa Trínita), 50123 Firenze. © 055-212-645. Fax 055-283-594. www.tornabuonihotels.com. 28 units. 280€ ($364) double; 350€ ($455) suite. Rates include buffet breakfast. AE, DC, MC, V. Parking 23€–25€ ($30–$33) in garage. Bus: 6, 11, 36, 37, or 68. **Amenities:** Restaurant; concierge; tour desk; 24-hr. room service; babysitting; laundry service; dry cleaning; Wi-Fi. *In room:* A/C, TV, minibar, hair dryer.

MODERATE

Hotel Alessandra ★ *(Value*   This old-fashioned *pensione* in a 1507 *palazzo* just off the river charges little for its simple comfort and kind hospitality. The rooms differ greatly in size and style, and while they won't win any awards from *Architectural Digest,* there are a few antique pieces and parquet floors to add to the charm. Air-conditioning is installed in 25 rooms. The bathrooms are outfitted with fluffy white towels, and the shared bathrooms are ample, clean, and numerous enough that you won't have to wait in line in the morning. They also rent out an apartment in a quiet section of the Oltrarno (across the bridge from the Santa Croce neighborhood) for 775€ ($1,008) per week for two people; check it out at **www. florenceflat.com**.

Borgo SS. Apostoli 17 (between Via dei Tornabuoni and Via Por Santa Maria), 50123 Firenze. © **055-283-438.** Fax 055-210-619. www.hotelalessandra.com. 27 units, 20 with private bathroom. 108€ ($140) double without bathroom; 145€ ($189) double with bathroom; 160€ ($208) double (with bathroom) overlooking river; 145€ ($189) triple without bathroom; 191€ ($248) triple with bathroom; 160€ ($208) quad without bathroom; 212€ ($276) quad with bathroom; 160€ ($208) junior suite; 200€ ($260) Baccio suite. Rates include breakfast. Ask about low-season rates. AE, MC, V. Parking in nearby garage 20€ ($26). Bus: B, 6, 11, 36, or 37. **Amenities:** Concierge; tour desk; limited room service (breakfast); massage; babysitting; laundry service; same-day dry cleaning; nonsmoking rooms (doubles overlooking river and suites). *In room:* A/C in most units, TV (PlayStation on request), hair dryer, safe in most units.

Hotel Torre Guelfa ★★   The Avuri family runs one of the most atmospheric hotels in Florence. The major reason to stay here is to drink in the breathtaking 360-degree view from the 13th-century tower, Florence's tallest privately owned tower. Although you're just steps from the Ponte Vecchio (and, unfortunately, the noise that comes along with it), you'll want to put sightseeing on hold and linger in your canopied iron bed. So many people request room no. 15, with a huge private terrace and a view similar to the tower's, they've had to tack 10€ ($13) onto the price. Follow the strains of classical music to the salon, whose vaulted ceilings and lofty proportions hark back to the *palazzo*'s 14th-century origins. Also ask them about their Tuscan hideaway, the **Villa Rosa di Boscorotondo** outside Panzano (p. 93).

Borgo SS. Apostoli 8 (between Via dei Tornabuoni and Via Por Santa Maria), 50123 Firenze. ℭ **055-239-6338.** Fax 055-239-8577. www.hoteltorreguelfa.com. 22 units. 155€–210€ ($202–$273) double; 190€–250€ ($247–$325) triple or junior suite. Rates include continental breakfast. Parking in nearby garage 30€ ($39). AE, MC, V. Bus: B, 6, 11, 36, or 37. **Amenities:** Concierge; tour desk; car-rental desk; courtesy car; limited room service; babysitting; laundry service; dry cleaning; Wi-Fi. *In room:* A/C, TV (in all but 6 1st-floor doubles), minibar, hair dryer.

5 South of Santa Maria Novella

MODERATE

Hotel Aprile   The Aprile fills a semirestored 15th-century palace on this busy hotel-laden street near the station. The corridors are hung with detached fresco fragments, notably ruined from centuries of exposure on the *palazzo*'s original facade. Portions of 16th- and 17th-century frescoes in much better shape grace many of the accommodations, and those on the ceiling of the breakfast room are beautifully intact (though in summer you can also breakfast in the garden out back). Aside from their antique touches, the simple guest rooms are nothing to write home about. The street noise gets through even the double glazing, so light sleepers will want to request a room off the road—besides, some of the back rooms have a breathtaking view of Santa Maria Novella. The frescoes and relative quiet of no. 16 make it an excellent choice. Historical footnote: Cavernous room no. 3 has had a bathroom attached to it since the 15th century, one of the first "rooms with bathroom" ever!

Via della Scala 6 (1½ blocks from the train station), 50123 Firenze. ℭ **055-216-237.** Fax 055-280-947. www.hotelaprile.it. 30 units. 270€ ($351) double; 290€ ($377) triple; 350€ ($455) junior suite. Rates include breakfast, and drop by about 50% in off season. AE, DC, MC, V. Parking 18€–26€ ($23–$34) in nearby garage. Bus: 1, 2, 12, 16, 17, 22, 29, or 30. **Amenities:** Concierge; tour desk; car-rental desk; babysitting; laundry service; same-day dry cleaning. *In room:* A/C (in all but 1 unit), TV, Wi-Fi, minibar, hair dryer.

Villa Azalee ⭐ *Finds*   The atmosphere of this 1870 villa on the historic center's edge, with its prizewinning flowers, soundproof rooms, and comfortable beds, makes you forget the eight lanes of traffic flowing a few dozen feet away along Florence's inner ring road. You'll find a sunroom in the main villa, tapestries on the walls, and a very friendly staff. The rooms are floral print–oriented—perfect for Laura Ashley buffs, but for others the pink taffeta and gauzy canopies might seem over-the-top. The old *scuderia* (stables) out back were reconstructed in a hybrid Italian-English style, and many of the rooms in it evoke a cozy Cotswalds cottage. The best accommodations are on the *scuderia*'s ground floor, with heavy beamed ceilings, and on the villa's first (upper) floor, with wood floors, sleigh beds, and Empire bathrooms. I'd give it another star if only it weren't so far from the action.

Viale Fratelli Rosselli 44 (at the end of Via della Scala, between the station and Cascine Park), 50123 Firenze. (✆) **055-214-242**. Fax 055-268-264. www.villa-azalee.it. 25 units. 90€ ($117) double; 173€ ($225) superior double; 100€ ($130) triple; 232€ ($302) superior triple. Rates include breakfast. AE, DC, MC, V. Parking 30€ ($39) in nearby garage. Bus: 1, 2, 9, 13, 16, 17, 26, 27, 29, 30, or 35. **Amenities:** Bike rental (3€/$3.90 a day); concierge; tour desk; car-rental desk; 24-hr. room service; laundry service; same-day dry cleaning. *In room:* A/C, TV, minibar, hair dryer.

6 Between Santa Maria Novella & Mercato Centrale

MODERATE

Hotel Mario's ⟨★★⟩ In a traditional Old Florence atmosphere, the Masieri and Benelli families run a first-rate ship. Your room might have a wrought-iron headboard and massive reproduction antique armoire, and look out onto a peaceful garden; the amenities include fresh flowers and fruit. The beamed ceilings in the common areas date from the 17th century, although the building became a hotel only in 1872. I'd award Mario's three stars if not for its location—it's a bit far from the Duomo nerve center. Hefty discounts during off-season months (as low as the lowest rates listed below) "de-splurge" this lovely choice.

Via Faenza 89 (1st floor; near Via Cennini), 50123 Firenze. (✆) **055-216-801**. Fax 055-212-039. www.hotelmarios.com. 16 units. 80€–165€ ($104–$215) double; 100€–210€ ($130–$273) triple. Rates include continental breakfast. AE, DC, MC, V. Valet parking 23€–28€ ($30–$36). Bus: 7, 10, 11, 12, 25, 31, 32, or 33. **Amenities:** Concierge; tour desk; limited room service (breakfast); babysitting; laundry service; dry cleaning; nonsmoking rooms. *In room:* A/C, TV, hair dryer, safe.

Hotel Nuova Italia ⟨★★⟩ ⟨Kids⟩ A Frommer's fairy tale: With her trusty Arthur Frommer's *Europe on $5 a Day* in hand, the fair Eileen left the kingdom of Canada on a journey to faraway Florence. At her hotel, Eileen met Luciano, her baggage boy in shining armor. They fell in love, got married, bought a castle (er, hotel) of their own— called the Nuova Italia—and their clients live happily ever after. . . . The staff here really puts itself out for guests, recommending restaurants, shops, day trips—they gave me tips the tourist office didn't know about. The rooms are board-rated two-star standard, medium to small, but the attention to detail makes the Nuova Italia stand out. Every room has a bathroom (with fuzzy towels), orthopedic mattress, and triple-paned windows (though some morning rumble from the San Lorenzo market street carts still gets through). It's also one of a handful of hotels in all Tuscany with mosquito screens in the windows. The family's love of art is manifested in framed posters and paintings, and Eileen is a great source about local exhibits.

Via Faenza 26 (off Via Nazionale), 50123 Firenze. ℭ 055-268-430 or 055-287-508. Fax 055-210-941. http://nuovaitalia.hotelinfirenze.com. 20 units. 125€ ($163) double; 145€ ($189) triple. Rates include continental breakfast. There are frequent discounts, so ask when booking. AE, DC, MC, V. Parking 25€ ($32) in nearby garage. Bus: 7, 10, 11, 12, 25, 31, 32, or 33. **Amenities:** Concierge; tour desk; car-rental desk; babysitting; laundry service; dry cleaning. *In room:* A/C, TV, hair dryer on request.

INEXPENSIVE

Albergo Azzi   Musicians Sandro and Valentino, the owners of this ex-*pensione* (also known as the Locanda degli Artisti/Artists' Inn), are creating here a haven for artists, artist *manqués,* and students. It exudes a relaxed bohemian feel—not all the doors hang straight and not all the bedspreads match, though strides are being made (and they've even recently discovered some old frescoes in rooms 3 and 4). You'll love the open terrace with a view where breakfast is served in warm weather, as well as the small library of art books and guidebooks so you can enjoy a deeper understanding of Florence's treasures.

Via Faenza 88r (1st floor), 50123 Firenze. ℭ/fax **055-213-806.** hotelazzi@hotmail. com. 16 units, 1 with shared bathroom. 70€–130€ ($91–$169) double with bathroom. Extra person 25€ ($33). Rates include breakfast. AE, DC, MC, V. Parking in nearby garage 16€ ($21). Bus: 7, 10, 11, 12, 25, 31, 32, or 33. **Amenities:** Concierge; tour desk. *In room:* Hair dryer on request, no phone.

Albergo Merlini ⍟ *Value*   Run by the Sicilian Gabriella family, this cozy third-floor walk-up boasts rooms appointed with wooden-carved antique headboards and furnishings (and a few modular pieces to fill in the gaps). It's one of only two hotels in all of Florence with mosquito screens. The optional breakfast is served on a sunny glassed-in terrace decorated in the 1950s with frescoes by talented American art students and overlooking a leafy large courtyard. Room nos. 1, 4 (with a balcony), and 6 through 8 all have views of the domes topping the Duomo and the Medici Chapels across the city's terra-cotta roofscape. A recent renovation tripled the number of private bathrooms and freshened up everything. This is a notch above your average board-rated one-star place, the best in a building full of tiny *pensioni.* Note that there's a 1am curfew.

Via Faenza 56 (3rd floor), 50123 Firenze. ℭ **055-212-848.** Fax 055-283-939. www.hotelmerlini.it. 10 units, 6 with private bathroom. 45€–65€ ($59–$85) double without bathroom; 50€–79€ ($65–$103) double with bathroom; 60€–90€

($78–$117) triple without bathroom; 80€–100€ ($104–$130) quad without bathroom. Breakfast 6€ ($7.80). MC, V. Bus: 7, 10, 11, 12, 25, 31, 32, or 33. **Amenities:** Concierge; tour desk; Internet connection in lobby. *In room:* Hair dryer on request, no phone.

Mia Cara/Archi Rossi Hostel *(Value)*   The only way you'll pay less than at the Mia Cara is at the Noto family's hostel on the ground floor. At the hotel you'll find double-paned windows, spacious no-frills rooms, renovated plumbing (no shower curtains), and attractive iron headboards. Now if they'd only up the wattage of the light fixtures. The rooms overlooking the small garden out back are more tranquil than those on the street side.

Angela, the English-speaking daughter, can be reached at the number below or at ℂ **055-290-804** for information on the downstairs **Archi Rossi Hostel** (www.hostelarchirossi.com), where units sleep four to six, without bathroom for 19€ ($25) per person, and with bathroom for 17€ to 19€ ($22–$25) depending on how many beds are in the room (there are also private, bathroomless singles in the hostel for 29€/$38 including breakfast, and family rooms sleeping three to five for 24€/$31 each including breakfast). The hotel is closed 11am to 2:30pm, with a 1am curfew. Both the hotel and the hostel have their own TV room and public phone. They are planning a renovation that will double the size of both hotel and hostel, and may turn the hotel into a moderate property, but just when this will happen is anybody's guess.

Via Faenza 58 (2nd floor), 50123 Firenze. ℂ **055-216-053.** Fax 055-230-2601. 22 units, 14 with private bathroom. 50€ ($65) double without bathroom; 60€ ($78) double with bathroom. Extra bed 35% more. Ask about off-season discounts. No breakfast offered in hotel (only in hostel). No credit cards. 4 parking spots; sometimes free, sometimes up to 8€ ($10). Bus: 7, 10, 11, 12, 25, 31, 32, or 33. **Amenities:** Concierge; tour desk; nonsmoking rooms. *In room:* No phone.

7 Near San Marco & Santissima Annunziata

VERY EXPENSIVE

Hotel Regency *✦✦*   The Regency, converted from two 19th-century mansions, is set on a wooded piazza at the edge of town that looks remarkably like a giant London residential square. The posh old England feel continues into the salon and bar lounge, furnished with worn antiques and darkly patterned carpets and wall fabrics. This decoration scheme dominates in the comfortable rooms as well, with a liberal use of mirrored wall panels in the smaller rooms (though none are tiny by any stretch). The marble-clad bathrooms feature heated towel racks, and the discreet service includes fresh fruit, sparkling wine, and candies left in your room and a complimentary *Herald Tribune* each morning.

Piazza Massimo d'Azeglio 3, 50121 Firenze. ✆ **055-245-247.** Fax 055-234-6735. www.regency-hotel.com. 35 units. 325€–430€ ($422–$559) classic double; 390€–490€ ($507–$537) deluxe double; 450€–600€ ($585–$780) junior suite. Rates include breakfast. AE, DC, MC, V. Valet parking 26€ ($34). Bus: 6, 31, or 32. **Amenities:** Justifiably famous Relais le Jardin restaurant; cozy bar; bike rental; concierge; tour desk; car-rental desk; 24-hr. room service; in-room massage; babysitting; laundry service; dry cleaning; nonsmoking rooms. *In room:* A/C, TV, minibar, hair dryer, safe.

EXPENSIVE

Hotel Loggiato dei Serviti ★★   The Loggiato is installed in the

building designed by Antonio da Sangallo the Elder in 1527 to mirror the Ospedale degli Innocenti across the piazza, forming part of one of Italy's most beautiful squares. As recently as the 1990s, this was a student *pensione,* but a renovation converted it into a board-rated three-star hotel and has restored the Renaissance aura. High vaulted ceilings in soft creams abound throughout and are particularly lovely supported by the gray columns of the bar/lounge. The wood or brick-tiled floors in the rooms are covered with rugs, and most of the beds have wood frames and fabric canopies for an antique feel. The rooms along the front can be a bit noisy in the evenings because traffic is routed through the edges of the piazza, but I usually reserve one anyway, just for the magical view.

Piazza Santissima Annunziata 3, 50122 Firenze. ✆ **055-289-592.** Fax 055-289-595. www.loggiatodeiservitihotel.it. 38 units. 205€ ($267) double; 266€ ($346) triple; 230€–380€ ($299–$494) suite. Rates include breakfast. AE, DC, MC, V. Parking 22€ ($29). Bus: 6, 31, or 32. **Amenities:** Concierge; tour desk; car-rental desk; limited room service; babysitting; laundry service; dry cleaning. *In room:* A/C, TV, minibar, hair dryer, safe.

MODERATE

Hotel Le Due Fontane   The only thing this place has over its

neighbor—the Hotel Loggiato dei Serviti (see above)—is that the rooms get a view of all three loggia-blessed sides of the harmonious piazza (in the Loggiato, you look out from one of them). Although installed in a 15th-century palace, both the accommodations and the public areas are done along clean lines of a nondescript modern style. Unless you get a room with the view of the piazza (along with unfortunate traffic noise), it might not be the most memorable place to stay.

Piazza Santissima Annunziata 14, 50122 Firenze. ✆ **055-210-185.** Fax 055-294-461. www.leduefontane.it. 57 units. 150€–180€ ($195–$235) double; 180€–230€ ($235–$269) triple. Rates include breakfast. AE, DC, MC, V. Parking 15€ ($20) in nearby garage. Bus: 6, 31, or 32. **Amenities:** Concierge; tour desk; car-rental desk;

courtesy car; limited room service; babysitting; laundry service; dry cleaning; non-smoking rooms. *In room:* A/C, TV, dataport, minibar, hair dryer.

Morandi alla Crocetta ★★ *(Finds)*   This subtly elegant *pensione* belongs to a different era, when travelers stayed in private homes filled with family heirlooms and well-kept antiques. Though the setting is indeed historic (it was a 1511 Dominican nuns' convent), many of the old-fashioned effects, such as the wood beam ceilings, 1500s artwork, and antique furnishings, are the result of a recent redecoration. It has all been done in good taste, however, and there are still plenty of echoes of the original structure, from exposed brick arches to one room's 16th-century fresco fragments.

Via Laura 50 (a block east of Piazza Santissima Annunziata), 50121 Firenze. © 055-234-4747. Fax 055-248-0954. www.hotelmorandi.it. 10 units. 177€ ($230) double; 220€ ($286) triple; 260€ ($338) quad. Breakfast 11€ ($14). AE, DC, MC, V. Parking 16€ ($21) in garage. Bus: 6, 31, or 32. **Amenities:** Concierge; tour desk; car-rental desk; limited room service; babysitting; laundry service; dry cleaning. *In room:* A/C, TV, dataport, minibar, hair dryer, safe.

8 Near Santa Croce
EXPENSIVE
Hotel Monna Lisa ★★   There's a certain old-world elegance to the richly decorated sitting and breakfast rooms and the gravel-strewn garden of this 14th-century *palazzo.* Among the potted plants and framed oils, the hotel has Giambologna's original rough competition piece for the *Rape of the Sabines,* along with many pieces by neoclassical sculptor Giovanni Duprè, whose family's descendants own the hotel. They try their best to keep the entire place looking like a private home, and many rooms have the original painted wood ceilings, as well as antique furniture and richly textured wallpaper or fabrics. In 2002, they restructured 15 additional rooms in another, recently acquired building bordering the courtyard and dubbed it "La Limonaia," with rooms overlooking the garden.

Borgo Pinti 27, 50121 Firenze. © 055-247-9751. Fax 055-247-9755. www.monna lisa.it. 45 units. 193€–370€ ($254–$421) double; 262€–460€ ($341–$598) triple; 438€–740€ ($569–$962) suite. Rates include breakfast. AE, DC, MC, V. Parking 11€ ($14) is very limited, so reserve ahead. Bus: B, 14, 23, or 71. **Amenities:** American bar; small gym; concierge; tour desk; car-rental desk; limited room service; babysitting; massage; laundry service and dry cleaning (not on weekends); high-speed Internet access. *In room:* A/C, TV, minibar, hair dryer, safe.

MODERATE
Hotel Ritz ★   One of the more intimate hotels along the Arno, the Ritz's walls are hung with reproductions of Italian art from the

Renaissance to Modigliani, and the reading room and bar are cozy. The room decor varies—some floors have wood or marble, others are carpeted. The mix-and-match furniture is mostly modern yet tasteful. Two rooms on the front have balconies to better enjoy the Arno view, and two on the back (nos. 37 and 38) have small private terraces, and there's a roof terrace with its view of Fiesole. The rather roomy bathrooms have been completely redone with new tile and heated towel racks.

Lungarno della Zecca Vecchia 24, 50122 Firenze. © 055-234-0650. Fax 055-240-863. www.florenceitaly.net/ritz. 30 units. 110€–180€ ($143–$234) double; 150€–230€ ($195–$299) triple; 170€–280€ ($221–$364) quad; 170€–330€ ($221–$429) family suite. Rates include breakfast. AE, DC, MC, V. Valet parking in garage 25€ ($33). Bus: B, 13, 14, or 23. **Amenities:** Bar; concierge; tour desk; car-rental desk; 24-hr. room service (breakfast and bar). *In room:* A/C, TV, high-speed Internet access, dataport, minibar, hair dryer, safe.

9 In the Oltrarno

MODERATE

Hotel La Scaletta ✿ *Kids*   Three partners, Andrea, Paolo, and Fabrizi, took over this well-worn old shoe of a place in 2005, one of the only remaining *palazzi* on this block between the Pitti Palace and Ponte Vecchio. The inn's star is the flower-bedecked, sun-kissed terrace offering a 360-degree vista over the Boboli Gardens, the Oltrarno rooftops, and (beyond a sea of antennas) the monumental heart of Florence. Return visitors book months in advance for the homey rooms that have tiny bathrooms and old tiled floors. Street-side accommodations have double-paned windows that really do block the noise, and the worn, dark wood lacquer furniture is pleasantly unassuming.

Via Guicciardini 13 (2nd floor; near Piazza de Pitti), 50125 Firenze. © 055-283-028. Fax 055-289-562. www.lascaletta.it. 13 units. 140€ ($182) double; 160€ ($208) triple; 180€ ($234) quad. Rates include continental breakfast. Ask about off-season discounts. AE, MC, V. Nearby parking 10€–28€ ($13–$36). Bus: D, 11, 36, or 37. **Amenities:** Concierge; tour desk; limited room service (breakfast); babysitting; laundry service; dry cleaning; computer w/Internet access. *In room:* A/C, TV, hair dryer on request.

Pensione Sorelle Bandini ✿ *Value*   This *pensione* occupies a landmark Renaissance *palazzo* on one of the city's great squares. You can live like the nobles of yore in rooms with 4.6m (15-ft.) ceilings, whose 3m (10-ft.) windows and oversize antique furniture are proportionately appropriate. Room no. 9 sleeps five people and offers a Duomo view from its bathroom window; room B is a double with a fantastic cityscape out the window. On closer inspection, you'll see that the resident cats have left their mark on common-area sofas, and everything seems a bit ramshackle and musty. But that seems to be the point. The highlight is the monumental roofed veranda where Mimmo, the English-speaking manager, oversees breakfast and encourages brown-bag lunches and the chance to relax and drink in the views. Franco Zeffirelli used the *pensione* for some scenes in *Tea with Mussolini*. Quite frankly, their fame as a "typical old-fashioned" *pensione* has allowed them to charge more than what might be expected from a budget hotel.

Piazza Santo Spirito 9, 50125 Firenze. © **055-215-308.** Fax 055-282-761. pensione bandini@tiscali.it. 13 units, 5 with private bathroom. 112€ ($146) double without bathroom; 135€ ($176) double with bathroom. Single rate on request. Extra person 35% more. Rates include continental breakfast (subtract about 9€/$12 per person if you opt out). No credit cards. Bus: D, 11, 36, or 37. **Amenities:** Concierge; tour desk; car-rental desk; limited room service (breakfast); babysitting. *In room:* No phone.

Silla ⭐   On a shaded riverside piazza, this 15th-century *palazzo*'s second-floor patio terrace is one of the city's nicest breakfast settings (in winter, there's a breakfast salon with chandeliers and oil paintings). The Silla's most recent renovation was in 2005, when they restored 10 rooms. Many overlook the Arno and, when winter strips the leaves off the front trees, the spire of Santa Croce on the opposite bank. Every room is unique; some have beamed ceilings and parquet floors, others floral wallpaper and stylish furnishings. The attention to detail and friendly skilled staff should make this hotel better known; word-of-mouth keeps it regularly full in pricey Florence despite its refreshing low profile.

Via dei Renai 5 (on Piazza Demidoff, east of Ponte delle Grazie), 50125 Firenze. © **055-234-2888.** Fax 055-234-1437. www.hotelsilla.it. 35 units. 170€ ($221) double; 220€ ($286) triple. Rates include buffet breakfast. Ask about off-season discounts. AE, DC, MC, V. Parking in hotel garage 16€ ($21). Often closes late Nov to late Dec. Bus: C, D, 12, 13, or 23. **Amenities:** Concierge; tour desk; limited room service; nonsmoking rooms. *In room:* A/C, TV, Wi-Fi, minibar, hair dryer, safe.

10 In the Hills

VERY EXPENSIVE

Villa San Michele ⭐   The peaceful ambience of this place recalls its origins in the 15th century as a Franciscan monastery, but I doubt the good friars had a heated outdoor pool or Jacuzzis in their cells. The facade was reputedly designed by Michelangelo, and everything is in shades of creamy yellow with soft gray *pietra serena* accents. The antique furnishings are the epitome of simple elegance, and some rooms come with canopied beds and linen sheets; others are fitted with wrought-iron headboards and antiques. The regular rooms are all in the main buildings, with modern junior suites dug into the hillside behind it, snuggled into the slopes between the terraces that host the swimming pool and formal gardens. (Several junior suites enjoy their own minigardens or terraces.) They've converted the tiny hillside chapel into a cozy honeymoon suite with sweeping views, and the *limonaia* (where potted citrus trees once spent the frosty winters) into a grander suite. The monks never had it this good.

Via Doccia 4 (just below Fiesole off Via Fra' Giovanni Angelico), 50014 Fiesole (FI). ℂ 800/237-1236 in the U.S., or 055-567-8200 in Italy. Fax 055-567-8250. www.villa sanmichele.com. 41 units. 840€–1,030€ ($1,092–$1,339) double; 1,300€–1,660€ ($1,690–$2,158) junior suite; 2,110€–3,000€ ($2,743–$3,900) suite. Rates include breakfast. For half-pension add 79€ ($103), full pension add 150€ ($195). AE, DC, MC, V. Closed mid-Nov to mid-Mar. Free parking. Bus: 7 (ask driver for stop, because you get off before Fiesole); free hourly shuttle bus from Piazza del Duomo. **Amenities:** Restaurant; piano bar; heated outdoor pool; bike rental; concierge; tour desk; car-rental desk; shuttle bus to/from town center; small business center and secretarial services; 24-hr. room service; massage; babysitting; laundry service; same-day dry cleaning; extensive park w/nature trails and jogging track. *In room:* A/C, TV/VCR (front desk has free movies), dataport, minibar, hair dryer.

EXPENSIVE

Torre di Bellosguardo ✹✹✹ *Finds*   This castle was built around a 13th-century tower sprouting from a hillside on the southern edge of Florence. Spend a few days here above the city heat and noise, lazing by the pool, hiking the olive orchard roads, or sitting on a garden bench to enjoy the intimate close-range vista of the city. Don't come expecting another climate-controlled and carpeted bastion of luxury. With its echoing halls, airy loggias, and imposing stone staircases, the Bellosguardo feels just a few flickering torches shy of the Middle Ages—exactly its attraction. It's packed with antiques, and the beds from various eras are particularly gorgeous. Some rooms have intricately carved wood ceilings, others sport fading frescoes, and many have views, including a 360-degree panorama in the romantic tower suite. It's a 15-minute stroll down the hill to Alla Vecchia Bettola (reviewed on p. 91).

Via Roti Michelozzi 2, 50124 Florence. ℂ 055-229-8145. Fax 055-229-008. www. torrebellosguardo.com. 16 units. 290€ ($377) double; 340€ ($442) suite. Breakfast 20€ ($26). AE, DC, MC, V. Free parking. Bus: 12 or 13 to Piazza Tasso (then taxi up hill). **Amenities:** Outdoor pool (June–Sept); small indoor pool; small exercise room; Jacuzzi; sauna; concierge; tour desk; car-rental desk; 24-hr. room service (bar, no food); massage; babysitting; laundry service; same-day dry cleaning. *In room:* A/C in 3 suites, dataport, hair dryer.

MODERATE

Pensione Benescistà ✶✶ *(Kids)*   This comfortable and quiet family-run *pensione* in a rambling 14th-century villa gets you the same view and escape from the city as the Villa San Michele above it at one-fifth the price. Antiques abound, and the elegantly cluttered salons are straight out of an E. M. Forster novel. Many accommodations have big old chests of drawers, and some open onto the pretty little garden. The dining room has a view of Florence, but in summer take in the vista by breakfasting on the terrace. Although service from the staff is occasionally offhanded, the owners are friendly and truly consider you a guest in their home. They also expect to be treated as hosts and require you to stay for most dinners. (I recommend trading one dinner for a lunch to try the nearby Trattoria le Cave di Maiano; see p. 94.)

Via Benedetto da Maiano 4 (just below Fiesole off the main road), 50014 Fiesole (FI). ✆/fax **055-59-163**. 40 units. 176€ ($229) double. Rates include required half pension (full pension available for small supplement). No credit cards. Free parking. Bus: 7 to Villa San Michele, then backtrack onto side road following signs. **Amenities:** Restaurant; limited room service (breakfast only). *In room:* Hair dryer.

11 Hostels & Camping

Both hostels below are immensely popular, especially in summer. If you aren't able to write or fax to reserve a space—months ahead, if possible—show up when they open. Also check out the private hostel Archi Rossi, listed earlier (along with its sister hotel Mia Cara) under the Santa Maria Novella/Mercato Centrale neighborhood.

Campeggio Michelangelo   Back in the good old days of yore, when my family was wont to do "Europe on $5 a Day in an Ugly Orange VW Camper-van," this was our Florentine parking spot *de choix*. Here we could sleep with a select 1,000 of our fellow campers and have almost the same vista that the tour buses get up above on Piazzale Michelangiolo. (Sadly, a stand of trees blocks the Duomo.) Of course, you're packed in like sardines on this small plateau with very little shade (in Aug, arrive early to fight for a spot along the tree-lined fringe), but you get a bar, a minimart, a Laundromat, and that killer view.

Viale Michelangelo 80 (about ²/₃ of the way up to Piazzale Michelangiolo), 50125 Firenze. ✆ **055-681-1977**. Fax 055-689-348. www.ecvacanze.it/ing/michelangelo_home.asp. Open camping (sleeps 1,000). 9.50€ ($12) per person, plus 6€ ($7.80) per tent and 5.50€ ($7.15) per car; rented tents 11€ ($14). No credit cards. Closed Nov–1 week before Easter. Bus: 12 or 13. **Amenities:** Bar; coin-op laundry.

Instituto Gould *Kids*   These are the best hostel-like accommodations in Florence, without a curfew, lockout period, or shower charge but with brand-new furnishings in plain but immaculate rooms—like a college dorm that's never seen a frat party. It's technically not a hostel, though it looks and operates like one. Most rooms are doubles or triples (all with buttonless phones to receive calls), and unless you opt for a five-person room, you're unlikely to bunk with strangers. The institute's real work is caring for orphans, and the proceeds from your room fee go to help needy children. Reception is open Monday through Friday from 9am to 1pm and 3 to 7pm, Saturday from 9am to 1pm. (You can stay over and prepay to check out during the weekend, but you can't check in.)

Via dei Serragli 49 (near Santo Spirito), 50124 Firenze. ✆ **055-212-576.** Fax 055-280-274. gould.reception@dada.it. 33 units, 27 with private bathroom. Depending on how many beds are in room (1–4): 17€–28€ ($22–$36) per person without bathroom; 20€–34€ ($26–$44) per person with bathroom. No credit cards. Bus: 11, 36, or 37. *In room:* No phone.

Villa Camerata (Ostello della Gioventù)   Florence's IYH hostel is a way outside the city center but worth it for the budget-minded. The name doesn't lie—this really is a countryside villa, with an outdoor loggia, and it's surrounded by greenery. The rooms are typically bland but livable. You can check in after the lockout (9am–2pm in summer, 9am–3pm in winter), and curfew is midnight. They also offer 180 tent sites for cool camping amid their wooded acres for 5€ ($6.50) per person plus 4€ to 6€ ($5.20–$7.80) per tent.

Viale Augusto Righi 2–4 (3.5km/2 miles northwest of the city center; above Campo di Marte), 50137 Firenze. ✆ **055-601-451.** Fax 055-610-300. www.ostellionline. org. 322 beds. 16€ ($21) per person; 17€ ($22) per person in 3-person family room; 19€ ($25) per person in 2-person family room. Lunch/dinner 8€ ($11). Rates include breakfast. No credit cards. Bus: 17B (30-min. ride; 17A and 17C take longer). **Amenities:** Coin-op laundry. *In room:* No phone.

12 Long-Term Stays

One of the most reputable specialists in Florence is **Florence and Abroad,** Via San Zanobi 58 (✆ **055-487-004;** fax 055-490-143; www.florenceandabroad.com), which matches different tastes and budgets to a wide range of apartments starting at about 500€ ($650) per week—though note that they take a commission (10% for 1-month rentals, less for longer periods). Another reputable agency for short-term apartment and house rentals (weekly and monthly) is **Windows on Tuscany,** Via Tornabuoni 2 or Via della Vigna Vecchia 2 (© **055-268-510;** fax 055-238-1524; www.windowson tuscany.com). To go it alone, check out the classifieds in the biweekly *Le Pulce,* available at newsstands.

Palazzo Antellesi   Many people passing through Piazza Santa Croce notice Giovanni di Ser Giovanni's 1620 graffiti frescoes on the overhanging facade of no. 21, but few realize they can actually stay there. The 16th-century *palazzo* is owned by Signora Piccolomini, who rents out truly extravagant apartments to anyone who has dreamed of lying in bed next to a roaring fire under a 17th-century frescoed ceiling (the Granduca, which sleeps two or three) or sipping tea in a living room surrounded by *trompe l'oeil* Roman ruins with a 16th-century wood ceiling above (the Donatello, which sleeps six to eight). Even in the more standard rooms the furnishings are tasteful, with wicker, wood, or wrought-iron bed frames; potted plants; and the occasional 18th-century inlaid wood dresser to go with the plush couches and chairs. The fourth-floor rooms (the Miravista and Mimi) are booked seasons in advance by those who love the private penthouse terraces overlooking the lively piazza. The kitchens are sizable and fully equipped. Author R. W. B. Lewis wrote extensively about the Antellesi in the final chapter of *The City of Florence.*

Piazza Santa Croce 21–22, 50122 Firenze. © **212/932-3480** in the U.S., or 055-244-456 in Italy. Fax 212/932-9039 in the U.S., or 055-234-5552 in Italy. www.palazzo antellesi.com. 13 apts, sleeping 2–6. 2,400€–5,200€ ($3,120–$6,760) per week. Heating included in some, but most utilities extra. No credit cards. Parking 16€ ($21) in garage. Bus: B, 13, 23, or 71. **Amenities:** Babysitting; nonsmoking rooms. *In room:* A/C, TV, VCR on request, dataport, kitchen, fridge, coffeemaker, hair dryer, safe.

4

Where to Dine in Florence

Florence is thick with restaurants, though many in the most touristy areas (around the Duomo and Piazza della Signoria) are low quality, high priced, or both. I'll point out the few that aren't. The highest concentrations of excellent *ristoranti* and *trattorie* are around Santa Croce and across the river in the Oltrarno. Bear in mind that menus at restaurants in Tuscany can change frequently: weekly, or even daily. Note, too, that reservations at the following restaurants are not required unless otherwise indicated.

1 Near the Duomo

MODERATE

Da Ganino FLORENTINE   The tiny family-run Ganino has long been a major destination for hungry tourists because it's across from the American Express office as well as halfway between the Duomo and the Uffizi. This has caused the place to jack its prices to eyebrow-raising levels but not sacrifice its friendly service and good food, from the big ol' chunk of *mortadella* that accompanies your bread basket through the tasty *ribollita* or *gnocchi al pomodoro* (ricotta-and-spinach gnocchi in tomato sauce) to the *filetto all'aceto basalmico* (veal filet cooked in balsamic vinegar) or *coniglio in umido* (rabbit with boiled potatoes on the side) that rounds out your meal.

Piazza de' Cimatori 4r (near the Casa di Dante). ℭ **055-214-125.** Reservations recommended. Primi 6€–12€ ($7.80–$16); secondi 10€–20€ ($13–$26). AE, DC, MC, V. Mon–Sat 12:30–3pm and 7:30–10pm. Closed Aug. Bus: 14.

Paoli TUSCAN   Paoli has one of the most *suggestivo* (oft-used Italian word for "evocative") settings in town, with tables under a 14th-century vaulted ceiling whose ribs and lunettes are covered with fading 18th-century frescoes. It's in the heart of the sightseeing zone, meaning the prices are as high as they can reasonably push them; very few Italians drop by, but the food is actually quite good. The *ravioli verdi alla casalinga* (spinach ravioli in tomato sauce) may not be inspiringly prepared, but it's freshly made and tasty. In mushroom season you can order *risotto ai funghi,* and year-round the scrumptious secondo *entrecôte di manzo arlecchino* (a thick steak in cognac-spiked cream sauce with peppercorns and sided with mashed potatoes).

Via dei Tavolini 12r. ℂ **055-216-215.** Reservations highly recommended. Primi 6€–12€ ($7.80–$16); secondi 14€–18€ ($18–$23); fixed-price menu with wine 20€ ($26). AE, MC, V. Wed–Mon noon–3pm and 7pm–midnight. Bus: A.

Ristorante Casa di Dante (da Pennello) ℛ TUSCAN/

ITALIAN   This is one of Florence's oldest restaurants, housed since the late 1400s in a *palazzo* that once belonged to Renaissance artist Albertinelli (Cellini, Pontormo, and Andrea del Sarto used to dine here). Its claim to fame is the antipasto table, groaning under the day's changing array of two dozen appetizers. Prices vary, but expect to spend 5€ to 8€ ($6.50–$11) for a good sampling. The best of the primi are under the handwritten *lo chef consiglia* (the chef recommends) and *pasta fresa* (handmade pasta) sections of the menu. They do a perfectly grilled pork chop and, if the antipasti and pasta have done you in, several light omelets for secondo.

Via Dante Alighieri 4r (between Via dei Calzaiuoli and Via del Proconsolo). ℂ **055-294-848.** Reservations suggested. Primi 5.50€–8€ ($7.15–$10); secondi 7.50€–13€ ($9.75–$17); *menù turistico* 20€ ($26) without wine. AE, DC, V. Tues–Sat noon–3pm and 7–10:30pm. Closed Aug.

INEXPENSIVE

Cantinetta del Verrazzano ℛ *Value* WINE BAR   Owned by the

Castello di Verrazzano, one of Chianti's best-known wine-producing estates, this wood-paneled *cantinetta* with a full-service bar/*pasticceria* and seating area helped spawn a revival of stylish wine bars as convenient spots for fast-food breaks. It promises a delicious self-service lunch or snack of focaccia, plain or studded with peas, rosemary, onions, or olives; buy it hot by the slice or as *farcite* (sandwiches filled with prosciutto, arugula, cheese, or tuna). Try a glass of their full-bodied chianti to make this the perfect respite. Platters of Tuscan cold cuts and aged cheeses are also available.

Via dei Tavolini 18–20r (off Via dei Calzaiuoli). ℂ **055-268-590.** Focaccia sandwiches 1€–3€ ($1.30–$3.90); glass of wine 1.30€–8€ ($1.70–$10). AE, DC, MC, V. Mon–Sat 8am–9pm.

I Fratellini ℛ SANDWICHES & WINE   Just off the busiest

tourist thoroughfare lies one of the last of a dying breed: a *fiaschitteria* (derived from the word for a flask of wine). It's the proverbial hole in the wall, a doorway about 1.5m (5 ft.) deep with rows of wine bottles against the back wall and Armando and Michele Perrino busy behind the counter, fixing sandwiches and pouring glasses of

Where to Dine in Florence

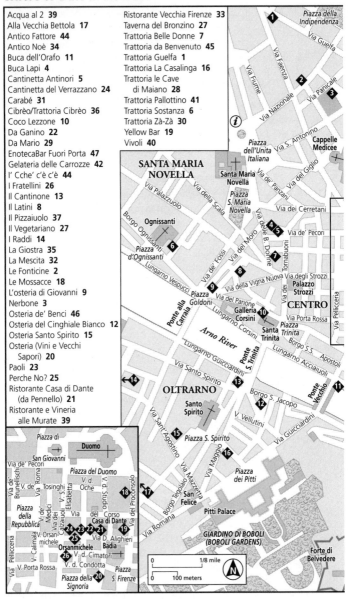

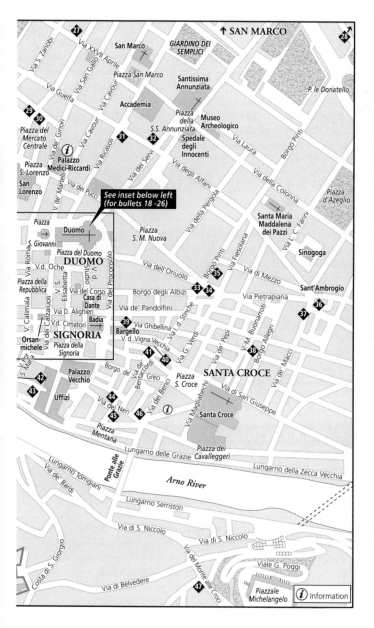

vino. You stand, munching and sipping, on the cobblestones of the narrow street surrounded by Florentines on their lunch break and a few bemused tourists. The *cinghiale piccante con caprino* (spicy raw wild boar sausage with creamy goat cheese) is excellent. Otherwise, choose your poison from among 30 stuffing combinations—the menu posted on the doorjamb has English translations—and accompany it with either a basic *rosso* (red) wine or point to any bottle to try *un bicchiere* (a glass).

Via dei Cimatori 38r (2 blocks from Piazza della Signoria, off Via Calzaiuoli). ✆ **055-239-6096.** Sandwiches 2.10€–2.60€ ($2.75–$3.40); wine from 1.30€ ($1.70) a glass. No credit cards. Daily 8am–8:30pm (July–Aug closed Sat–Sun). Closed Aug 10–20 and 2 weeks in Mar. Bus: 14, 23, or 71.

Le Mossacce FLORENTINE   Delicious, cheap, abundant, fast home cooking: This tiny *osteria,* filled with lunching businesspeople, farmers in from the hills, locals who've been coming since 1942, and a few knowledgeable tourists, is authentic to the bone. The waiters hate breaking out the printed menu, preferring to rattle off a list of such Florentine faves as *ribollita, spaghetti alle vongole, crespelle,* and *lasagne al forno.* Unlike in many cheap joints catering to locals, the secondi are pretty good. You could try the *spezzatino* (goulashy beef stew) or a well-cooked, and for once cheap, *bistecca alla fiorentina,* but I put my money on the excellent *involtini* (thin slices of beef wrapped tightly around a bread stuffing and artichoke hearts, then cooked to juiciness in tomato sauce).

Via del Proconsolo 55r (a block south of the Duomo). ✆ **055-294-361.** Reservations suggested for dinner. Primi 4.20€–4.70€ ($5.45–$6.10); secondi 4.70€–14€ ($6.10–$18). AE, MC, V. Mon–Fri noon–2:30pm and 7–9:30pm.

2 Near Piazza Della Signoria

MODERATE

Acqua al 2 ITALIAN   Under a barrel-vaulted ceiling and dim sconce lights, diners sit elbow-to-elbow at tightly packed tables to sample this innovative restaurant's *assaggi* (tastings) courses. Acqua al 2 is proud of its almost cultish status, attained through the success of its *assaggio di primi,* which offers you a sampling of five flavorful pastas or *risotti.* If you order the *assaggio* for two, you both just may have room left over for a grilled portobello mushroom "steak," one of the many veal dishes, or something more cross-cultural, such as *couscous d'agnello* (lamb). They also offer *assaggi* of salads, cheese, and desserts. Tour companies have started bringing in tourists by the busload on occasion, but the crowd still remains a good mix of locals and travelers.

Via della Vigna Vecchia 40r (at Via dell'Acqua). ✆ **055-284-170**. www.acquaal2.
com. Reservations required. Primi 7€–8€ ($9.10–$10); secondi 7€–17€ ($9.10–
$22); *assaggio* 8€ ($10) for pasta, 5€ ($6.50) for dessert. AE, MC, V. Daily
7:30pm–1am. Closed 1 week in Aug. Bus: 14.

Antico Fattore FLORENTINE   The Antico Fattore was a literary watering hole early in the 20th century and remained a favorite
trattoria just a few steps from the city's premier museum until the
1993 Uffizi bomb went off a few feet from its doors. The interior has
been rebuilt and the restaurant reopened, but many claim it isn't
what it used to be. You can't deny that they still make a tantalizing
lombatina all'aceto basalmico (one of the thickest and most tender
veal chops you'll ever find, cooked in balsamic vinegar). You can pre-
cede this with a *ribollita* (more souplike than usual) or a traditional
Tuscan *pappardelle sul cinghiale* (wide noodles in wild boar sauce). If
veal's not your style, try their specialty *piccione* (grilled pigeon).

Via Lambertesca 1–3r (between the Uffizi and the Ponte Vecchio). ✆ **055-288-975**.
www.mega.it/antico.fattore. Reservations recommended. Primi 5.70€–8€ ($7.40–
$10); secondi 8.80€–14€ ($11–$18). AE, DC, MC, V. Mon–Sat 12:15–3pm and
7:15–10:30pm. Bus: 23 or 71.

Buca dell'Orafo FLORENTINE   A *buca* is a cellar joint with half
a dozen crowded tables serving good, basic Florentine fare. A few
locals come here every night, but Orafo's years in the guidebooks
have made Americans its primary customers—Florentines aren't
willing to give this place up yet, though, and you can still find it
packed with locals if you reserve a late seating. However, the heavy
tourism has jacked its prices above what you'd expect for peasant
food. That food is still very well prepared, however, and the location
can't be beat. You can't go wrong with the thick *ribollita*. If it's on the
menu, go for the *paglia e fieno alla boscaiola* (a "hay and straw" mix
of both egg and spinach fettuccine in mushroom-meat sauce).
Orafo's best secondo is *arista di maiale con patate* (roast pork loin with
potatoes), while candied stewed pears round out the meal nicely.

Volta dei Girolami 28r (under the arched alley left of the Ponte Vecchio). ✆ **055-
213-619**. Reservations strongly recommended (or show up early for a spot at a
communal table). Primi 6€–10€ ($7.80–$13); secondi 11€–20€ ($14–$26). No
credit cards. Tues–Sat noon–2:30pm and 7:30–9:45pm. Bus: 23 or 71.

I' Cche' c'è c'è ✶✶ TUSCAN   The name is a dialect variant on
"What you see is what you get." What you see is a room with modern art prints and shelves of ancient wine bottles on the walls. What
you get is good Tuscan cooking from Gino Noci, who trained in
the kitchens of London before returning here to open a traditional

(Kids) Family-Friendly Restaurants

It'd be a sin for any family to visit Florence and not drop by one of its premier gelato parlors to sample the rich Italian equivalent of ice cream. See "A Big Step above Ice Cream: Florentine Gelato," on p. 82. If the kids mutiny and absolutely insist on a hamburger, try the slightly American-style restaurant **Yellow Bar**, Via del Proconsolo 39r (© **055-211-766**). But be warned: The hamburger doesn't come with a bun (a form of blasphemy among certain preteens). The Yellow Bar also serves pizzas.

Il Cantinone (p. 91)   This noisy old wine cellar is popular with students and has long tables where your family can spread out and bite deep into *crostone* (slabs of peasant bread piled with your choice of toppings, like a pizza).

Il Latini (p. 84)   This can be one of the most fun places to eat in Florence—you're seated at communal tables under battalions of hanging ham hocks and treated to huge portions of the Tuscan bounty. No food is too fancy or oddball to offend suspicious young palates, the waiters love to ham it up, and a festive atmosphere prevails.

Il Pizzaiuolo (p. 88)   When the kids are hankering for a pizza, turn it into a learning experience by visiting the

trattoria. There's no telling what he might come up with for an appetizer: The most recent treat was a *sformatino* with pears, while for a first dish, the scrumptious *ravioli rosée* (in creamy tomato sauce) faces serious competition from the *tagliatelle all boscaiola* (same sauce with giant slices of forest mushrooms added). *Topini* are Florentine potato gnocchi, topped with spinach and cream or four cheeses. Follow up with the grilled salmon or one of their specialties, *stracotto al chianti* (beef stuffed with celery and carrot and smothered in a chianti gravy served with fried polenta and an artichoke heart).

Via Magalotti 11r (just east of Via Proconsolo, 2 blocks from the Arno). © **055-216-589**. Reservations recommended (not available for set-price menu at lunch). Primi 4€–9€ ($5.20–$12); secondi 9€–15€ ($12–$20); fixed-price menu without wine 11€ ($14). AE, MC, V. Tues–Sun 12:30–2:30pm and 7:30–10:30pm. Closed a week in late Jan and a week in Aug.

Osteria (Vini e Vecchi Sapori)   FLORENTINE/TUSCAN

Within a block of the Palazzo Vecchio is an authentic *osteria* with a

only pizza parlor in Florence run by a Neapolitan. The "plain pizza," called *pizza margherita* in Italy, was invented about 100 years ago by a Naples chef who wanted to honor Italy's Queen Margherita with a pizza done in patriotic colors. For the newly created Kingdom of Italy, this meant red (tomatoes), white (mozzarella), and green (fresh basil)—the colors of the new flag. If someone at the table prefers pepperoni, order the pizza with *salame piccante* (hot salami slices); *pepperoni* in Italian are bell peppers.

Ristorante Vecchia Firenze (p. 89) This roomy restaurant has a long menu sure to satisfy everyone's appetites. They love children here, and this was my family's favorite Florentine restaurant when I was 12. The owner, tickled pink one night that a little American boy was struggling to speak Italian, took over our meal, had all the wonders of Tuscan cuisine brought to our table, introduced us to grappa, and kept me up well past my bedtime.

Trattoria da Benvenuto (p. 78) The dishes here are simple and homey—they're sure to have a plate of plain spaghetti and tomato sauce to please finicky youngsters.

wood-beamed ceiling, brick floor, the end of a giant chianti barrel embedded in one wall, and a handwritten menu that starts *Oggi C'è* ("Today we got . . ."). As the sign proudly proclaims, this one-room joint is devoted to "wine and old flavors," which means lunch could consist of anything from a rib-sticking stewlike *ribollita* and a *frittata rustica* (a darkly fried omelet thick with potatoes and vegetables) to an excellent crostini assortment and *scamorza e speck al forno* (smoked mozzarella melted with ham in a bowl, to scoop out and slather onto bread). The paunchy owner will continue pacing back and forth, passing around the lone menu, and welcoming people in off the street until he feels like going home.

Via dei Magazzini 3r (the alley off Piazza della Signoria to the left of the Palazzo Vecchio). © 055-293-045. Primi 6€–8€ ($7.80–$10); secondi 10€–14€ ($13–$18). No credit cards. Tues–Sat 9am–11pm; Sun noon–2:30pm. Bus: 14, 23, or 71.

Trattoria da Benvenuto ✦ *Kids* TUSCAN HOME COOKING
This is a no-nonsense place, simple and good; and Gabriella is a no-
nonsense lady who'll get exasperated if you're not ready with your
order when she's ready to take it. Da Benvenuto's is basically a neighborhood hangout that somehow found its way into every guidebook
over the years. Yet it continues to serve adequate helpings of tasty
Florentine home cooking to travelers and locals seated together at
long tables in two brightly lit rooms. This is always my first stop on
any trip to Florence, where I usually order ravioli or *gnocchi* (potato-
dumpling pasta)—both served in tomato sauce—and follow with a
veal scaloppa alla Livornese or a *frittata* (an omelet filled at the whim
of Loriano, Gabriella's husband and cook).

Via Mosca 16r (at the corner of Via dei Neri; walk around the right of the Palazzo
Vecchio, under the arch, and it's in front of you after 4 short blocks). ℰ **055-214-
833.** Primi 4.50€–9.50€ ($5.85–$12); secondi 5.50€–15€ ($7.15–$20). AE, MC, V.
Mon–Tues and Thurs–Sat 12:30–3pm and 7–10:30pm. Bus: 23 or 71.

3 Near San Lorenzo & the Mercato Centrale
MODERATE
Da Mario ✦ *Value* FLORENTINE This is down-and-dirty Florentine lunchtime at its best, an *osteria* so basic that the little stools
don't have backs, and a communal spirit so entrenched that the wait-
resses will scold you if you try to take a table all to yourself. Since
1953, their stock in trade has been feeding market workers, and you
can watch the kitchen through the glass as they whip out a wipe-
board menu of simple dishes at lightning speed. Hearty primi
include *tortelli di patate al ragù* (ravioli stuffed with potato in ragù),
minestra di farro e riso (emmer-and-rice soup), and *penne al
pomodoro* (pasta quills in fresh tomato sauce). The secondi are basic
but good; try the *coniglio arrosto* (roast rabbit) or go straight for the
Fiorentina steak, often priced to be the best deal in town.

Via Rosina 2r (at the north corner of Piazza Mercato Centrale). ℰ **055-218-550.**
Reservations not accepted. Primi 3.10€–3.40€ ($4.05–$4.40); secondi 4€–11€
($5.20–$14). No credit cards. Mon–Sat noon–3:30pm. Closed Aug. Bus: 10, 12, 25,
31, 32, or 91.

Le Fonticine BOLOGNESE/TUSCAN Modern paintings carpet
the walls like a jigsaw puzzle here. Over the past 4 decades, Silvano
Bruci has taken as much care in selecting the works of art as his
Bologna-born wife, Gianna, has in teaching these Tuscans the finer
points of Emilia-Romagna cuisine. Even with the art, this place still
feels a bit like a country trattoria. Ask to sit *in dietro* (in the back), if
only so you get to walk past the open kitchen and grill. There are so

many good primi it's hard to choose, but you can't go wrong with lasagne, *penne al prosciutto punte d'asparagi* (stubby pasta with diced prosciutto and wild asparagus tips), or *ribollita*. Afterward, set to work on the *cinghiale maremmana cipolline* (stewed wild boar with caramelized baby onions) or *baccalà alla livornese* (salt cod covered in tomatoes and served with chickpeas in oil).

Via Nazionale 79r (at Via dell'Ariento, north end of the Mercato San Lorenzo). ℂ 055-282-106. www.lefonticine.com. Reservations recommended. Primi 6€–12€ ($7.80–$16); secondi 8€–16€ ($11–$21). AE, DC, MC, V. Tues–Sat noon–2:30pm and 7–10pm. Closed July 25–Aug 25. Bus: 12, 25, 31, or 32.

Trattoria Zà-Zà ☜ TUSCAN CASALINGA (HOME COOK-ING)   This place serves a lot of the food-market workers from across the way, as well as so many foreigners with particular eating schedules that the owners have started serving meals all day long, 7 days a week—a true rarity in Florence. Ask to sit downstairs in the brick barrel vault of the old *cantina* if you want some privacy; if you want company (they make even the small wooden tables commu-nal), sit upstairs, where you can gaze at the dozens of photos of the restaurant's more (but mostly less) famous patrons. Securing outdoor seating, which spills over with customers, will require some patience at lunchtime. The *antipasto caldo alla Zà-Zà* has a bit of everything. If you don't want *ravioli strascicati* (in creamy ragù), brace yourself for a *tris di minestre* (three soups: *ribollita, pappa al pomodoro,* and *fagioli con farro*). *Bocconcini di vitella alla casalinga con fagioli all'uc-celletto* (veal nuggets with tomato-stewed beans) makes an excellent second course.

Piazza Mercato Centrale 26r. ℂ 055-215-411. www.trattoriazaza.it. Reservations recommended. Primi 5.30€–10€ ($6.90–$13); secondi 10€–18€ ($13–$23); *menù turistico* without wine 13€ ($17). AE, DC, MC, V. Daily 11am–11pm. Closed Aug. Bus: 10, 12, 25, 31, 32, or 91.

INEXPENSIVE

Nerbone ☜ 𝓜𝓸𝓶𝓮𝓷𝓽𝓼 FLORENTINE   Nerbone has been stuffing stall owners and market patrons with excellent Florentine *cucina povera* ("poor people's food") since the Mercato Centrale opened in 1874. You can try *trippa alla fiorentina, pappa al pomodoro,* or a plate piled with boiled potatoes and a single fat sausage. But the mainstay here is a *panino con bollito,* a boiled beef sandwich that's *bagnato* (dipped in the meat juices). Eat standing with the crowd of old men at the side counter, sipping glasses of wine or beer, or fight for one of the few tables against the wall.

In the Mercato Centrale, entrance on Via dell'Ariento, stand no. 292 (ground floor). 𝒞 055-219-949. All dishes 3.50€–7€ ($4.55–$9.10). No credit cards. Mon–Sat 7am–2pm. Bus: 10, 12, 25, 31, 32, or 91.

4 Near Piazza Santa Trínita

VERY EXPENSIVE

Cantinetta Antinori FLORENTINE/TUSCAN   The Antinori *marchesi* started their wine empire 26 generations ago, and, taking their cue from an ancient vintner tradition, installed a wine bar in their 15th-century *palazzo* 30 years ago. Most ingredients come fresh from the Antinori farms, as does all the fine wine. Start with the *fettucini all'anatra* (noodles in duck sauce) or the *ribollita*, and round out the meal with the *trippa alla fiorentina* or the mighty *gran pezzo* (thick slab of oven-roasted Chiana beef). If you choose this worthy splurge as a secondo, skip the first course and instead follow your steak with *formaggi misti,* which may include pecorino and mozzarella made fresh that morning. Their *cantucci* (Tuscan biscotti) come from Prato's premier producer.

Palazzo Antinori, Piazza Antinori 3 (at the top of Via Tornabuoni). 𝒞 **055-292-234.** www.antinori.it. Reservations strongly recommended. Primi 10€–16€ ($13–$21); secondi 14€–24€ ($18–$31). AE, DC, MC, V. Mon–Fri 12:30–3pm and 6:30–10:30pm. Closed Aug and Dec 24–Jan 6. Bus: 6, 11, 36, 37, or 68.

EXPENSIVE

Buca Lapi TUSCAN   The vaulted ceiling is carpeted with travel posters, the cuisine is carefully prepared, and the wine comes from the Antinori vineyards (this was once part of their cellars). This place's prices have risen astronomically, for no apparent reason, but the quality is still spot-on. An interesting start is the *filetto di cinghiale all'olio di rosmarino* (wild boar slices cured like prosciutto and served with rosemary-scented olive oil). One specialty is the *cannelloni gratinati alla Buca Lapi* (pasta canapés stuffed with ricotta and spinach served in a cream sauce of boar and mushrooms). A light secondo could be *coniglio disossato ripieno* (stuffed rabbit), or you can go all out on a masterful *bistecca chianina* (grilled steak, for two only). The desserts are homemade, including a firm and delicate *latte portugese* (a kind of crème caramel) and a richly dense chocolate torte.

Via del Trebbio, 1r (just off Piazza Antinori at the top of Via Tornabuoni). 𝒞 **055-213-768.** Reservations essential. Primi 10€–12€ ($13–$16); secondi 20€–25€ ($26–$33). AE, DC, MC, V. Tues–Sat 12:30–2:30pm; Mon–Sat 7:30–10:30pm. Bus: 6, 11, 14, 17, 22, 36, 37, or 68.

Coco Lezzone FLORENTINE   This tiny trattoria hidden in a tangle of alleys near the Arno consists of long communal tables in a couple of pocket-size rooms wrapped around a cubbyhole of a kitchen, whose chef, according to the restaurant's dialect name, is a bit off his rocker. The place is popular with local intellectuals, journalists, and the city soccer team. While enjoying your *ribollita* (known here as a "triumph of humility") or *rigatoni al sugo* (in a chunky ragù), look at where the yellow paint on the lower half of the wall gives way to white: That's how high the Arno flooded the joint in 1966. If you want a *bistecca alla fiorentina,* call ahead first. Friday is *baccalà* (salt cod) day, and every day their *involtini* (thin veal slice wrapped around vegetables) and *crocchette di filetto* (veal-and-basil meatloaf smothered in tomato sauce) are good.

Via del Parioncino 26r (at the corner of Via Purgatorio). (C) **055-287-178.** Reservations recommended. Primi 6.50€–13€ ($8.45–$17); secondi 9.50€–16€ ($12–$21). No credit cards. Mon and Wed–Sat noon–2:30pm and 7–10pm; Tues noon–2:30pm. Closed late July to Aug and Dec 23–Jan 7. Bus: C, 6, 11, 14, or 17.

L'osteria di Giovanni 𝕣𝕣 TUSCAN   Giovanni Latini comes from one of Florence's best-known culinary clans, whose homonymous eatery on Via del Palchetti is a household name in Florence. In the 1990s, Giovanni left Il Latini to start his own restaurant in the countryside and in 2004 made a triumphant return to his old neighborhood. He bought what was once known as Osteria No. 1 and started offering refined Tuscan cuisine at honest prices. His two half-American daughters—Caterina, the chef, and Chiara, the sommelier—practice their crafts while Giovanni attends to his guests. It is a sophisticated but social atmosphere, with well-dressed Italians and tourists sharing either the quiet front room or the more communal back room. For starters, try the *insalata tiepida di piccione con spinaci e nocciole* (pigeon with spinach and hazelnuts, dressed with raspberry vinaigrette) or the sautéed squid with asparagus and cherry tomatoes; and don't miss the *involtini di vitello con pecorino fresco, melanzane e funghi* (sliced veal wrapped around fresh pecorino, eggplant, and mushrooms). Even if you're on a diet, allow yourself just this once the pleasure of Caterina's *tortelli ripieni di radicchio e ricotta con melanzane ed olive* (radicchio-stuffed tortelli, with eggplant and olives). Chiara will recommend the perfect *digestif* to accompany your chocolate mousse.

Via del Moro 22 (near the Ponte alla Carraia). (C) **055-284-897.** www.osteriadi giovanni.com. Reservations recommended. Primi 9€–12€ ($12–$16); secondi 15€–25€ ($20–$33). AE, DC, MC, V. Tues–Sat noon–2:30pm and 7–11pm; Mon 7pm–12:30am. Closed Aug. Bus: A, C, 6, 9, 11, 36, 37, or 68.

A Big Step above Ice Cream: Florentine Gelato

Gelato is a Florentine institution—a creamy, sweet, flavorful food item on a different level entirely from what Americans call "ice cream." Making fine Florentine gelato is a craft taken seriously by all except the tourist-pandering spots around major attractions that serve air-fluffed bland "vanilla" and nuclear-waste pistachio so artificially green it glows.

Here's how to order gelato: First, pay at the register for the size of *coppa* (cup) or *cono* (cone) you want, then take the receipt up to the counter to select your flavors (unlike in America, they'll let you stuff multiple flavors into even the tiniest cup). Prices are fairly standardized, with the smallest serving at around 1.50€ ($1.95) or 2€ ($2.60) and prices going up in .50€ (65¢) increments for six or eight sizes. *Warning:* Gelato is denser than ice cream and richer than it looks. There's also a concoction called *semifreddo,* somewhere on the far side of the mousse family, in which standard Italian desserts, such as tiramisù, are creamed with milk and then partially frozen.

There are plenty of quality *gelaterie* besides the ones listed here. A few rules of thumb: Look for a sign that proudly proclaims *PRODUZIONE PROPRIA* (homemade) and take a look at the gelato itself—no matter what kind you plan to order, make sure the banana is gray, the egg-based *crema* (egg-based "vanilla," though there's nary a vanilla bean in it) yellow, and the pistachio a natural, pasty pale olive.

Of all the centrally located *gelaterie,* **Festival del Gelato,** Via del Corso 75r, just off Via dei Calzaiuoli ((✆ **055-239-4386**), is one of the few serious contenders to the premier Vivoli (see below), offering about 50 flavors along with pounding pop music and colorful neon. It's open Tuesday through Sunday: summer 8am to 1am and winter 11am to 1am.

Vivoli, Via Isole delle Stinche 7r, a block west of Piazza Santa Croce ((✆ **055-239-2334**), is still the city's institution. Exactly how renowned is this bright gelateria? Taped to the wall is a postcard bearing only "Vivoli, Europa" for the address, yet it was successfully delivered to this world capital of ice cream. It's open Tuesday through Sunday 9am to 1am (closed Aug and Jan to early Feb).

One of the major advantages of the always crowded **Gelateria delle Carrozze,** Piazza del Pesce 3–5r (℃ 055-23-96-810), is its location at the foot of the Ponte Vecchio—if you're coming off the bridge and about to head on to the Duomo, this gelateria is immediately off to your right on a small alley that forks off the main street. In summer, it's open daily 11am to 1am; in winter, hours are Thursday through Tuesday 11am to 8pm.

A block south of the Accademia (pick up a cone after you've gazed upon *David*'s glory) is what some local purists insist is Vivoli's only deserving contender to the throne as gelato king: **Carabé,** Via Ricasoli 60r (℃ **055-289-476**). It offers genuine homemade Sicilian gelato in the heart of Florence, with ingredients shipped in from Sicily by the hardworking Sicilian owners. Taste for yourself and see if Florentines can hope to ever surpass such scrumptiousness direct from the island that first brought the concept of ice cream to Europe. May 16 through September, it's open daily 10am to midnight; February 15 through May 15 and October through November 15, hours are Tuesday through Sunday 10am to 8pm.

In 1946, the first ice-cream parlor in the city's heart, **Perche No?** ⚡, Via dei Tavolini 19r, off Via del Calzaiuoli (℃ **055-239-8969**; bus: 14, 23, or 71), introduced a novelty: the glass display case filled with tubs of flavors that have become standard in ice-cream stores the world over. Wedged into an alley off Via dei Calzaiuoli between Piazza della Signoria and the Duomo, Perche No? has done an admirable job over the years of being many a harried tourist's first introduction to quality Florentine gelato. During World War II, when the American army reached Florence after the Nazi withdrawal, they had the power grid specially reconnected so that Perche No?'s gelato production—and G.I. consumption—could continue. Try their *ciocolato bianco* (white chocolate, studded with chunks of the main ingredient) or one of the *semifreddi*, a moussing process they helped invent. It's open Wednesday through Monday from 10am to midnight.

MODERATE

Il Latini *Kids Kids Kids* FLORENTINE   Narciso Latini opened this cheap locals' eatin' joint in 1950, though it now gets as many tourists as Florentines. Now in his mid-90s, Narciso still stops by to lend a hand. For dinner, arrive at 7:30pm to get in the crowd massed at the door, for even with a reservation you'll have to wait as they skillfully fit parties together at the communal tables. In fact, getting thrown together with strangers and sharing a common meal is part of the fun here. Under hundreds of hanging prosciutto ham hocks, the waiters try their hardest to keep a menu away from you and serve instead a filling, traditional set meal with bottomless wine. This usually kicks off with *ribollita* and *pappa al pomodoro* or *penne strascicate* (in a ragù mixed with cream). If everyone agrees on the *arrosto misto,* you can get a table-filling platter heaped high with assorted roast meats. Finish off with a round of *cantucci con vin santo* for everyone.

Via del Palchetti 6r (off Via della Vigna Nuova). ✆ **055-210-916.** Reservations strongly recommended. Primi 6€ ($7.80); secondi 8€–16€ ($10–$21); unofficial fixed-priced full meal with limitless wine 30€–35€ ($39–$46). AE, DC, MC, V. Tues–Sun 12:30–2:30pm and 7:30–10:30pm. Closed 15 days in Aug and Dec 24–Jan 6. Bus: C, 6, 11, 36, 37, or 68.

Trattoria Belle Donne TUSCAN   Tucked away on a narrow street (whose name refers to the women of the night who once worked this then-shady neighborhood) parallel to exclusive Via dei Tornabuoni, this packed-to-the-gills lunch spot (with no identifying sign) immediately drew the area's chic boutique owners and sales staff. It now tries to accommodate them and countless others in a rather brusque style—no lingering over lunch; dinner isn't as rushed. Tuscan cuisine gets reinterpreted and updated by the talented young chef, who placates the local palate without alienating it: Traditional dishes appear in the company of innovative alternatives such as cream of zucchini and chestnut soup or lemon-flavored chicken.

Via delle Belle Donne 16r (north off Via della Vigna Nuova). ✆ **055-238-2609.** Reservations not accepted. Primi 7€–11€ ($9–$14); secondi 9€–16€ ($12–$21). MC, V. Mon–Fri 12:30–2:30pm and 7:15–10:30pm. Closed most of Aug.

5 Near Santa Maria Novella

MODERATE

Trattoria Guelfa FLORENTINE/TUSCAN   Always crowded and always good, the Guelfa has lots of paintings hanging on its walls and a random trattoria decor—pendulous gourds, wine bottles, and an old oxen yoke rule over the tightly packed, noisy tables. The kitchen is very traditional, offering *spaghetti alla rustica* (in a cheesy, creamy tomato sauce) and *risotto ai quattro formaggi* (a gooey rice dish made with four cheeses) as proud primi. For a main course, you can go light with the *pinzimonio di verdure crude* (a selection of seasonally fresh raw veggies with oil to dip them in) or indulge your taste buds with the *petti di pollo alla Guelfa* (a chicken breast rolled around a stuffing of prosciutto, cheese, and truffled cream served with a side of olive oil–drenched oven-roasted potatoes).

Via Guelfa 103r (near the Fortezza, beyond Via Nazionale). ℭ **055-213-306.** Reservations strongly recommended. Primi 5€–8€ ($6.50–$10); secondi 6€–15€ ($7.80–$20); *menù turistico* with wine 9€ ($12). AE, MC, V. Thurs–Tues noon–2:30pm and 7–10:30pm. Bus: 4, 10, 13, 14, 23, 25, 28, 31, 32, 33, 67, or 71.

Trattoria Sostanza FLORENTINE   Sostanza is popularly called "Il Troia" (The Trough) because people have been lining up at the long communal tables since 1869 to enjoy huge amounts of some of the best traditional food in the city. The primi are very simple: pasta in sauce, *tortellini in brodo* (meat-stuffed pasta in chicken broth), and *zuppa alla paesana* (peasant soup *ribollita*). The secondi don't steer far from Florentine traditions either, with *trippa alla fiorentina* or their mighty specialty *petti di pollo al burro* (thick chicken breasts fried in butter). It's an extremely unassuming place, so laid-back you may not realize you're meant to be ordering when the waiter wanders over to chat. They also frown on anybody trying to cheat his or her own taste buds out of a full Tuscan meal.

Via Porcellana 25r (near the Borgo Ognissanti end). ℭ **055-212-691.** Reservations strongly recommended. Primi 7€–8€ ($9–$10); secondi 7€–18€ ($9.10–$23). No credit cards. Mon–Fri noon–2:15pm and 7:30–9:45pm. Closed Aug. Bus: A, C, 6, 9, 11, 36, 37, or 68.

6 Near San Marco & Santissima Annunziata
MODERATE
Il Vegetariano VEGETARIAN   Come early to one of Florence's only vegetarian restaurants and use your coat to save a spot at one of the communal wood tables before heading to the back to get your food. You pay at the start of the meal, after choosing from the daily selections penned on the wipe board, and take your dishes self-service style from the workers behind the counter. The menu changes constantly but includes such dishes as risotto with yellow squash and black cabbage; a soupy, spicy Tunisian-style couscous with vegetables; a quichelike *pizza rustica* of ricotta, olives, tomatoes, and mushrooms; or a plate with *farro* (emmer) and a hot salad of spinach, onions, sprouts, and bean-curd chunks sautéed in soy sauce. You can

mix and match your own salad, and they make a good chestnut flour cake stuffed with hazelnut cream for dessert.

Via delle Ruote 30r (off Via Santa Reparata near Piazza Indipendenza). © **055-475-030**. Reservations not accepted. Primi 5€–6€ ($6.50–$7.80); secondi 7.50€–8€ ($9.75–$10). No credit cards. Tues–Fri 12:30–2:30pm; Tues–Sun 7:30pm–midnight. Closed 2–3 weeks in Aug and Dec 24–Jan 2. Bus: 12, 91, or anything to San Marco.

La Mescita HOME COOKING/SANDWICHES This tiny *fiaschetteria* is immensely popular with local businesspeople and students from the nearby university. Lunch can be a crushing affair, and they have signs admonishing you to eat quickly to give others a chance to sit. You'll be eating with Italians, and it's not for the timid because you have to take charge yourself: securing a seat, collecting your own place setting, and getting someone's attention to give your order before going to sit down. They offer mainly sandwiches, though there are always a few simple meat and pasta dishes ready as well. *Melanzana* (eggplant) is overwhelmingly the side dish of choice, and you can look to the cardboard lists behind the counter to select your wine—the house wine is very good, and a quarter liter of it is cheaper than a can of soda.

Via degli Alfani 70r (near the corner of Via dei Servi). © **347-795-1604**. All sandwiches and dishes 4€–7€ ($5.20–$9.10). No credit cards. Mon–Sat 11am–4pm. Closed Aug. Bus: 6, 31, or 32.

Taverna del Bronzino TUSCAN The 1580 house where Santi di Tito spent the last years of his life painting is now inhabited by polite, efficient, and very accommodating waiters who will show you to a table in the vaulted-ceiling dining room or on the arbor-shaded patio. Among the delectable antipasti are *salmone Scozzese selvatica* (wild Scottish salmon) and *petto d'oca affumicato e carciofi* (thin slices of smoked goose breast on a bed of sliced artichokes drowned in olive oil). The *risotto agli asparagi* is a bit light on the asparagus but still very creamy and tasty. You can also try the excellent *ravioli alla Senese* (ricotta and spinach–stuffed pasta in creamy tomato sauce) or *tagliolini ai pesci* (noodles with fish). To stick with the sea you can order *branzino* (sea bass simmered in white wine) next or select the *paillard di vitella all'ortolana* (a grilled veal steak wrapped around cooked vegetables).

Via delle Ruote 27r (between Piazza Indipendenza and San Marco). © **055-495-220**. Reservations strongly recommended. Primi 12€–15€ ($16–$20); secondi 21€–25€ ($27–$33). AE, DC, MC, V. Mon–Sat 12:30–2:30pm and 7:30–10:30pm. Closed 3 weeks in Aug. Bus: 12, 91, or anything to San Marco.

7 Near Santa Croce
VERY EXPENSIVE

Cibrèo ✦ TUSCAN There's no pasta and no grilled meat—can this be Tuscany? Rest assured that while Benedetta Vitale and Fabio Picchi's culinary creations are a bit out of the ordinary, most are based on antique recipes. Cibrèo actually has a split personality; this is a review not of the trattoria branch (p. 90), but of the fan-cooled main restaurant room, full of intellectual babble, where the elegance is in the substance of the food and the service, not in surface appearances. Waiters pull up a chair to explain the list of daily specials, and those garlands of hot peppers hanging in the kitchen window are a hint at the cook's favorite spice. All the food is spectacular, and dishes change regularly, but if they're available try the yellow pepper soup drizzled with olive oil, the soufflé of potatoes and ricotta spiced and served with pecorino shavings and ragù, or the roasted duck stuffed with minced beef, raisins, and pinoli.

Via Andrea del Verrocchio 8r (at the San Ambrogio Market, off Via de' Macchi). ℂ 055-234-1100. Reservations required. Primi 18€ ($23); secondi 34€ ($44). AE, DC, MC, V. Tues–Sat 12:30–2:30pm and 7:30–11:15pm. Closed July 26–Sept 6. Bus: B or 14.

Ristorante e Vineria alle Murate CUCINA CREATIVA/ TUSCAN Soft illumination, soft jazz, and soft pastels rule in this trendy spot owned by Chef Umberto Montano. Alle Murate was one of the first places in the city to experiment with nouvelle cuisine. It tries, however, to balance *cucina creativa* with traditional Tuscan techniques and dishes. You could start with *zuppa di fagioli e gamberi* (soup of creamed white beans with shrimp) or the lasagne. The best fish dish is sea bass on a bed of fried potatoes topped with diced tomatoes; and, for a main course, you could go in for the *anatra disossata alle erbete e scorze di arancia* (duck à l'orange). The *brasato di Chiana* (steak) in Brunello wine, however, was disappointing. For these prices, the portions could be larger and the presentation better, but the food is good and the antipasti, *contorni* (side dishes), aperitifs, and dessert wines are included in the price of your meal. The *vineria* half—really just a small room off the main one—offers an abbreviated menu at abbreviated prices.

Via Ghibellina 52r (near Borgo Allegri). ℂ 055-240-618. www.caffeitaliano.it. Reservations strongly recommended (specify *vineria* or *ristorante*). Primi 18€ ($23); secondi with side dish 22€–24€ ($29–$31); *menù degustazione* without wine 52€–60€ ($68–$78). AE, DC, MC, V. Tues–Sun 7:30–11pm. Bus: 14.

EXPENSIVE

Antico Noè SANDWICHES/WINE   A *fiaschitteria* with superior sandwiches masquerading as a regular bar, the Antico Noè is popular with students and shopkeepers for its well-stuffed panini and cheap glasses of quaffable wine—perfect for a light lunch on the go. The place is rather hidden, but you'll know you've found it when you see a small crowd gathered around a door in the shade of a covered alley—though, I should warn you, the alley and adjacent tiny piazza have of late begun hosting a small community of vagrants and bums. You can order your sandwich from the list, invent your own, or (better yet) let them invent one for you. The sit-down *osteria* next door serves simple Tuscan dishes.

Volta di San Piero 6r (the arched alley off Piazza San Pier Maggiore). ℭ **055-234-0838**. Sandwiches 2.50€–5€ ($3.25–$6.50); wine .75€–2€ ($1–$2.60) per glass; primi and secondi 7€–15€ ($9.10–$20). No credit cards. Mon–Sat 8am–midnight (often open Sun, too). Bus: B, 14, 23, or 71.

La Giostra ✿✿✿ TUSCAN   The chef/owner is Dimitri d'Asburgo Lorena, a Habsburg prince (with some local Medici blood for good measure), who opened this restaurant merely to indulge his love of cooking. They start you off with a complimentary flute of *spumanti* before you plunge into the tasty *crostini misti* and exquisite primi. Among my favorites are *tortelloni alla Mugellana* (handmade potato-stuffed pasta in ragù), *gnocchetti alla Lord Reinolds* (potato dumplings in a sauce of stilton and Port), homemade *tagliatelle* with tiny wild asparagus spears, and ravioli stuffed with brie in a sauce with thinly sliced, lightly fried artichokes. For an encore, try the *nodino di vitella ai tartufi bianchi* (veal slathered in eggy white-truffle sauce with fresh truffle grated on top) or the lighter *spianata alle erbe aromatiche di Maremma* (a huge platter of spiced beef pounded flat and piled with a salad of rosemary sprigs, sage, and other herbs). Don't leave without sampling the sinfully rich Viennese Sachertorte, made from an old Habsburg family recipe. This place has become (justifiably) popular, and even with a reservation there's often a short wait—laudably, they don't rush anybody to empty up tables—but it's worth it.

Borgo Pinti 10r (off Piazza Salvemini). ℭ **055-241-341**. www.ristorantelagiostra. com. Reservations recommended. Primi 10€–14€ ($13–$18); secondi 14€–21€ ($18–$27). AE, DC, MC, V. Daily noon–2:30pm and 7pm–midnight. Bus: A, B, C, 6, 14, 23, 31, 32, or 71.

MODERATE

Il Pizzaiuolo ✿ *Kids* NEAPOLITAN/PIZZA   Despite their considerable skill in the kitchen, Florentines just can't make a decent pizza. It takes a Neapolitan to do that, so business has been booming ever since Naples-born Carmine opened this pizzeria. Even with a reservation, you'll probably have to wait for a spot at a long, crowded, and noisy marble table. Save the pizza for a main dish; start instead with a Neapolitan first course such as *fusilli c'a ricotta* (homemade pasta spirals in creamy tomato-and-ricotta sauce). Of the pizzas, you can't go wrong with a classic *margherita* (mozzarella, tomatoes, and fresh basil), or spice up your evening with a *pizza diavola,* topped with hot salami and olives.

Via de' Macci 113r (at the corner of Via Pietrapiana). (*C*) **055-241-171.** Reservations required for dinner. Pizza 4.50€–10€ ($5.85–$13); primi 6.50€–13€ ($8.45–$17); secondi 7.50€–13€ ($9.75–$17). No credit cards. Mon–Sat 12:30–3pm and 7:30pm–midnight. Closed Aug. Bus: B or 14.

Osteria de' Benci INVENTIVE TUSCAN   This popular trattoria serves enormous portions (especially of secondi) on beautiful hand-painted ceramics under high ceiling vaults echoing with the conversation of Florentine trendoids. The menu changes monthly, but you can always be assured of excellent *salumi*—they come from Falorni, the famed butcher of the Chianti. The *eliche del profeta* are fusiloni tossed with ricotta, olive oil, oregano, and fresh tomatoes sprinkled with *parmigiano.* The unique *spaghetti dell'ubriacone* is bright crimson spaghetti that takes its color from being cooked in red wine, sauced with garlic, pepperoncini, and parsley sautéed in olive oil. And the *cibrèo delle regine* is a traditional rich Florentine dish of chopped chicken livers and gizzards served on toast.

Via de' Benci 13r (at the corner of Via de' Neri). (*C*) **055-234-4923.** Reservations highly recommended. Primi 6€–9€ ($7.80–$12); secondi 5€–16€ ($6.50–$21). AE, DC, MC, V. Mon–Sat 1–2:45pm and 7:45–10:45pm. Bus: B, 23, or 71.

Ristorante Vecchia Firenze ✿ *Kids* FLORENTINE/TUSCAN   It's set in a 15th-century *palazzo,* so avoid sitting in the boring front room in favor of the more intimate back rooms or the rowdier stone-lined *cantina* downstairs full of Florentine students. The *zuppa pavese* is a good vegetable soup, but try the *penne Vecchia Firenze* (pasta quills in a subtle creamy mushroom sauce with tomatoes). By all means order the *bistecca alla fiorentina,* but if your appetite runs more to *coniglio alla griglia* (grilled rabbit) or *branzino alla griglia* (grilled sea bass), you won't be disappointed.

Borgo degli Albizi 76–78r. (*C*) **055-234-0361.** Primi 5€–7€ ($6.50–$9.10); secondi 7€–10€ ($9.10–$13); pizza 5€–7€ ($6.50–$9.10); fixed-price menus without wine 13€–15€ ($17–$20). AE, DC, MC, V. Tues–Sun 11am–3pm and 7–10pm. Bus: 14, 23, or 71.

Trattoria Cibrèo FLORENTINE   This is the casual trattoria of celebrated chef-owner Fabio Picchi; its limited menu comes from the same creative kitchen that put on the map his premier and more than twice as expensive *ristorante* next door. The trattoria moved from its back alley location to the main street in 1999, and this higher visibility has only made the lines longer. Picchi takes his inspiration from traditional Tuscan recipes, and the first thing you'll note is the absence of pasta. After you taste the velvety *passata di peperoni gialli* (yellow bell-pepper soup), you won't care much. The stuffed roast rabbit demands the same admiration. My only complaint: They rush you through your meal in an un-Italian fashion in order to free up tables. Enjoy your after-dinner espresso at the Caffè Cibrèo across the way.

Via de' Macci 122r. ✆ **055-234-1100.** Primi 6€ ($7.80); secondi 13€ ($17). AE, DC, MC, V. Tues–Sat 1–2:30pm and 7–11:15pm. Closed July 26–Sept 6. Bus: B or 14.

Trattoria Pallottino FLORENTINE   One long room with a few long tables on the cobblestone floor and a second room on the side are all there is to this local cafeteria-like setting, and don't expect anything too fancy on the menu, either. The cook makes a mean *bruschetta al pomodoro* (toasted bread topped with tomatoes over which you are invited to drizzle the olive oil liberally). For a first course, look no farther than the *spaghetti alla fiaccheraia,* with a tomato sauce mildly spiked with hot peppers. You might follow it with the *peposo* (beef stew loaded with black pepper). Skip dessert and pop next door for a Vivoli gelato (see the box, "A Big Step above Ice Cream: Florentine Gelato," on p. 82).

Via Isola delle Stinche 1r. ✆ **055-289-573.** Reservations required for dinner. Primi 5€–8€ ($6.50–$10); secondi 7€–14€ ($9.10–$18). AE, DC, MC, V. Tues–Sun 12:30–2:30pm and 7:30–10:30pm. Closed Aug 5–21.

8 In the Oltrarno

EXPENSIVE

Osteria Santo Spirito *(Overrated)* NOUVELLE TUSCAN   It's hard to miss this hip place right on the square—funk and dance music pounds from the speakers and the tables are packed—but the staff might not notice you. Now bordering on becoming a tourist trap, the wait can be extraordinarily long here (I recently waited a full 2 hrs. before anything arrived at the table), but the food is interesting at least. You can start with a salad such as *pollo pinoli e uvetta con dressing* (chicken, pine nut, and raisin), or for pasta try *orecchiette Santo Spirito* (pasta in spicy tomato sauce with ricotta) or *gnocchi di patate gratinati* (oven-baked gnocchi swimming in a bubbling hot mix of soft cheeses flavored with truffle). Afterward, fill up on *filetto di manzo à tartufo* (beef filet with truffles) or the *coscie d'anatre con la panna* (very meaty roasted duck in cream sauce with carrots and bacon).

Piazza Santo Spirito 16r. (C) **055-238-2383.** Reservations recommended. Primi 6€–14€ ($7.80–$18); secondi 12€–25€ ($16–$33). AE, DC, MC, V. Daily 12:45–2:30pm and 8pm–midnight. Bus: B, 11, 36, 37, or 68.

MODERATE

Alla Vecchia Bettola FLORENTINE   Founded by the owners of Nerbone in the Mercato Centrale (see review on p. 79), this simple room right on the piazza may not look it, but it's one of the city's premier restaurants in town for ultratraditional Florentine food. It fills up very early with food-loving Florentines, who choose from an always-changing menu that may include *penne alla Bettola* in spicy cream tomato sauce, rigatoni dressed with crushed olives, or *riso sulle testicciole d'agnello* (a "local's" rice dish cooked in a halved sheep's head). Secondi range from *anatra ripiena tartufata* (stuffed duck in truffle sauce) to the superlative *carpaccio con rucola*—pounded disks of beef piled high with arugula and tissue-thin slices of pecorino cheese. As far as wine goes, you simply pay for however much you finish of the light and tangy house wine on the table.

Viale Vasco Pratolini 3/7 (on Piazza Tasso). (C) **055-224-158.** Reservations required. Primi 6€–7€ ($7.80–$9.10); secondi 8€–12€ ($10–$16). No credit cards. Tues–Sat noon–2:30pm and 7:30–10:30pm. Closed 3 weeks in Aug, Dec 23–Jan 2, and Easter. Bus: 12 or 13.

Il Cantinone 𝔉 *(Kids)* TUSCAN   With tourists and large groups of locals all seated at long tables under the low arc of a brick ceiling, the convivial noise can sometimes get a bit overwhelming. But the feeling of having walked into a party is part of the charm of this place. The specialty is *crostini,* slabs of peasant bread that act as vehicles for toppings such as prosciutto, tomatoes, mozzarella, and sausage. You and your companion get an antipasto, two primi (usually pasta dishes), and a secondo, which might be a tender and tasty wild boar stew. With each course you get a different wine, building from something like a light Orvieto *secco* through a well-chosen chianti to a brawny Brunello for the meat dish. The *ribollito* is great, but is usually only served in winter, when black cabbage is in season.

Via Santo Spirito 6r (off Piazza Santa Trinita). (C) **055-218-898** or 055-225-955 www.ilcantinonedifirenze.it. Primi and *crostoni* 5.50€–8€ ($7.15–$10); secondi 6€–20€ ($7.80–$26). AE, MC, V. Tues–Sun 12:30–2:30pm and 7:30–10:30pm. Bus: D, 8, 11, 36, or 37.

I Raddi ⭐ TUSCAN   Luccio's trattoria, hidden in the heart of the Oltrarno, is a true find—excellent cooking at reasonable prices, which is unusual now in Florence. The beamed ceiling and Tuscan standbys on the menu ground it in tradition, while the young staff and light touch in the kitchen lend a fresh bohemian air. The specialty is *tagliolini ardiglione* (with sausage and aromatic herbs), but they also make a mean *crespelle alla fiorentina* (pasta crepes layered with cheese). They do a fine *cibrèo*, a tasty *peposo alla fornacina con spinaci* (beef baked in wine with lots of pepperoncini and served with spinach), and a spicy *fagioli all'uccelleto con salsiccia.*

Via Ardiglione 47r (off Via dei Serragli, near Piazza delle Carmine). ℂ **055-211-072.** Reservations recommended. Primi 7€ ($9.10); secondi 10€–15€ ($13–$20). AE, MC, V. Mon–Sat noon–3pm and 7–11pm. Closed 10 days in Feb and a week in mid-Aug. Bus: D, 11, 36, 37, or 68.

Osteria del Cinghiale Bianco TUSCAN   Massimo Masselli will sooner turn people away at the door than rush you though your meal. The place does a good repeat business of locals (including cooks from other restaurants) and tourists alike who come for the delicious *taglierini* (wide noodles) with pesto or the famous *strozzapreti* ("priest-chokers" made of the spinach-and-ricotta mix normally found inside ravioli, served with melted butter). You can't go wrong ordering anything made of the restaurant's namesake *cinghiale* (wild boar)—from the cold boar slices as an appetizer to *cinghiale alla maremmana con polenta* (wild boar stew, cozying up to creamy, firm polenta) as a main course. Set in the base of a 12th-century tower, this place milks its medieval look with exposed stone, odd iron implements hanging everywhere, and lights hidden in suspended cauldrons or the pigeonholed walls. Note that dishes with truffles might raise the maximum prices listed below by about 5€ ($6.50).

Borgo Sant' Jacopo 43r. ℂ **055-215-706.** www.cinghialebianco.it. Reservations required on weekends. Primi 5€–10€ ($6.50–$13); secondi 9.50€–16€ ($12–$21). MC, V. Thurs–Tues 6:30–10:30pm (Sat–Sun also noon–3pm). Closed July 10–Aug 1. Bus: D, 8, 11, 36, or 37.

INEXPENSIVE

EnotecaBar Fuori Porta CROSTONI/ENOTECA   You can dine out on the sidewalk in nice weather, or sit on the benches at tiny wooden tables inside to taste the excellent pizzalike crostini here. Start with the *pappa al pomodoro* or gnocchi with broccoli rabe and sausage. The *crostoni* are divided by cheese—mozzarella, sharp pecorino, creamy goat-cheese *caprino*—along with a list of the toppings to accompany them. My favorite is *caprino con prosciutto arrosto e pomodori secchi* (with goat cheese, roasted prosciutto, and

Cook like a True Tuscan

Take a walk down Via dei Velluti in the Oltrarno, peek into the furniture restoration studios, watch the artisans practicing their ancient craft, and soon you'll stumble upon another studio devoted to a time-honored art: cooking. For 25€ ($33) per person, **"In Tavola,"** Via dei Velluti 18/20r (© **055-217-672;** www.intavola.org), will get you started on your Tuscan culinary quest by showing you how to prepare such staples as *crostini, zuppa di faro,* and *cantucci,* while you work your way through a complimentary bottle of chianti.

In Tavola has taken to the city what *agriturismi* have been doing for a few years now in the countryside, especially in Chianti. Another good beginner's course is offered by the **Villa Rosa di Boscorotondo,** Via S. Leonino 59, Pannzano Greve in Chianti (© **055-852-577;** www.resortvilla rosa.it), near Radda-in-Chianti. For 90€ ($117) per person, Vincenzo Regoli shows you the ins and outs of bruschetta, *panzanella, spezzatino del Chianti* and tiramisù.

At the high-end of the spectrum are programs offered by **Villa San Michele,** Via Doccia 4, Fiesole (© **055-567-8200;** www.villasanmichele.com). These are weeklong seminars with famous chefs, incorporated in a package deal with the luxury villa: a 5-night stay and cooking class runs about 3,200€ ($4,160) per person.

For a full-immersion course in a place that raises its own meat and vegetables, check out **La Petraia,** 53017 Radda-in-Chianti (© **0577-738-582;** www.lapetraia.com), where award-winning chef Susan McKenna Grant will help you make an elegant Tuscan dish with whatever vegetables and herbs are in season. The price is 150€ ($195) for visitors, 100€ ($130) for guests of the *agriturismo.*

Most farm resorts and luxury hotels throughout Tuscany and Umbria are affiliated with some sort of cooking class these days—be sure to inquire at the front desk.

sun-dried tomatoes). The wine is a key part of the meal; the list draws from the more interesting vineyards in Tuscany and beyond. This place is a bit out-of-the-way but worth the trip.

Via del Monte alle Croci 10r (near San Niccolò, through the gate at Via San Miniato). ℂ 055-234-2483. www.fuoriporta.it. Sandwiches and appetizers 2€–7€ ($2.60–$9.10). AE, MC, V. Mon–Sat 12:30–3:30pm and 7pm–1am. Bus: C, D, 12, 13, or 23.

Trattoria La Casalinga FLORENTINE   Their recent expansion sadly removed the last wisps of Renaissance aura from La Casalinga, replacing it with a crowded, almost cafeteria-like feeling—but the home cooking of its name is still some of the most genuine in town. The *ribollita* is thick, the *ravioli al sugo di coniglio* (in a rabbit sauce) rich, and the *pasta della nonna* (short, hollow pasta in a sauce of tomatoes, sausage, and onions) excellent. Don't expect anything fancy in the secondi department, either—just solid favorites such as *bollito misto* (a mix of boiled meats with green sauce), *trippa alla fiorentina,* and *galletto ruspante al forno* (half a young oven-baked chicken). The starving artists and local artisans have been all but driven out by the tourist hordes, but if you want to stuff yourself on huge portions of Oltrarno workmen's food, this is the place to come.

Via Michelozzi 9r (between Via Maggio and Piazza Santo Spirito). ℂ 055-267-9243. Primi 3.50€–4€ ($4.55–$5.20); secondi 5€–10€ ($6.50–$13). AE, DC, MC, V. Mon–Sat noon–2:30pm and 7–10pm. Bus: D, 8, 11, 36, or 37.

9 In the Hills
MODERATE
Trattoria le Cave di Maiano ⓕ TUSCAN   This converted farmhouse is the countryside restaurant of choice for Florentines wishing to escape the city heat on a summer Sunday afternoon. You can enjoy warm-weather lunches on the tree-shaded stone terrace with a bucolic view. In cooler weather, you can dine inside several large rustic rooms with haphazard paintings scattered on the walls. The *antipasto caldo* of varied *crostini* and fried polenta is a good way to kick off a meal, followed by a *misto della casa* (for two only) that gives you a sampling of primi. This may include *penne strascicate* (stubby pasta in cream sauce and tomato ragù) or *riso allo spezzacamino* (rice with beans and black cabbage). The best secondo is the *pollastro al mattone* (chicken roasted under a brick with pepper) or the *lombatina di vitello alla griglia* (grilled veal chop).

Via Cave di Maiano 16 (in Maiano, halfway between Florence and Fiesole east of the main road). ℂ 055-59-133. Reservations required. Primi 7€–10€ ($9.10–$13); secondi 10€–15€ ($13–$20). AE, DC, MC, V. Daily 12:30–3:30pm and 7:30pm–midnight. Bus: 7 (get off at Villa San Michele, then turn around and take the road branching to the left of the winding one your bus just took; continue on about ¾ mile up this side road, past the Pensione Benecistà); a taxi is a better idea.

5

Exploring Florence

Florence is the Renaissance city—home to Michelangelo's *David,* Botticelli's *Birth of Venus,* and Raphael's Madonnas. It's where Fra' Angelico painted delicate *Annunciations* in bright primary colors and Giotto frescoed monks wailing over the *Death of St. Francis.* The city is so dense in art, history, and culture that even a short visit can wear out the best of us. Take a hint from that great pragmatist Mark Twain, who, after acknowledging the genius of Michelangelo, said "I do not want Michelangelo for breakfast—for luncheon—for dinner—for tea—for supper—for between meals. I like a change occasionally."

Don't necessarily pass up the Uffizi or take a rain check on *David* and the Accademia, but do take the time to enjoy the simple pleasures of Florence—wander the medieval streets in Dante's old neighborhood, sip a cappuccino on Piazza della Signoria and people-watch, haggle for a leather jacket at the street market around San Lorenzo, or immerse yourself in the greenery of the Boboli Gardens.

1 On Piazza Del Duomo

The cathedral square is filled with tourists and caricature artists during the day, strolling crowds in the early evening, and knots of students strumming guitars on the Duomo's steps at night. Though it's always crowded, the piazza's vivacity and the glittering facades of the cathedral and the baptistery doors keep it an eternal Florentine sight.

At the corner of the busy pedestrian main drag, Via Calzaiuoli, sits the pretty little **Loggia del Bigallo** (1351–58). Inside is a small museum of 14th-century works, which is unfortunately almost always closed. Call © **055-215-440** if you're interested in trying to make an appointment to get in to see the 1342 *Madonna della Misericordia* by the school of Bernardo Daddi, which features the earliest known cityscape view of Florence.

Note that just south of the Duomo, hidden in the tangle of medieval streets toward Piazza della Signoria, is a 14th-century Florentine house restored and converted into the **Casa di Dante** (© **055-219-416**), a small museum chronicling the life and times of the great

What to See & Do in Florence

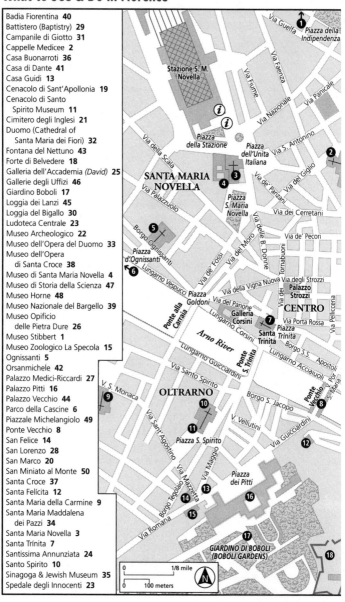

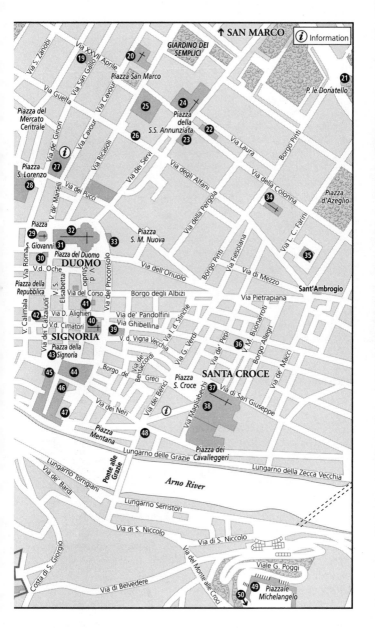

> ### *Tips* The Best Times to Sightsee
>
> **Museums Open on Mondays:** Palazzo Vecchio, Museo Bar-
> dini, Museo di Firenze Com'Era, Museo di Santa Maria
> Novella, Casa Buonarroti, Casa di Dante, Opera di Santa
> Croce, Museo dell'Opera del Duomo, Campanile di Giotto,
> Duomo's cupola, Opificio Pietre Dure, Museo Stibbert,
> Instituto e Museo di Storia di Scienza, Palazzo Medici-Ric-
> cardi, Museo Horne, Cappella Brancacci, Synagogue,
> Spedale degli Innocenti, Roman Amphitheater, and Museo
> Archeologico (Fiesole).
>
> **Sights Open During Il Riposo (1–4pm):** Uffizi, Accademia,
> Palazzo Vecchio, Duomo and its cupola, Museo dell'Opera
> del Duomo, Campanile di Giotto, Baptistery, Palazzo Vec-
> chio, Santa Croce, Galleria Palatina (Pitti Palace), Forte di
> Belvedere and Boboli Gardens, Cappella Brancacci, Roman
> Amphitheater, and Museo Archeologico (Fiesole).

poet. But, this isn't likely the poet's actual house. The entrance is up the side alley of Via Santa Margherita, and it's open Monday and Wednesday through Saturday from 10am to 6pm (to 4pm in winter) and Sunday from 10am to 2pm. Admission has nearly tripled to a ludicrous 6.50€ ($8.45), so only die-hard fans should bother.

Duomo (Cathedral of Santa Maria dei Fiori) ☆☆   For cen-
turies, people have commented that Florence's cathedral is turned inside out, its exterior boasting Brunelleschi's famous dome, Giotto's bell tower, and a festive cladding of white, green, and pink marble, but its interior left spare, almost barren.

By the late 13th century, Florence was feeling peevish: Its archri-
vals Siena and Pisa sported huge new Duomos filled with art, while it was saddled with the tiny 5th- or 6th-century Santa Reparata as a cathedral. So, in 1296, the city hired Arnolfo di Cambio to design a new Duomo, and he began raising the facade and the first few bays before his death in 1302. Work continued under the auspices of the Wool Guild and architects Giotto di Bondone (who concentrated on the bell tower) and Francesco Talenti (who finished up to the drum of the dome and in the process greatly enlarged Arnolfo's original plan). The facade we see today is a neo-Gothic composite designed by Emilio de Fabris and built from 1871 to 1887. (For its story, see the Museo dell'Opera del Duomo, below.)

The Duomo's most distinctive feature is its enormous **dome** ✷✷✷, which dominates the skyline and is a symbol of Florence itself. The raising of this dome, the largest in the world in its time, was no mean architectural feat, tackled admirably by Filippo Brunelleschi between 1420 and 1436 (see "A Man & His Dome," below). You can climb up between the two shells of the cupola for one of the classic panoramas across the city. At the base of the dome, just above the drum, Baccio d'Agnolo began adding a balcony in 1507. One of the eight sides was finished by 1515, when someone asked Michelangelo—whose artistic opinion was by this time taken as cardinal law—what he thought of it. The master reportedly scoffed, "It looks like a cricket cage." Work was immediately halted, and to this day the other seven sides remain rough brick.

The Duomo was actually built around **Santa Reparata** so it could remain in business during construction. For more than 70 years, Florentines entered their old church through the free-standing facade of the new one, but in 1370 the original was torn down when the bulk of the Duomo—except the dome—was finished. Ever the fiscal conservatives, Florentines started clamoring to see some art as soon as the new facade's front door was completed in the early 1300s—to be sure their investment would be more beautiful than rival cathedrals. Gaddo Gaddi was commissioned to mosaic an *Enthronement of Mary* in the lunette above the inside of the main door, and the people were satisfied. The stained-glass windows set in the facade were designed by Lorenzo Ghiberti, and Paolo Uccello, a painter obsessed by the newly developed perspective, frescoed the huge *hora italica* clock with its four heads of Prophets in 1443.

At a right-aisle pier are steps leading down to the excavations of the old Santa Reparata. In 1972, a tomb slab inscribed with the name Filippo Brunelleschi was discovered there (visible through a gate). Unless you're interested in the remains of some ancient Roman houses and parts of the paleo-Christian mosaics from Santa Reparata's floor, the 3€ ($3.90) admission isn't worth it.

Against the left-aisle wall are the only frescoes besides the dome in the Duomo. The earlier one to the right is the greenish *Memorial to Sir John Hawkwood* ✷ (1436), an English *condottiere* (mercenary commander), whose name the Florentines mangled to Giovanni Acuto when they hired him to rough up their enemies. Before he died, or so the story goes, the mercenary asked that a bronze statue of him riding his charger be raised in his honor. Florence solemnly promised to do so; but, in typical tightwad style, after Hawkwood's death, the city hired the master of perspective and illusion, Paolo

Uccello, to paint an equestrian monument instead—much cheaper than casting a statue in bronze. Andrea del Castagno copied this painting-as-equestrian-statue idea 20 years later when he frescoed a *Memorial to Niccolò da Tolentino* next to Uccello's work. Near the end of the left aisle is Domenico di Michelino's *Dante Explaining the Divine Comedy* (1465).

In the back left corner of the sanctuary is the **New Sacristy.** Lorenzo de' Medici was attending Mass in the Duomo one April day in 1478 with his brother Giuliano when they were attacked in the infamous Pazzi Conspiracy. The conspirators, egged on by the pope and led by a member of the Pazzi family, old rivals of the Medici, fell on the brothers at the ringing of the sanctuary bell. Giuliano was murdered on the spot—his body rent with 19 wounds—but Lorenzo vaulted over the altar rail and sprinted for safety into the New Sacristy, slamming the bronze doors behind him. Those doors were cast from 1446 to 1467 by Luca della Robbia, his only significant work in the medium. Earlier, Luca had provided a lunette of the *Resurrection* (1442) in glazed terra cotta over the door, as well as the lunette *Ascension* over the south sacristy door. The interior of the New Sacristy is filled with beautifully inlaid wood cabinet doors.

The frescoes on the **interior of the dome** were designed by Giorgio Vasari but painted mostly by his less-talented student Federico Zuccari by 1579. The frescoes were subjected to a thorough cleaning, completed in 1996, which many people saw as a waste of restoration lire when so many more important works throughout the city were waiting to be salvaged. The scrubbing, however, did bring out Zuccari's only saving point—his innovative color palette.

Piazza del Duomo. ℂ 055-230-2885. www.operaduomo.firenze.it. Admission to church free; Santa Reparata excavations 3€ ($3.90); cupola 6€ ($7.80), free for children under 6. Church Mon–Wed and Fri 10am–5pm; Thurs 10am–3:30pm; 1st Sat of month 10am–3:30pm, other Sat 10am–4:45pm; Sun 1:30–4:30pm. Free tours every 40 min. daily, 10:30am–noon and 3–4:20pm. Cupola Mon–Fri 8:30am–6:20pm; Sat 8:30am–5pm (1st Sat of month to 3:20pm). Bus: 1, 6, 17, 14, 22, 23, 36, 37, or 71.

Battistero (Baptistery) 𝕬𝕬𝕬   In choosing a date to mark the beginning of the Renaissance, art historians often seize on 1401, the year Florence's powerful wool merchant's guild held a contest to decide who would receive the commission to design the **North Doors** 𝕬 of the Baptistery to match the Gothic **South Doors,** cast 65 years earlier by Andrea Pisano. The era's foremost Tuscan sculptors each designed and cast bas-relief bronze panels depicting his vision of The Sacrifice of Isaac. Twenty-two-year-old Lorenzo Ghiberti, competing against the likes of Donatello, Jacopo della Quercia, and Filippo Brunelleschi, won hands down. He spent the next 21 years casting 28 bronze panels and building his doors. Although limited by his contract to design the scenes within Gothic frames as on Pisano's doors, Ghiberti infused his figures and compositions with an unmatched realism and classical references that helped define Renaissance sculpture. (Ghiberti stuck a self-portrait in the left door, the fourth head from the bottom of the middle strip, wearing a turban.)

The result so impressed the merchant's guild—not to mention the public and Ghiberti's fellow artists—they asked him in 1425 to do the **East Doors** ✸✸✸, facing the Duomo, this time giving him the artistic freedom to realize his Renaissance ambitions. Twenty-seven years later, just before his death, Ghiberti finished 10 dramatic lifelike Old Testament scenes in gilded bronze, each a masterpiece of Renaissance sculpture and some of the finest low-relief perspective in Italian art. The panels now mounted here are excellent copies; the originals are displayed in the Museo dell'Opera del Duomo (see below). Years later, Michelangelo was standing before these doors and someone asked his opinion. His response sums up Ghiberti's life accomplishment as no art historian ever could: "They are so beautiful that they would grace the entrance to Paradise." They've been called the Gates of Paradise ever since.

The Baptistery is one of Florence's oldest, most venerated buildings. Florentines long believed it was originally a Roman temple, but it most likely was raised somewhere between the 4th and 7th centuries on the site of a Roman palace. The octagonal drum was rebuilt in the 11th century, and by the 13th century it had been clad in its characteristic green-and-white Romanesque stripes of marble and capped with its odd pyramid-like dome.

The interior is ringed with columns pilfered from ancient Roman buildings and is a spectacle of mosaics above and below. The floor was inlaid in 1209, and the ceiling was covered between 1225 and the early 1300s with glittering **mosaics** ✸✸. Most were crafted by Venetian or Byzantine-style workshops, which worked off designs drawn by the era's best artists. Coppo di Marcovaldo drew sketches for the over 7.8m (26-ft.) high, ape-toed Christ in Judgment and the Last Judgment that fills over a third of the ceiling.

To the right of the altar is the 1425 wall **tomb of Antipope John XXIII,** designed by Michelozzo and Donatello, who cast the bronze effigy of the deceased, deposed pontiff.

Piazza di San Giovanni. ℂ **055-230-2885.** www.operaduomo.firenze.it. Admission 3€ ($3.90), free for children under 6. Mon–Sat noon–6:30pm; Sun 8:30am–1:30pm. Bus: 1, 6, 17, 14, 22, 23, 36, 37, or 71.

A Man & His Dome

Filippo Brunelleschi, a diminutive man whose ego was as big as his talent, managed in his arrogant, quixotic, suspicious, and brilliant way to literally invent Renaissance architecture. Having been beaten by Lorenzo Ghiberti in the famous contest to cast the baptistery doors (see below), Brunelleschi resolved he'd rather be the top architect than the second-best sculptor and took off for Rome to study the buildings of the ancients. On returning to Florence, he combined subdued gray *pietra serena* stone with smooth white plaster to create airy arches, vaults, and arcades of classically perfect proportions in his own special variant on the ancient Roman orders of architecture. Apart from designing the serene San Lorenzo, Santo Spirito, and the elegant Ospedale degli Innocenti, his greatest achievement by far was erecting the dome over Florence's cathedral.

The Duomo, then the world's largest church, had already been built, but nobody had been able to figure out how to cover the daunting space over its center without spending a fortune and without filling the church with the necessary scaffolding—plus no one was sure whether they could create a dome that would hold up under its own weight. One of the many ridiculous solutions was making it of pumice (so it would be light) and filling the church with dirt studded with small coins. (After the work was done, the populace would be invited to dig for the money and thus remove the dirt.) Brunelleschi kept insisting he had the answer, but he wouldn't share it, fearful others would use his ideas and get the job over him.

After becoming so heated during several meetings of the Dome Erection Committee that he had to be carried out, he finally came in bearing an egg and issued a challenge (or so Vasari says). He bet he was the only one of the learned

Campanile di Giotto (Giotto's Bell Tower) 🐦🐦 In 1334, Giotto started the cathedral bell tower (clad in the same three colors of marble gracing the Duomo) but completed only the first two levels before his death in 1337. He was out of his league with the engineering aspects of architecture, and the tower was saved from falling in on itself by Andrea Pisano, who doubled the thickness of the

architects and councilmen in the room who could make an egg stand on its end. A marble slab was procured for the balancing act but, try as they might, the others couldn't get the egg to stay vertical. Brunelleschi took the egg in his hand, and with one quick movement slammed it down on the marble, smashing its end—but leaving it standing. The others protested that they, too, could have easily done that, to which Brunelleschi replied they would say the same thing if he showed them his plans for the dome. He was granted the commission and revealed his ingenious plan—which may have been inspired by close study of Rome's Pantheon.

He built the dome in two shells, the inner one thicker than the outer, both shells thinning as they neared the top, thus leaving the center hollow and removing a good deal of the weight. He also planned to construct the dome of giant vaults with ribs crossing over them, with each of the stones making up the actual fabric of the dome being dovetailed. In this way, the walls of the dome would support themselves as they were erected. In the process of building, Brunelleschi found himself as much an engineer as architect, constantly designing remarkable new winches, cranes, and hoists to carry the materials faster and more efficiently up to the level of the workmen. He was even farsighted enough to build in drainage systems for the rain and iron hooks to support interior scaffolding for future cleanings or paint jobs.

His finished work speaks for itself, 45m (148 ft.) wide at the base and 90m (295 ft.) high from drum to lantern—Florentines proudly claim they've lived their entire lives within sight of the dome. For his achievement, Brunelleschi was accorded a singular honor: He's the only person ever buried in Florence's cathedral, under his ingenious and revolutionary dome.

walls. Andrea, a master sculptor of the Pisan Gothic school, also changed the design to add statue niches—he even carved a few of the statues himself—before quitting the project in 1348. Francesco Talenti finished the job between 1350 and 1359—he exchanged the heavy solidity of the base for a lighter, airier effect.

The **reliefs** and **statues** in the lower levels—by Andrea Pisano, Donatello, and others—are all copies, the weatherworn originals now housed in the Museo dell'Opera del Duomo (see below). You can climb the 414 steps to the top of the tower. The two things that make the 84m-high (276-ft.) view different from what you get out of the more popular climb up the cathedral dome, besides a cityscape vista, are great views of the Baptistery as you ascend and the best close-up shot in the entire city of Brunelleschi's dome.

Piazza del Duomo. © 055-230-2885. www.operaduomo.firenze.it. Admission 6€ ($7.80). Daily 8:30am–6:50pm. Bus: 1, 6, 17, 14, 22, 23, 36, 37, or 71.

Museo dell'Opera del Duomo (Duomo Works Museum) 𝕲

This museum exists mainly to house the sculptures removed from the niches and doors of the Duomo group for restoration and preservation from the elements. The dusty old museum was completely rearranged from 1998 to 2000.

The courtyard has now been enclosed to show off—under natural daylight, as they should be seen—Lorenzo Ghiberti's original gilded bronze panels from the Baptistery's *Gates of Paradise* 𝕲𝕲𝕲, which are being displayed as they're slowly restored. Ghiberti devoted 27 years to this project (1425–52), and you can now admire up close his masterpiece of *schiacciato* (squished) relief—using the Donatello technique of almost sketching in perspective to create the illusion of depth in low relief.

On the way up the stairs, you pass **Michelangelo's *Pietà*** 𝕲 (1548–55), his second and penultimate take on the subject, which the sculptor probably had in mind for his own tomb. The face of Nicodemus is a self-portrait, and Michelangelo most likely intended to leave much of the statue group only roughly carved, just as we see it. Art historians inform us that the polished figure of Mary Magdalene on the left was finished by one of Michelangelo's students, while storytellers relate that part of the considerable damage to the group was inflicted by the master himself when, in a moment of rage and frustration, he took a hammer to it.

The top floor of the museum houses the **Prophets** carved for the bell tower, the most noted of which are the remarkably expressive figures carved by Donatello: the drooping aged face of the *Beardless Prophet;* the sad fixed gaze of *Jeremiah;* and the misshapen ferocity of the bald ***Habakkuk*** 𝕲 (known to Florentines as *Lo Zuccone*—pumpkin head). Mounted on the walls above are two putty-encrusted marble ***cantorie*** **(choir lofts).** The slightly earlier one (1431) on the entrance wall is by Luca della Robbia. His panels (the originals now displayed at eye level, with plaster casts set in the actual frame above) are in perfect early Renaissance harmony, both within themselves and with each other, and they show della Robbia's mastery of creating great depth within a shallow piece of stone. Across the room, Donatello's *cantoria* ✿ (1433–38) takes off in a new artistic direction as his singing cherubs literally break through the boundaries of the "panels" to leap and race around the entire *cantoria* behind the mosaicked columns.

The room off the right stars one of Donatello's more morbidly fascinating sculptures: a late work in polychrome wood of *The Magdalene* ✿ (1453–55), emaciated and veritably dripping with penitence.

The new exit corridor leading off from the Prophets room houses some of the **machines** used to build the cathedral dome, **Brunelleschi's death mask** as a grisly reminder of its architect, and the **wooden model proposals** for the cupola's drum and for the facade. The original Gothic facade was destroyed in 1587 to make room for one done in High Renaissance style, but the patron behind the work—Grand Duke Francesco de' Medici—died before he could choose from among the submissions by the likes of Giambologna and Bernardo Buontalenti. The Duomo remained faceless until purses of the 18th century, heavy with money and relentless bad taste, gave it the neo-Gothic facade we see today.

Piazza del Duomo 9 (directly behind the dome end of the cathedral). ✆ 055-230-2885. www.operaduomo.firenze.it. Admission 6€ ($7.80), free for children under 6. Mon–Sat 9am–7:30pm; Sun 9am–2pm; last admission 30 min. before close. Bus: 6, 11, 14, 17, or 23.

2 Around Piazza Della Signoria

When the medieval Guelf party finally came out on top of the Ghibellines, they razed part of the old city center to build a new palace for civic government. It's said the Guelfs ordered architect Arnolfo di Cambio to build what we now call the Palazzo Vecchio in the corner of this space, but to be careful that not 1 inch of the building sat on the cursed former Ghibelline land. This odd legend was probably fabricated to explain Arnolfo's quirky off-center architecture.

The space around the *palazzo* became the new civic center of town, the L-shaped **Piazza della Signoria** ✿✿, named after the oligarchic ruling body of the medieval city. Today, it's an outdoor sculpture gallery, teeming with tourists, postcard stands, horses and buggies, and outdoor cafes.

The statuary on the piazza is particularly beautiful, starting on the far left (as you're facing the Palazzo Vecchio) with Giambologna's equestrian statue of *Grand Duke Cosimo I* (1594). To its right is one of Florence's favorite sculptures to hate, the *Fontana del Nettuno* (*Neptune Fountain;* 1560–75), created by Bartolomeo Ammannati as a tribute to Cosimo I's naval ambitions but nicknamed by the Florentines *Il Biancone,* "Big Whitey." Michelangelo, to whom many a Renaissance quip is attributed, took one look at it and shook his head, moaning "Ammannato, Ammannato, what a beautiful piece of marble you've ruined." The highly Mannerist bronzes surrounding the basin are much better, probably because a young Giambologna had a hand in most of them.

Note the **porphyry plaque** set in the ground in front of the fountain. This marks the site where puritanical monk Savonarola held the Bonfire of the Vanities: With his fiery apocalyptic preaching, he whipped the Florentines into a reformist frenzy, and hundreds filed into this piazza, arms loaded with paintings, clothing, and other effects that represented their "decadence." They consigned it all to the flames of a roaring pile. However, after a few years the pope (not amused by Savonarola's criticisms) excommunicated first the monk and then the entire city for supporting him. On May 23, 1498, the Florentines decided they'd had enough of the rabid-dog monk, dragged him and two followers to the torture chamber, pronounced them heretics, and led them into the piazza for one last day of fire and brimstone. In the very spot where they once burned their luxurious belongings, they put the torch to Savonarola himself. The event is commemorated by an anonymous painting kept in Savonarola's old cell in San Marco and by the plaque here.

To the right of the Neptune Fountain is a long, raised platform fronting the Palazzo Vecchio known as the *arringheria,* from which soapbox speakers would lecture to crowds before them (we get our word "harangue" from this). On its far left corner is a copy (original in the Bargello) of Donatello's **Marzocco,** symbol of the city, with a Florentine lion resting his raised paw on a shield emblazoned with the city's emblem, the *giglio* (lily). To its right is another Donatello replica, **Judith Beheading Holofernes.** Farther down is a man who needs little introduction, Michelangelo's **David,** a 19th-century copy of the original now in the Accademia. Near enough to David to look truly ugly in comparison is Baccio Bandinelli's **Heracles** (1534). Poor Bandinelli was trying to copy Michelangelo's muscular male form, but made Heracles merely lumpy.

At the piazza's south end, beyond the long U that opens down the Uffizi, is one of the square's earliest and prettiest embellishments, the **Loggia dei Lanzi** ✮✮ (1376–82), named after the Swiss guard of

> ## (Tips) Reserving Tickets for the Uffizi & Other Museums
>
> You can bypass the hours-long ticket line at the **Uffizi Galleries** by reserving a ticket and an entry time in advance by calling **Firenze Musei** at ℂ **055-294-883** (Mon–Fri 8:30am–6:30pm, Sat until 12:30pm) or visiting **www.firenzemusei.it**. By March, entry times can be booked more than a week in advance. You can also reserve for the **Accademia Gallery** (another interminable line, to see *David*), as well as the **Galleria Palatina** in the Pitti Palace, the **Bargello,** and several others. There is a 1.55€ ($2.85) fee (worth every penny), and you can pay by credit card.

lancers *(lanzi)* Cosimo de' Medici stationed here. The airy loggia was probably built on a design by Andrea Orcagna—spawning another of its many names, the Loggia di Orcagna (another is the Loggia della Signoria). The three huge arches of its simple, harmonious form were way ahead of the times, an architectural style that really belongs to the Renaissance. At the front left corner stands Benvenuto Cellini's masterpiece in bronze, *Perseus* ⋆⋆ (1545), holding out the severed Medusa's head before him, restored from 1996 to 2000. On the far right of the loggia has stood Giambologna's *Rape of the Sabines* ⋆⋆, one of the most successful Mannerist sculptures in existence, a piece you must walk all the way around to appreciate, catching the action and artistry from different angles. Sadly, once it was boxed up and examined for restoration, authorities determined that the outdoors had wreaked intolerable damage, and the original statue has been moved to the Accademia (taking the place of its plaster model long anchoring the museum's first room) with a marble copy to substitute for it here.

Gallerie degli Uffizi (Uffizi Galleries) ⋆⋆⋆   The Uffizi is one of the world's great museums, and the single best introduction to Renaissance painting, with works by Giotto, Masaccio, Paolo Uccello, Sandro Botticelli, Leonardo da Vinci, Perugino, Michelangelo, Raphael Sanzio, Titian, Caravaggio, and the list goes on. The museum is deceptively small. What looks like a small stretch of gallery space can easily gobble up half a day—many rooms suffer the fate of containing nothing but masterpieces.

The Uffizi

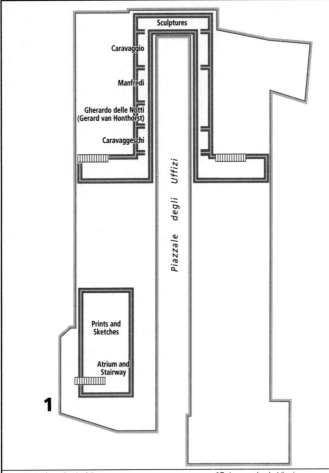

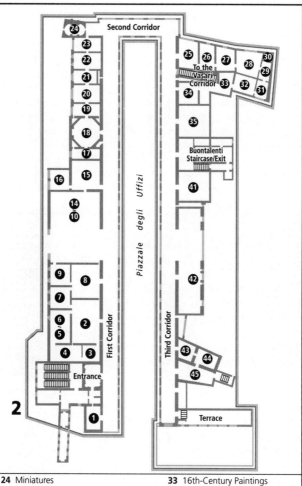

24 Miniatures	**33** 16th-Century Paintings
25 Michelangelo & Florentine Artists	**34** Lombard School
26 Raphael & Andrea del Sarto	**35** Barocci
27 Pontormo & Rosso Fiorentino	**41** Rubens & Flemish Paintings
28 Tiziano & Sebastiano del Piombo	**42** Niobe
29 Parmigianino & Dosso Dossi	**43** 17th Century Painters
30 Emilian Paintings	**44** Rembrandt
31 Veronese	**45** 18th-Century Paintings
32 Tintoretto	

Tips for Seeing the Uffizi

If you have the time, make two trips to the museum. On your first, concentrate on the first dozen or so rooms and pop by the Greatest Hits of the 16th Century, with works by Michelangelo, Caravaggio, Raphael, and Titian. Return later for a brief recap and continue with the rest of the gallery.

Be aware that the **gift shop** at the end of the galleries closes 20 minutes before the museum. You can visit it without reentering the museum at any time; if you plan to stay in the collections until closing, go down to the shop earlier during your visit and get the guards' attention before you pass through the exit turnstile, so they'll know you're just popping out to buy a few postcards and will recognize you when you ask to be let back in.

Know before you go that the Uffizi regularly shuts down rooms for crowd-control reasons—especially in summer, when the bulk of the annual 1.5 million visitors stampedes the place. Of the more than 3,100 artworks in the museum's archives, only about 1,700 are on exhibit.

The painting gallery is housed in the structure built to serve as the offices (*uffizi* is Florentine dialect for *uffici,* or "offices") of the Medici, commissioned by Cosimo I from Giorgio Vasari in 1560—perhaps his greatest architectural work. The painting gallery was started by Cosimo I as well and is now housed in the second-floor rooms that open off a long hall lined with ancient statues and frescoed with grotesques.

The first room off to your left after you climb Vasari's monumental stairs (**Room 2;** Room 1 is perennially closed) presents you with a crash course in the Renaissance's roots. It houses three huge altarpieces by Tuscany's greatest late-13th-century masters. On the right is Cimabue's *Santa Trínita Maestà* (1280), still very much rooted in the Byzantine traditions that governed painting in the early Middle Ages—gold-leaf crosshatching in the drapery, an Eastern-style inlaid throne, spoonlike depressions above the noses, highly posed figures, and cloned angels with identical faces stacked up along the sides. On the left is Duccio's *Rucellai Maestà* (1285), painted by the master who studied with Cimabue and eventually founded the Sienese school of painting. The style is still thoroughly medieval but introduces innovations into the rigid traditions. There's a little more weight to the Child Madonna and the Madonna's face has a more human, somewhat sad, expression.

In the center of the room is Giotto's incredible ***Ognissanti Maestà*** ☆☆☆ (1310), by the man who's generally credited as the founding father of Renaissance painting. It's sometimes hard to appreciate just how much Giotto changed when he junked half the traditions of painting to go his own way. It's mainly in the very simple details, the sorts of things we take for granted in art today, such as the force of gravity, the display of basic emotions, the individual facial expressions, and the figures that look like they have an actual bulky body under their clothes. Giotto's Madonna sways slightly to one side, the fabric of her off-white shirt pulling realistically against her breasts as she twists. Instead of floating in mysterious space, Giotto's saints and angels stand on solid ground.

Room 3 pays homage to the 14th-century Sienese school with several delicately crafted works by Simone Martini and the Lorenzetti brothers. Here is Martini's ***Annunciation*** ☆ (1333). Note that Mary, who in so much art both before and after this period is depicted as meekly accepting her divine duty, looks reluctant, even disgusted, at the news of her imminent Immaculate Conception. Pietro and Ambrogio Lorenzetti helped revolutionize Sienese art and the Sienese school before succumbing to the Black Death in 1348. Of their work here, Ambrogio's 1342 *Presentation at the Temple* is the finest, with a rich use of color and a vast architectural space created to open up the temple in the background.

Room 4 houses the works of the 14th-century Florentine school, where you can clearly see the influence Giotto had on his contemporaries. **Rooms 5 and 6** represent the dying gasps of International Gothic, still grounded in medievalism but admitting a bit of the emergent naturalism and humanist philosophy into their works. Lorenzo Monaco's *Coronation of the Virgin* (1413) is particularly beautiful, antiquated in its styling but with a delicate suffused coloring.

In **Room 7,** the Renaissance proper starts taking shape, primarily driven by Paolo Uccello and Masaccio, two artists on a quest for perfect perspective. On the left wall is Uccello's *Battle of San Romano* (1456), famously innovative but also rather ugly. This painting depicts one of Florence's great victories over rival Siena, but for Uccello it was more of an excuse to explore perspective—with which this painter was, by all accounts, positively obsessed.

Rising from the Blast

On May 27, 1993, a car bomb ripped through the west wing of the Uffizi, seriously damaging it and some 200 works of art and destroying three (thankfully lesser) Renaissance paintings. The bomb killed five people inside, including the museum curator and her family. While everything from a Mafia hit to a government conspiracy was blamed, the motive for the bombing, and the perpetrators, remain unknown to this day.

In December 1998, Italy unveiled what it called the New Uffizi, a $15-million renovation that repaired all damaged rooms, added more than 20,000 square feet of new museum space, and displayed more than 100 works that had never been seen before—part of a larger project to triple exhibit space. Several branches of the book/gift shop were added to the ticketing areas on the ground floor, and the old outdoor cafe at the end of the galleries, atop the Loggia dei Lanzi with a view of the Palazzo Vecchio's tower, was reopened.

In the far corner is the only example of Masaccio's art here (he died at 27), the *Madonna and Child with St. Anne,* which he helped his master, Masolino, paint in 1424. Masaccio's earthy realism and sharp light are evident in the figures of Mary and the Child, as well as in the topmost angel peeking down. In the center of the room is Piero della Francesca's **Portrait of Federico da Montefeltro and Battista Sforza** ⭐⭐, painted around 1465 or 1470 and the only work by this remarkable Sansepolcran artist to survive in Florence. The fronts of the panels depict the famous duke of Urbino and his wife, while on the backs are horse-drawn carts symbolic of the pair's respective virtues. Piero's incredibly lucid style and modeling and the detailed Flemish-style backgrounds need no commentary, but do note that he purposefully painted the husband and wife in full profile—without diluting the realism of a hooked nose and moles on the duke—and mounted them face to face, so they'll always gaze into each other's eyes.

Room 8 is devoted to Filippo Lippi, with more than half a dozen works by the lecherous monk who turned out rich religious paintings with an earthy quality and a three-dimensionality that make them immediately accessible. His most famous painting here is the *Madonna and Child with Two Angels* (1455–66). Also here are a few works by Filippo's illegitimate son, Filippino. **Room 9** is an interlude of virtuoso paintings by Antonio del Pollaiolo, plus a number of large Virtues by his less-talented brother, Piero. These two masters of anatomical verisimilitude greatly influenced the young Botticelli, three of whose early works reside in the room. This introduction to Botticelli sets us up for the next room, invariably crowded with tour-bus groups.

The walls separating **Rooms 10 to 14** were knocked down in the 20th century to create one large space to accommodate the resurgent popularity of Sandro Filipepi—better known by his nickname, Botticelli ("little barrels")—master of willowy women in flowing gowns. Fourteen of his paintings line the walls, along with works by his pupil (and illegitimate son of his former teacher) Filippino Lippi and Domenico Ghirlandaio, Michelangelo's first artistic master. But everybody flocks here for just two paintings, Botticelli's *Birth of Venus* and his *Primavera (Allegory of Spring)*. Though, in later life, Botticelli was influenced by the puritanical preaching of Savonarola and took to cranking out boring Madonnas, the young painter began in grand pagan style. Both paintings were commissioned between 1477 and 1483 by a Medici cousin for his private villa, and they celebrate not only Renaissance art's love of naturalism but also the humanist philosophy permeating 15th-century Florence, a neo-Platonism that united religious doctrine with ancient ideology and mythological stories.

In the ***Birth of Venus*** 🎨🎨, the love goddess is born of the sea on a half shell, blown to shore by the Zephyrs. Ores, a goddess of the seasons, rushes to clothe her. Some say the long-legged goddess was modeled on Simonetta Vespucci, a renowned Florentine beauty, cousin to Amerigo (the naval explorer after whom America is named) and not-so-secret lover of Giuliano de' Medici, Lorenzo the Magnificent's brother. The ***Primavera*** 🎨🎨 is harder to evaluate, since contemporary research indicates it may not actually be an allegory of spring influenced by the humanist poetry of Poliziano but rather a celebration of Venus, who stands in the center, surrounded by various complicated references to Virtues through mythological characters. Also check out Botticelli's *Adoration of the Magi,* where the artist painted himself in the far right side, in a great yellow robe and golden curls.

Room 15 boasts Leonardo da Vinci's ***Annunciation*** 🎨🎨🎨, which the young artist painted in 1472 or 1475 while still in the workshop of his master, Andrea del Verrocchio; however, he was already fully developed as an artist. The solid yet light figures and sfumato airiness blurring the distance render remarkably lifelike figures somehow suspended in a surreal dreamscape. Leonardo helped Verrocchio on the *Baptism of Christ*—most credit the artist-in-training with the angel on the far left as well as the landscape, and a few art historians think they see his hand in the figure of Jesus as well. The *Adoration of the Magi,* on which Leonardo didn't get much beyond the sketching stage, shows how he could retain powerful compositions even when creating a fantasy landscape of ruinous architecture and incongruous horse battles. The room also houses works by Lorenzo di Credi and Piero di Cosimo, fellow 15th-century maestros, and a *Pietà* that shows Perugino's solid plastic style of studied simplicity. (This Umbrian master would later pass it on to his pupil Raphael.) Uffizi officials use **Room 18, the Tribune,** as a crowd-control pressure valve. You may find yourself stuck shuffling around it slowly, staring at the mother-of-pearl discs lining the domed ceiling; studying the antique statues, such as the famous *Medici Venus* (a 1st-c.-B.C. Roman copy of a Greek original); and scrutinizing the Medici portraits wallpapering the room. The latter include many by the talented early baroque artist Agnolo Bronzino, whose portrait of **Eleonora of Toledo** ⚔, wife of Cosimo I, with their son Giovanni de' Medici (1545), is particularly well worked. It shows her in a satin dress embroidered and sewn with velvet and pearls. At the time the Medici tombs were opened in 1857, her body was found buried in this same dress. (It's now in the Pitti Palace's costume museum.)

Also here are Raphael's late *St. John the Baptist in the Desert* (1518) and Mannerist Rosso Fiorentino's 1522 *Angel Musician,* where an insufferably cute little *putto* (cherub) plucks at an oversize lute—it's become quite the Renaissance icon in the recent spate of angel mania.

Room 19 is devoted to both Perugino, who did the luminous *Portrait of Francesco delle Opere* (1494), and Luca Signorelli, whose *Holy Family* (1490–95) was painted as a tondo set in a rectangle, with allegorical figures in the background and a torsion of the figures that were to influence Michelangelo's version (in a later room). **Room 20** is devoted to Dürer, Cranach, and other German artists who worked in Florence, while **Room 21** takes care of 16th-century Venetians Giovanni Bellini, Giorgione, and Carpaccio. In **Room 22** are Flemish and German works by Hans Holbein the Younger, Hans Memling, and others, and **Room 23** contains Andrea Mantegna's triptych of the *Adoration of the Magi, Circumcision, and Ascension*

(1463–70), showing his excellent draftsmanship and fascination with classical architecture. Now we move into the west wing, still in the throes of restoration following the bombing (see "Rising from the Blast," above). **Room 25** is overpowered by Michelangelo's *Holy Family* 🌟🌟🌟 (1506–08), one of the few panel paintings by the great master. The glowing colors and shocking nudes in the background seem to pop off the surface, and the torsion of the figures was to be taken up as the banner of the Mannerist movement. Michelangelo also designed the elaborate frame.

Room 26 is devoted to Andrea del Sarto and High Renaissance darling Raphael. Of Raphael we have the *Madonna of the Goldfinch* (1505), a work he painted in a Leonardesque style for a friend's wedding, and several important portraits, including *Pope Leo X with Cardinals Giulio de' Medici and Luigi de' Rossi* and *Pope Julius II,* as well as a famous *Self-portrait.* Del Sarto was the most important painter in Florence in the early 16th century, while Michelangelo and Raphael were off in Rome. His consciously developed Mannerist style is evident in his masterful *Madonna of the Harpies* (1515–17).

Room 27 is devoted to works by Del Sarto's star Mannerist pupils, Rosso Fiorentino and Pontormo, and by Pontormo's adopted son, Bronzino. Fiorentino's *Moses Defends the Daughters of Jethro* 🌟 (1523) owes much to Michelangesque nudes but is also entirely original in the use of harsh lighting that reduces the figures to basic shapes of color.

Room 28 honors the great Venetian Titian, of whose works you'll see a warm full-bodied *Flora* 🌟🌟 and a poetic *Venus of Urbino* 🌟 languishing on her bed; Sienese High Renaissance painter Sebastiano del Piombo (his *Death of Adonis* and *Portrait of a Woman* are both strong works); and a few mediocre works by Palma il Vecchio.

Tiny **rooms 29 and 30,** ostensibly honoring works by several Emilian artists, are totally dominated by late Mannerist master Il Parmigianino, who carried the Mannerist movement to its logical extremes with the almost grotesquely elongated bodies of the *Madonna of the Long Neck* 🌟 (1534). **Room 31** continues to chart the fall of painting into decorative grace with Paolo Veronese's *Martyrdom of St. Justine* (1573), which is less about the saint being stabbed than it is a sartorial study in fashion design.

Room 32 is a nice break provided by the dramatic and visible brush strokes that boldly swirled rich, somber colors of several lesser works by Venetian master Tintoretto. All the better, as these must see you through the treacle and tripe of **rooms 33 to 34,** stuffed with substandard examples of 16th-century paintings by the likes of Vasari, Alessandro Allori, and other chaps who grew up in Michelangelo's shadow and desperately wished they could paint like him. (*Note:* They couldn't.)

Popping back out in the main corridor again, you visit the last several rooms one at a time as each opens off the hall. **Room 35** features the taffeta, cotton-candy oeuvre of baroque weirdo Federico Barocci (whose works are currently coming into vogue—why, I've no idea). Continue right past that exit staircase, because they save a few eye-popping rooms for the very end.

Room 41 is all about Rubens and his famously ample nudes, along with some works by his Flemish cohorts (Van Dyck, Sustermans). **Room 42** is a lovely side hall flooded with sunlight and graced by more than a dozen Roman statues that are copies of Hellenic originals, most of them of the dying Niobids.

And so we come to **Room 43,** previously home to Caravaggio before he and his students were moved to the expanded exhibition space downstairs. Now the room hosts a collection of 17th-century paintings by such artists as il Guercino and il Domenichino.

Duck through the end of this room to pay your respects to Rembrandt in **Room 44,** where he immortalized himself in two *Self-portraits,* one done as a youth and the other as an old man. Hang a right to exit back into the corridor again via **Room 45,** a bit of a letdown after the last two rooms, but still engaging (if you've any art-appreciation energies left after all this) for its "Greatest Hits of the 18th Century" artists—Giuseppe Maria Crespi, Giovanni Paolo Pannini, Il Canaletto, Francesco Guardi, and Tiepolo—plus a Spanish twist to end it all with two paintings by Francisco Goya.

Now it's time to move downstairs toward the exit, but not before you visit five recently added rooms on the ground floor, starting with the space devoted to Caravaggio in **Room 5.** Caravaggio was the baroque master of *chiaroscuro*—painting with extreme harsh light and deep shadows. The Uffizi preserves his painting of the severed head of *Medusa,* a *Sacrifice of Isaac,* and his famous ***Bacchus*** ✿✿. Caravaggio's work influenced a generation of artists—including Artemisia Gentileschi, the only female painter to make a name for herself in the late Renaissance/early baroque. Artemisia was eclipsed in fame by her slightly less talented father, Orazio, and she was the victim and central figure in a sensational rape trial brought against Orazio's one-time collaborator. It evidently had an effect on her professional life; the violent *Judith Slaying Holofernes,* is featured here, in all its gruesome detail.

Rooms 6 and 7 are devoted to two followers of Caravaggio: respectively, Bartolomeo Manfredi and Gerrit von Honthorst, known in Italy as Gherardo delle Notti. Paintings by both artists were destroyed in the 1993 car bomb; the ones on display here were previously safeguarded in storage. Manfredi will be forever remembered for bringing plebian life to the canvas, with scenes in taverns and featuring card-playing soldiers, although those in the Uffizi's collection focus on more religious and ancient Roman subjects. Gherardo delle Notti, as his nickname might suggest, was famous for his bright illumination of subjects by sources of light seen and unseen, and the paintings here, especially his adoration of the baby Jesus, will not disappoint.

Room 8 is dedicated to other European students of Caravaggio, including Matthias Stomer, Francesco Rustici, and Nicolas Regnier, while **Room 9** is dedicated to Guido Reni, perhaps best known for his collaboration with Annibale Caracci on the Farnese Palace in Rome, but also noted for his paintings betraying the influence of Caravaggio. His rendering of a triumphant David admiring the slain head of Goliath, upon your exit, is a fitting tribute to your conquest of this overwhelming gallery—because that's it. The Uffizi is finished. Treat yourself to a cappuccino alfresco. You've earned it.

Piazzale degli Uffizi 6 (off Piazza della Signoria). © 055-238-8651, or 055-294-883 to reserve tickets. www.uffizi.firenze.it (gallery info), or www.firenzemusei.it (to reserve tickets). Admission 6.50€ ($8.45). Tues–Sun 8:15am–7pm. Ticket window closes 45 min. before museum. Bus: A, B, 23, or 71.

Palazzo Vecchio ✪ Florence's imposing fortresslike town hall was built from 1299 to 1302 on the designs of Arnolfo di Cambio, Gothic master builder of the city. Arnolfo managed to make it solid and impregnable-looking yet still graceful, with thin-columned Gothic windows and two orders of crenellations—square for the main rampart and swallow-tailed on the 94m-high (308-ft.) bell tower.

The palace was once home to the various Florentine republican governments (and today to the municipal government). Cosimo I and his ducal Medici family moved to the *palazzo* in 1540 and engaged in massive redecoration. Michelozzo's 1453 **courtyard,** just through the door, was left architecturally intact but frescoed by Vasari with scenes of Austrian cities to celebrate the 1565 marriage of Francesco de' Medici and Joanna of Austria. The grand staircase leads up to the **Sala dei Cinquecento,** named for the 500-man assembly that met here in the pre-Medici days of the Florentine Republic and site of the greatest fresco cycle that ever wasn't. Leonardo da Vinci was commissioned in 1503 to paint one long wall with a battle scene celebrating a famous Florentine victory. He was always trying new methods and materials and decided to mix wax into his pigments. Leonardo had finished painting part of the wall, but it wasn't drying fast enough, so he brought in braziers stoked with hot coals to try to hurry the process. As others watched in horror, the wax in the fresco melted under the intense heat and the colors ran down the walls to puddle on the floor. Michelangelo never even got past making the preparatory drawings for the fresco he was supposed to paint on the opposite wall—Pope Julius II called him to Rome to paint the Sistine Chapel, and the master's sketches were destroyed by eager young artists who came to study them and took away scraps. Eventually, the bare walls were covered by Vasari and assistants from 1563 to 1565 with blatantly subservient frescoes exalting Cosimo I de' Medici and his dynasty.

Off the corner of the room (to the right as you enter) is the **Studiolo di Francesco I,** a claustrophobic study in which Cosimo's eldest son and heir performed his alchemy and science experiments and where baroque paintings hide secret cupboards. Against the wall of the Sala dei Cinquecento, opposite the door you enter, is Michelangelo's statue of **Victory** ✿, carved from 1533 to 1534 for the Julius II tomb but later donated to the Medici. Its extreme torsion—the way the body twists and spirals upward—was to be a great influence on the Mannerist movement.

The first series of rooms on the second floor is the **Quartiere degli Elementi,** again frescoed by Vasari. The **Terrazza di Saturno,** in the corner, has a view over the Uffizi to the hills across the Arno. Crossing the balcony overlooking the Sala dei Cinquecento, you enter the **Apartments of Eleonora di Toledo,** decorated for Cosimo's Spanish wife. Her small private chapel is a masterpiece of mid–16th-century painting by Bronzino. Farther on, under the sculpted ceiling of the **Sala dei Gigli,** are Domenico Ghirlandaio's fresco of *St. Zenobius Enthroned* with ancient Roman heroes and Donatello's original *Judith and Holofernes* ✿ bronze (1455), one of his last works.

During the summer evening hours, the following sections, normally closed, are open: the **Loeser Collections,** with paintings by Pietro Lorenzetti and Bronzino and sculptures by Tino di Camaino and Jacopo Sansovino, and, perhaps more fun, the outdoor **Balustrade** running around the roof behind the crenellations—it offers a unique panorama of the city and the piazza below.

Piazza della Signoria. ✆ **055-276-8465.** Admission 6€ ($7.80). Fri–Wed 9am–7pm; Thurs 9am–2pm. Bus: A, B, 23, or 71.

Ponte Vecchio (Old Bridge) ✮✮✮   The oldest and most famous bridge across the Arno, the Ponte Vecchio we know today was built in 1345 by Taddeo Gaddi to replace an earlier version. The characteristic overhanging shops have lined the bridge since at least the 12th century. In the 16th century, it was home to butchers until Cosimo I moved into the Palazzo Pitti across the river. He couldn't stand the stench as he crossed the bridge from on high in the Corridorio Vasariano every day, so he evicted the meat cutters and moved in the classier gold- and silversmiths, tradesmen who occupy the bridge to this day.

A bust of the most famous Florentine goldsmith, the swashbuckling autobiographer and *Perseus* sculptor Benvenuto Cellini, stands off to the side of the bridge's center, in a small piazza overlooking the Arno. From this vantage point Mark Twain, spoiled by the mighty Mississippi, once wryly commented, "It is popular to admire the Arno. It is a great historical creek, with four feet in the channel and some scows floating about. It would be a very plausible river if they would pump some water into it. They call it a river, and they honestly think it is a river. . . . They even help out the delusion by building bridges over it. I do not see why they are too good to wade."

The Ponte Vecchio's fame saved it in 1944 from the Nazis, who had orders to blow up all the bridges before retreating out of Florence as Allied forces advanced. They couldn't bring themselves to reduce this span to rubble—so they blew up the ancient buildings on either end instead to block it off. The Arno flood of 1966 wasn't so discriminating, however, and severely damaged the shops. Apparently, a private night watchman saw the waters rising alarmingly and called many of the goldsmiths at home, who rushed to remove their valuable stock before it was washed away.

Via Por Santa Maria/Via Guicciardini. Bus: B or D.

Museo di Storia della Scienza (Science Museum) ✮   The mainframe computer and multifunction calculator don't hold a candle to this collection's beautifully engraved intricate mechanical instruments. Galileo and his ilk practiced a science that was an art form of the highest aesthetic order. The cases display such beauties as a mechanical calculator from 1664—a gleaming bronze sandwich of engraved disks and dials—and an architect's compass and plumb disguised as a dagger, complete with sheath.

In the field of astronomy, the museum has the lens with which Galileo discovered four of the moons of Jupiter (which he promptly

and prudently named after his Medici patrons) and, alongside tele-
scopes of all sizes and complexity, a tiny "lady's telescope" made of
ivory that once came in a box of beauty products. There's also a
somewhat grisly room devoted to medicine, with disturbingly realistic wax models of just about everything that can go wrong during
childbirth. And what Italian institution would be complete without
a holy relic? In this case, it's the middle finger of Galileo's right hand,
swiped while he was en route to reinterment in Santa Croce. He was
allowed burial in a Christian church only in the 18th century, after
he was posthumously vindicated against the Inquisition for supporting a heliocentric view of the universe.

Piazza dei Giudici 1 (next to the Uffizi at the Arno end of Via dei Castellani). ℂ 055-
265-311. www.imss.fi.it. Admission 7.50€ ($9.75), 4.50€ ($5.85) ages 15–25, free
for ages 6–14 and over 65. June–Sept Mon and Wed–Fri 9:30am–5pm, Tues and Sat
9:30am–1pm, last Thurs of June and Aug, and 1st Thurs of July and Sept 9–11pm;
Oct–May Mon and Wed–Sat 9:30am–5pm, Tues 9:30am–1pm, and 2nd Sun of every
month 10am–1pm. Bus: 23.

Orsanmichele 𝕽𝕽   This tall structure halfway down Via dei
Calzaiuoli looks more like a Gothic warehouse than a church—which
is exactly what it was, built as a granary/grain market in 1337. After
a miraculous image of the Madonna appeared on a column inside,
however, the lower level was turned into a chapel. The city's merchant
guilds each undertook the task of decorating one of the outside niche-
like Gothic tabernacles around the lower level with a statue of their
guild's patron saint. Masters such as Ghiberti, Donatello, Verrocchio,
and Giambologna all cast or carved masterpieces to set here. Since
1984, these have been removed and are being replaced by casts as the
originals are slowly cleaned and exhibited up on the second story.

Unfortunately, the church now keeps erratic hours due to a lack
of personnel, so there are no set opening hours; however, you may
get lucky and find the doors thrown open when you pass by (or,
though this may take even more luck, someone might actually
answer the phone number below and give you details on when it will
next open). Since it's pretty nifty, and there's a chance you'll be able
to pop in, I'll go ahead and describe it all.

In the chapel's dark interior (emerged in 1999 from a long restoration and entered around the "back" side on Via dell'Arte della Lana)
are recently restored 14th- to 16th-century paintings by the likes of
Lorenzo di Credi and Il Poppi. The elaborate Gothic *Tabernacle* 𝕽
(1349–59) by Andrea Orcagna looks something like a miniature
church, covered with statuettes, enamel, inset colored marbles and
glass, and reliefs. It protects a luminous 1348 *Madonna and Child*

painted by Giotto's student Bernardo Daddi. The prominent statue of the *Madonna, Child, and St. Anne* to its left is by Francesco da Sangallo (1522).

Across Via dell'Arte della Lana from the Orsanmichele's main entrance is the 1308 Palazzo dell'Arte della Lana. This Gothic palace was home to medieval Florence's most powerful body, the guild of wool merchants, which employed about one-third of Florence in the 13th and 14th centuries. Up the stairs inside you can cross over the hanging walkway to the first floor (American second floor) of Orsanmichele. These are the old granary rooms, now housing a **museum of the statues** ✦ that once surrounded the exterior. A few are still undergoing restoration, but eight of the original sculptures are here, well labeled, including Donatello's marble *St. Mark* (1411–13); Ghiberti's bronze *St. John the Baptist* (1413–16), the first life-size bronze of the Renaissance; and Verrocchio's *Incredulity of St. Thomas* (1473–83). This museum, too, does not always adhere to its posted hours, as those are dependent on someone being around to honor them. Still, it's at least worth a try.

Via Arte della Lana 1/Via de' Calzaiuoli. ℂ **055-284-944.** Free admission. Church open erratic hours (though never open during *riposo*). Museum daily 9–9:45am, 10–10:45am, and 11–11:45am (plus Sat–Sun 1–1:45pm); closed the 1st and last Mon of month. Bus: A.

Museo Nazionale del Bargello (Bargello Museum) ✦✦
Inside this 1255 Gothic *palazzo* is Florence's premier sculpture museum, with works by Michelangelo, the della Robbias, and Donatello.

In the *palazzo*'s old **armory** are 16th-century works, including some of Michelangelo's earliest sculptures. Carved by a 22-year-old Michelangelo while he was visiting Rome, *Bacchus* ✦✦ (1497) was obviously inspired by the classical antiquities he studied there but is also imbued with his own irrepressible Renaissance realism—here is a (young) God of Wine who's actually drunk, reeling back on unsteady knees and holding the cup aloft with a distinctly tipsy wobble. Michelangelo polished and finished this marble in the traditional manner, but from 1503 to 1505, soon after finishing his famous *David* with a high polish, he carved the *Pitti Tondo* ✦ here, a *schiacciato* Madonna and Child scene in which the artist began using the textures of the partially worked marble itself to convey his artistic message. One of his weaker works here is the so-called *Apollo-David* (art historians can't agree on which hero the unfinished work was meant to be), but the master is back in top form with the bust of *Brutus* (ca. 1539). Some people like to see in this sculpture an idealized portrait of Michelangelo himself; a more accurate and less contentious representation sits nearby, the famous and oft-cast bronze bust of *Michelangelo* by his pupil Daniele da Volterra. Also in this room is Giambologna's ***Flying Mercury*** ⊛ (ca. 1564), looking for all the world as if he's on the verge of taking off from the ground—justifiably one of this Mannerist's masterpieces.

The *palazzo's* inner **courtyard**—one of the few medieval *cortile* in Florence to survive in more-or-less its original shape—is studded with the coats of arms of various past *podestà* (mayors) and other notables. The grand stairwell leads up to a second-story loggia filled with a flock of whimsical bronze birds cast by Giambologna for the Medici's gardens. The doorway leads into the old **Salone del Consiglio Generale (General Council Room)** ⊛⊛, a vast space with a high ceiling filled with glazed terra-cotta Madonnas by Luca della Robbia and his clan, and some of the most important sculptures of the early Renaissance.

Donatello dominates the room, starting with a mischievously smiling *Cupid* (ca. 1430–40). Nearby is his polychrome bust of *Niccolò da Uzzano,* a bit of hyperrealism next to two much more delicate busts of elfin-featured characters by Desiderio da Settignano. Donatello sculpted the *Marzocco,* lion symbol of the Florentine Republic, out of *pietra serena* between 1418 and 1420. The marble *David* (1408) is an early Donatello, but the bronze ***David*** ⊛⊛ (1440–50) beyond it is a much more mature piece, the first freestanding nude since antiquity. The figure is an almost erotic youth, with a shy, detached air that has little to do with the giant severed head at his feet. Against the far wall is ***St. George*** ⊛, carved in 1416 for a niche of Orsanmichele. The relief below it of the saint slaying his dragon is an early example of the sculptor's patented *schiacciato* technique, using thinly etched lines and perspective to create great depth in a very shallow space.

In the back right corner of this room are two bronze relief panels by Brunelleschi and Ghiberti of the *Sacrifice of Isaac,* finalists in the famous 1401 competition for the commission to cast the Baptistery's doors (see "A Man & His Dome," on p. 102). Ghiberti's panel won, as there was greater dynamism and flowing action in his version.

Out the other end of the room is the **Islamic Collection,** a testament to Florence's wide and profitable trade network. Decorative arts from the Roman era through the 16th century fill the long corridor, at the end of which is the small **Cappella Maddalena,** where condemned prisoners spent their last moments praying for their souls; it was frescoed by Giotto's studio. A perpendicular corridor houses the largest collection of ivories in the world, from the 5th to 17th centuries.

Upstairs are rooms with glazed terra cottas by Andrea and Giovanni della Robbia and another room devoted to the sculptural production of Leonardo da Vinci's teacher Verrocchio, including yet another *David* (1465), a haughty youth with a tousle of hair inspired by the Donatello version downstairs.

Via del Proconsolo 4. © **055-238-8606.** www.sbas.firenze.it. (Reserve tickets at © 055-294-883 or www.firenzemusei.it.) Admission 4€ ($5.20). Daily 8:30am– 1:50pm. Closed 2nd and 4th Mon and 1st, 3rd, and 5th Sun of each month. Bus: A, 14, or 23.

Badia Fiorentina   The slender pointed bell tower of this Benedictine abbey, founded in A.D. 978, is one of the landmarks of the Florentine skyline. Sadly, the bells Dante wrote of in his *Paradiso* no longer toll the hours. Serious structural problems have silenced the tower. In the now-baroque interior, some say Dante first laid eyes on his beloved Beatrice, and Boccaccio, of *Decameron* fame, used to lecture on Dante's Divine Comedy here. The church's most arresting sight is a 1485 Filippino Lippi painting of the *Madonna Appearing to St. Bernard.* The box used to shed light on it parcels out a measly 10 seconds for each coin, so feed it only the smallest denominations. For a nominal "donation," the sacristan will throw on the lights to the *trompe l'oeil* ceiling.

Via Dante Alighieri and Via del Proconsolo. © **055-287-389.** Free admission. Thurs–Tues 5–7pm (sometimes also in the morning). Bus: A, 14, or 23.

Santa Trínita ⚓   Beyond Bernardo Buontalenti's late-16th-century **facade** lies a dark church, rebuilt in the 14th century but founded by the Vallombrosans before 1177. The third chapel on the right has what remains of the detached frescoes by Spinello Aretino (viewable by push-button light), which were found under Lorenzo Monaco's excellent 1422 frescoes covering the next chapel down.

In the right transept, Domenico Ghirlandaio frescoed the **Cappella Sassetti** ⚓ in 1483 with a cycle on the *Life of St. Francis* (coinop lights), but true to form he set all the scenes against Florentine backdrops and peopled them with portraits of the notables of the day. The most famous is *Francis Receiving the Order from Pope Honorius,* which in this version takes place under an arcade on the north side of Piazza della Signoria—the Loggia dei Lanzi is featured in the middle, and on the left is the Palazzo Vecchio. (The Uffizi between them hadn't been built yet.) It's also full of contemporary portraits: In the little group on the far right, the unhandsome man with the light red cloak is Lorenzo the Magnificent.

The chapel to the right of the main altar houses the miraculous *Crucifix* that once hung in San Miniato al Monte. One day the nobleman Giovanni Gualberto was storming up the hillside in a rage, on his way to wreak revenge on his brother's murderer. Gualberto paused at San Miniato and after some reflection decided to pardon the assassin, whereupon this crucifix bowed its head in approval. Gualberto went on to found the Vallombrosan order of monks, who later established this church.

The south end of the piazza leads to the **Ponte Santa Trínita,** one of Italy's most graceful bridges. In 1567, Ammannati built a span here that was set with four 16th-century statues of the seasons in honor of the marriage of Cosimo II. After the Nazis blew up the bridge in 1944, it was rebuilt, and all was set into place again—save the head on the statue of Spring, which remained lost until a team dredging the river in 1961 found it by accident. From the bridge you get a great view upriver of the Ponte Vecchio and downriver of the **Ponte alla Carraia** (another postwar reconstruction), where, in 1304, so many people gathered to watch a floating production of Dante's *Inferno* that it collapsed and all were drowned. Florentine wits were quick to point out that all the people who went to see Hell that day found what they were looking for.

Piazza Santa Trínita. © **055-216-912.** Free admission. Mon–Sat 8am–noon and 4–6pm; Sun 4–6pm. Bus: A, B, 6, 11, 36, 37, or 68.

3 Around San Lorenzo & the Mercato Centrale

The church of San Lorenzo is practically lost behind the leather stalls and souvenir carts of Florence's vast **San Lorenzo street market** (p. 162). In fact, the hawking of wares and bustle of commerce characterize all the streets of this neighborhood, centered on both the church and the nearby **Mercato Centrale food market.** This is a colorful scene, but one of the most pickpocket-happy in the city, so be wary.

San Lorenzo ☞ A rough-brick antifacade and the undistinguished stony bulk of a building surrounded by the stalls of the leather market hide what is most likely the oldest church in Florence, founded in A.D. 393. San Lorenzo was the city's cathedral until the bishop's seat moved to Santa Reparata (later to become the Duomo) in the 7th century. More important, it was the Medici family's parish church, and as those famous bankers began to accumulate their vast fortune, they started a tradition of lavishing it on this church that lasted until the clan died out in the 18th century. Visiting the entire church complex at once is tricky: Though interconnected, the church proper, the Old Sacristy, and the Laurentian Library have different open hours. The Medici tombs, listed separately below, have a separate entrance around the back of the church and have still different hours.

The first thing Giovanni di Bicci de' Medici, founder of the family fortune, did for the church was hire Brunelleschi to tune up the **interior,** rebuilding according to the architect's plans in 1426. At the end of the aisle is a Desiderio da Settignano marble tabernacle that's a mastery of *schiacciato* relief and carefully incised perspective. Across the aisle is one of the two bronze 1460 **pulpits** ✹✹—the other is across the nave—that were Donatello's last works. His patron and the first great consolidator of Medici power, which at this early stage still showed great concern for protecting the interests of the people, was Cosimo il Vecchio, Lorenzo the Magnificent's grandfather. Cosimo, whose wise behind-the-scenes rule made him popular with the Florentines, died in 1464 and is buried in front of the high altar. The plaque marking the spot is simply inscribed PATER PATRIE— father of his homeland.

Off the left transept is the **Sagrestia Vecchia (Old Sacristy)** ✹, one of Brunelleschi's purest pieces of early Renaissance architecture. In the center of the chapel Cosimo il Vecchio's parents, Giovanni di Bicci de' Medici and his wife, Piccarda Bueri, rest in peace.

On the wall of the left aisle is Bronzino's huge fresco of the *Martyrdom of San Lorenzo* ✹. The 3rd-century namesake saint of this church, San Lorenzo was a flinty early Christian and the treasurer of the Roman church. When commanded by the Romans to hand over the church's wealth, Lorenzo appeared before Emperor Valerian's prefect with "thousands" of sick, poor, and crippled people saying "Here is all the church's treasure." The Romans weren't amused and decided to martyr him on a gridiron over hot coals. Feisty to the last, at one point while Lorenzo lay there roasting he called out to his tormentors through gritted teeth, "Turn me over, I'm done on this side."

Near this fresco is an entrance to the cloister and just inside it a stairwell to the right leading up to the **Biblioteca Laurenziana (Laurentian Library)** ✹✹, which can also be entered admission free without going through—and paying for—the church (the separate entrance is just to the left of the church's main doors). Michelangelo designed this library in 1524 to house the Medici's manuscript collection, and it stands as one of the most brilliant works of Mannerist architecture. The vestibule is a whacked-out riff on the Renaissance, all *pietra serena* and white plaster walls like a good Brunelleschi piece, but turned inside out. There are phony piers running into each other in the corners, pilaster strips that support nothing, and brackets that exist for no reason. On the whole, however, it manages to remain remarkably coherent. Its star feature is a *pietra serena* flight of curving stairs flowing out from the entrance to the reading room. This actual library part, however—filled with intricately carved wood and handsomely illuminated manuscripts—was closed indefinitely in 1999 until "urgent maintenance" is completed.

Piazza San Lorenzo. ✆ **055-216-634.** Admission 2.50€ ($3.25). Church Mon–Sat 10am–5pm. Old Sacristy (usually) Sept–July Mon, Wed, Fri, and Sat 10–11:45am; Tues and Thurs 4–5:45pm. Laurentian Library Mon–Sat 9am–1pm. Bus: 1, 6, 7, 11, 14, 17, 23, 67, 68, 70, or 71.

Cappelle Medicee (Medici Chapels) ✹✹ When Michelangelo built the New Sacristy between 1520 and 1533 (finished by Vasari in 1556), it was to be a tasteful monument to Lorenzo the Magnificent and his generation of fairly pleasant Medici. When work got underway on the Chapel of the Princes in 1604, it was to become one of the world's most god-awful and arrogant memorials, dedicated to the grand dukes, some of Florence's most decrepit tyrants. The **Cappella dei Principi (Chapel of the Princes)** ✹ is an exercise in bad taste, a mountain of cut marbles and semiprecious stones—jasper, alabaster, mother-of-pearl, agate, and the like—slathered onto the walls and ceiling with no regard for composition and still less for chromatic unity. The pouring of ducal funds into this monstrosity began in 1604 and lasted until the rarely conscious Gian Gastone de' Medici drank himself to death in 1737 without an heir—but teams kept doggedly at the thing, and they were still finishing the floor in 1962. The tombs of the grand dukes in this massive marble mistake were designed by Pietro Tacca in the 17th century, and off to the left and right of the altar are small treasuries full of gruesome holy relics in silver-bedecked cases. The dome of the structure, seen from the outside, is one of Florence's landmarks, a kind of infant version of the Duomo's.

Michelangelo's **Sagrestia Nuova (New Sacristy)** ✹✹, built to jibe with Brunelleschi's Old Sacristy in San Lorenzo proper, is much calmer. (An architectural tidbit: The dome's windows taper as they get near the top, which fools you into thinking the dome is higher.)

The Master's Doodles

On the walls around the small altar in the Medici Chapels are some recently uncovered architectural graffiti that have been attributed to Michelangelo. Even more important are some 50 charcoal drawings and sketches the master left on the walls in the sepulchral chamber below. The drawings include a sketch of the legs of Duke Giuliano, Christ risen, and the Laocoön. Michelangelo found himself hiding out here after the Medici reconquered the city in 1530—he had helped the city keep the dukes out with his San Miniato defenses and, probably rightly, feared a reprisal. You need an appointment to see the sketches; ask at the ticket office.

Michelangelo was supposed to produce three tombs here (perhaps four) but ironically got only the two less important ones done. So Lorenzo de' Medici the Magnificent—wise ruler of his city, poet of note, grand patron of the arts, and moneybags behind much of the Renaissance—ended up with a mere inscription of his name next to his brother Giuliano's on a plain marble slab against the entrance wall. Admittedly, they did get one genuine Michelangelo sculpture to decorate their slab, a *Madonna and Child* that's perhaps the master's most beautiful version of the theme. (The other two statues are later works by less talented sculptors.)

On the left wall of the sacristy is Michelangelo's **Tomb of Lorenzo** ✵, duke of Urbino (and Lorenzo the Magnificent's grandson), whose seated statue symbolizes the contemplative life. Below him on the elongated curves of the tomb stretch *Dawn* (female) and *Dusk* (male), a pair of Michelangelo's most famous sculptures, where he uses both high polish and rough cutting to impart strength, texture, and psychological suggestion to the allegorical works. This pair mirrors the similarly fashioned and equally important *Day* (male) and *Night* (female) across the way. One additional point *Dawn* and *Night* brings out is that Michelangelo really wasn't too adept at the female body—he just produced softer, less muscular men with slightly elongated midriffs and breasts sort of tacked on at funny angles.

Piazza Madonna degli Aldobrandini (behind San Lorenzo, where Via Faenza and Via del Giglio meet). ✆ **055-238-8602**. Admission 6€ ($7.80); call Firenze Musei ✆ 055-294-883 for reservations. Daily 8:15am–5pm. Closed 1st, 3rd, and 5th Mon and 2nd and 4th Sun of each month. Bus: 1, 6, 7, 11, 14, 17, 23, 67, 68, 70, or 71.

Palazzo Medici-Riccardi ⟨⟩   The Palazzo Medici-Riccardi was built by Michelozzo in 1444 for Cosimo de' Medici il Vecchio; it's the prototype Florentine *palazzo*, on which the more overbearing Strozzi and Pitti palaces were later modeled. It remained the Medici private home until Cosimo I more officially declared his power as duke by moving to the city's traditional civic brain center, the Palazzo Vecchio. A door off the right of the entrance courtyard leads up a staircase to the **Cappella dei Magi,** the oldest chapel to survive from a private Florentine palace; its walls are covered with gorgeously dense and colorful Benozzo Gozzoli **frescoes** (1459–63). Rich as tapestries, the walls depict an extended *Journey of the Magi* to see the Christ child, who's being adored by Mary in the altarpiece. Gozzoli is at his decorative best here, inheriting an attention to minute detail in plants and animals from his old teacher Fra' Angelico.

Via Cavour 3. ⓒ **055-276-0340.** Admission 4€ ($5.20). Thurs–Tues 9am–7pm. Number of visitors limited; arrive early or call to book a time to visit. Bus: 1, 6, 7, 11, 14, 17, 23, 67, 68, 70, or 71.

4 On or Near Piazza Santa Maria Novella

Piazza Santa Maria Novella boasts patches of grass and a central fountain. The two squat obelisks, resting on the backs of Giambologna tortoises, once served as the turning posts for the "chariot" races held here from the 16th to the mid–19th century. However, these days the piazza sees more action as a roving ground for the few gypsies picking tourists' pockets in Florence and as the hangout for the city's economically depressed small immigrant population and even smaller cache of itinerants. Several bars and pubs have tried to infuse the area with some life, but the night still leans toward the seedy around here.

Santa Maria Novella ⟨⟩⟨⟩   Of all Florence's major churches, the home of the Dominicans is the only one with an original **facade** ⟨⟩ that matches its era of greatest importance. The lower Romanesque half was started in the 14th century by architect Fra' Jacopo Talenti, who had just finished building the church itself (started in 1246). Leon Battista Alberti finished the facade, adding a classically inspired Renaissance top that not only went seamlessly with the lower half but also created a Cartesian plane of perfect geometry.

The church's interior underwent a massive restoration in the late 1990s, returning Giotto's restored *Crucifix* to pride of place, hanging in the nave's center—and becoming the first church in Florence to charge admission. Against the second pillar on the left of the nave is the pulpit from which Galileo was denounced for his heretical theory that Earth revolved around the sun. Just past the pulpit, on the left wall, is **Masaccio's *Trinità*** ⊛⊛⊛ (ca. 1428), the first painting ever to use perfect linear mathematical perspective. Florentine citizens and artists flooded in to see the fresco when it was unveiled, many remarking in awe that the coffered ceiling seemed to punch a hole back into space, creating a chapel out of a flat wall. The **transept** is filled with spectacularly frescoed chapels. The **sanctuary** ⊛ behind the main altar was frescoed after 1485 by Domenico Ghirlandaio with the help of his assistants and apprentices, probably including a very young Michelangelo. The left wall is covered with a cycle on *The Life of the Virgin* and the right shows the *Life of St. John the Baptist.* The works have a highly polished decorative quality and are less biblical stories than snapshots of the era's fashions and personages, full of portraits of the Tornabuoni family who commissioned them.

Restoration workers in 2005 found a fresco hidden behind one of the lesser-known works here—by 16th-century Veronese painter Jacopo Ligozzi—and the mystery of who created it is the talk of local art circles. As of the printing of this edition, it remains unknown.

The **Cappella Gondi** to the left of the high altar contains the *Crucifix* carved by Brunelleschi to show his buddy Donatello how it should be done (see the Santa Croce review, on p. 139, for the story). At the end of the left transept is a different **Cappella Strozzi,** covered with restored **frescoes** ⊛ (1357) by Nardo di Cione, early medieval casts of thousands where the saved mill about Paradise on the left and the damned stew in a Dantean inferno on the right.

Piazza Santa Maria Novella. ℂ **055-215-918.** Admission 2.50€ ($3.25) adults, 1.50€ ($1.95) ages 12–18. Mon–Thurs and Sat 9am–5pm; Fri and Sun 1–5pm. Bus: A, 6, 11, 12, 36, 37, or 68.

Museo di Santa Maria Novella ⊛   The cloisters of Santa Maria Novella's convent are open to the public as a museum. The **Chiostro Verde,** with a cypress-surrounded fountain and chirping birds, is named for the greenish tint in the pigment used by Paolo Uccello in his **frescoes** ⊛⊛. His works line the right wall of the first walkway; the most famous is the confusing, somewhat disturbing first scene you come to, where the *Flood and Recession of the Flood and the Drunkenness and Sacrifice of Noah* (1446) are all squeezed onto one panel as the story lines are piled atop one another and Noah appears several times. The two giant wooden walls on either side are meant to be the Ark, shown both before and after the Flood, seen in extreme, distorting perspective.

⟨Tips⟩ Seeing *David*

The wait to get in to see *David* can be up to an hour if you
didn't reserve ahead. Try getting there before the museum
opens in the morning or an hour or two before closing time.

The **Cappella degli Spagnoli (Spanish Chapel)** 𝕬 got its name
when it became the private chapel of Eleonora of Toledo, recently
arrived in Florence to be Cosimo de' Medici's bride. The pretty
chapel was entirely frescoed by Andrea da Firenze and his assistants
in a kind of half Florentine–half Sienese style around 1365.

Piazza Santa Maria Novella (entrance to the left of the church facade). ℭ **055-282-
187**. Admission 1.40€ ($1.80). Sat and Mon–Thurs 9am–2pm; Sun 8am–1pm. Bus:
A, 6, 11, 12, 36, 37, or 68.

Ognissanti 𝕬   Founded in 1256 by the Umiliati, a wool-weaving
sect of the Benedictines whose trade helped establish this area as a
textile district, the present Ognissanti was rebuilt by its new Franciscan owners in the 17th century. It has the earliest baroque **facade** in
Florence, designed by Matteo Nigetti in 1627 and rebuilt in traver-
tine in 1872.

Ognissanti was the parish church of the Vespucci family, agents of
the Medici bank in Seville. A young Domenico Ghirlandaio por-
trayed several of the family members in his *Madonna della Misericordia* (1470) on the second altar to the right. The lady under the
Madonna's left hand may be Simonetta Vespucci, renowned beauty
of her age, mistress of Giuliano de' Medici (Lorenzo's brother), and
the possible model for Venus in Botticelli's *Birth of Venus*. The young
man with black hair to the Madonna's right is said to be Amerigo
Vespucci (1454–1512), whose letters about exploring the New
World in 1499 and again from 1501 to 1502 would become so popular that a cartographer used a corruption of Amerigo's name on an
influential set of maps to describe the newly discovered continent.
Sorry, Columbus. The family tombstone (America's namesake rests
in peace underneath) is to the left of this altar.

Between the third and fourth altars is Botticelli's fresco of a pen-
sive *St. Augustine in His Study* (1480), a much more intense work
than its matching *St. Jerome in His Study*, by Ghirlandaio, across the
nave. Botticelli, whose real name was Sandro Filipepi, is buried
under a round marker in the second chapel in the right transept. In
the left transept's second chapel is the habit St. Francis was wearing

when he received the stigmata. You can enter the convent to the left of the church facade at Borgo Ognissanti 42. In the refectory here is Domenico Ghirlandaio's *Last Supper* ✸, painted in 1480 with a background heavy on Christian symbols.

Piazza Ognissanti. ② **055-239-8700.** Free admission. Church daily 8am–noon and 4–6:30pm. Convent Mon, Tues, and Sat 9am–noon. Bus: B, D, or 12.

5 Near San Marco & Santissima Annuziata

Galleria dell'Accademia (Academy Gallery) ✸✸ Though tour-bus crowds flock here just for Michelangelo's *David,* anyone with more than a day in Florence can take the time to peruse some of the Accademia's paintings as well.

The first long hall is devoted to Michelangelo and, though you pass his *Slaves* and the entrance to the painting gallery, most visitors are immediately drawn down to the far end, a tribune dominated by the most famous sculpture in the world: **Michelangelo's *David*** ✸✸✸. A hot young sculptor fresh from his success with the *Pietà* in Rome, Michelangelo offered in 1501 to take on a slab of marble that had already been worked on by another sculptor (who had taken a chunk out of one side before declaring it too strangely shaped to use). The huge slab had been lying around the Duomo's work yards so long it earned a nickname, *Il Gigante* (The Giant), so it was with a twist of humor that Michelangelo, only 29 years old, finished in 1504 a Goliath-size David for the city.

There was originally a vague idea that the statue would become part of the Duomo, but Florence's republican government soon wheeled it down to stand on Piazza della Signoria in front of the Palazzo Vecchio to symbolize the defeated tyranny of the Medici, who had been ousted a decade before (but would return with a vengeance). During a 1527 anti-Medicean siege on the *palazzo,* a bench thrown at the attackers from one of the windows hit David's left arm, which reportedly came crashing down on a farmer's toe. (A young Giorgio Vasari came scurrying out to gather all the pieces for safekeeping, despite the riot going on around him, and the arm was later reconstituted.) Even the sculpture's 1873 removal to the Accademia to save it from the elements (a copy stands in its place) hasn't kept it entirely safe—in 1991, a man threw himself on the statue and began hammering at the right foot, dislodging several toes. The foot was repaired, and *David*'s Plexiglas shield went up.

The hall leading up to *David* is lined with perhaps Michelangelo's most fascinating works, the four famous *nonfiniti* ("unfinished")

Slaves, or *Prisoners* ✸✸✸. Like no others, these statues symbolize Michelangelo's theory that sculpture is an "art that takes away super-fluous material." The great master saw a true sculpture as something that was already inherent in the stone, and all it needed was a skilled chisel to free it from the extraneous rock. That certainly seems to be the case here, as we get a private glimpse into Michelangelo's work-ing technique: how he began by carving the abdomen and torso, going for the gut of the sculpture and bringing that to life first so it could tell him how the rest should start to take form. Whether he intended the statues to look the way they do now or in fact left them only half done has been debated by art historians to exhaustion. The result, no matter what the sculptor's intentions, is remarkable, a sym-bol of the master's great art and personal views on craft as his Slaves struggle to break free of their chipped stone prisons.

Nearby, in a similar mode, is a statue of *St. Matthew* ✸✸ (1504–08), which Michelangelo began carving as part of a series of Apostles he was at one point going to complete for the Duomo. (The *Pietà* at the end of the corridor on the right is by one of Michelan-gelo's students, not by the master as was once thought.)

Off this hall of *Slaves* is the first wing of the painting gallery, which includes a panel, possibly from a wedding chest, known as the *Cassone Adimari* ✸, painted by Lo Scheggia in the 1440s. It shows the happy couple's promenade to the Duomo, with the green-and-white marbles of the baptistery prominent in the background.

In the wings off *David*'s tribune are large paintings by Michelan-gelo's contemporaries, Mannerists over whom he had a very strong influence—they even say Michelangelo provided the original draw-ing from which Pontormo painted his amorous *Venus and Cupid.* Off the end of the left wing is a long 19th-century hall crowded wall-to-wall and stacked floor-to-ceiling with **plaster casts** of hundreds of sculptures and busts—the Accademia, after all, is what it sounds like: an academy for budding young artists, founded in 1784 as an off-shoot of the Academy of Art Design that dates from Michelangelo's time (1565).

Via Ricasoli 58–60. ℂ **055-238-8609** or 055-238-8612. www.sbas.firenze.it/accademia. (Reserve tickets at ℂ **055-294-883** or www.firenzemusei.it.) Admis-sion 6.50€ ($8.45) adults, 3.25€ ($4.25) children. Tues–Sun 8:15am–6:50pm; last admission 30 min. before close. Bus: 1, 6, 7, 10, 11, 17, 25, 31, 32, 33, 67, 68, or 70.

San Marco ✸✸   In 1437, Cosimo de' Medici il Vecchio, grandfa-ther of Lorenzo the Magnificent, had Michelozzo convert a medieval monastery here into a new home for the Dominicans, in which

Cosimo also founded Europe's first public library. From 1491 until he was burned at the stake on Piazza della Signoria in 1498, this was the home base of puritanical preacher Girolamo Savonarola. The monastery's most famous friar, though, was early Renaissance painter Fra' Angelico, and he left many of his finest works, devotional images painted with the technical skill and minute detail of a miniaturist or an illuminator but on altarpiece scale. While his works tended to be transcendently spiritual, Angelico was also prone to filling them with earthly details with which any peasant or stonemason could identify.

The museum rooms are entered off a pretty cloister. The old Pilgrim's Hospice has been converted into a **Fra' (Beato) Angelico Gallery** 𝒜𝒜, full of altarpieces and painted panels. Also off the cloister is the **Reffetorio Grande (Great Refectory),** with 16th- and 17th-century paintings, and the **Sala del Capitolo (Chapter House),** frescoed from 1441 to 1442 with a huge *Crucifixion* by Fra' Angelico and his assistants. The door next to this leads past the staircase up to the Dormitory (see below) to the **Sala del Cenacolo (Small Refectory),** with a long fresco of the *Last Supper* by Domenico Ghirlandaio.

The **Dormitorio (Dormitory)** 𝒜𝒜 of cells where the monks lived is one of Fra' Angelico's masterpieces and perhaps his most famous cycle of frescoes. In addition to the renowned *Annunciation* 𝒜𝒜 at the top of the stairs to the monks' rooms, Angelico painted the cells themselves with simple works to aid his fellow friars in their meditations. One of these almost anticipates surrealism—a flagellation where disembodied hands strike at Christ's face and a rod descends on him from the blue-green background. Angelico's assistants carried out the repetitious Crucifixion scenes in many of the cells. At the end of one of the corridors is the suite of cells occupied by Savonarola when he was here prior. In the first are two famous portraits of him by his devout follower and talented painter Fra' Bartolomeo, along with an anonymous 16th-century painting of *Savonarola Burned at the Stake* on Piazza della Signoria. The **Biblioteca (Library)** off the corridor to the right of the stairs was designed by Michelozzo in 1441 and contains beautifully illuminated choir books.

Piazza San Marco 3. ☎ **055-238-8608.** Admission 4€ ($5.20) adults, 2€ ($2.60) children. Mon–Fri 8:30am–1:50pm; Sat–Sun 8:15am–7pm. Closed 1st, 3rd, and 5th Sun and 2nd and 4th Mon of each month. Bus: 1, 6, 7, 10, 11, 17, 20, 25, 31, 32, 33, 67, 68, or 70.

Cenacolo di Sant'Apollonia 𝒜   There are no lines at this former convent and no crowds. Few people even know to ring the bell at the

Michelangelo: The Making of a Renaissance Master

Irascible, moody, and manic-depressive, Michelangelo was quite simply one of the greatest artists of all time. Many feel he represents the pinnacle of the Italian Renaissance, a genius at sculpture, painting, and architecture, and even a master poet.

In 1475, Michelangelo Buonarroti was born near Arezzo in the tiny town of Caprese, where his Florentine father was serving a term as a *podestà* (visiting mayor). He grew up on the family farm at Settignano, outside Florence, and was wet-nursed by the wife of a local stonecutter—he used to joke that he sucked his skill with the hammer and chisel along with the mother's milk. He was apprenticed early to the fresco studio of Domenico Ghirlandaio who, while watching the young apprentice sketching, once remarked in shock, "This boy knows more about it than I do." After just a year at the studio, Michelangelo was recruited by Lorenzo the Magnificent de' Medici to become part of his new school for sculptors.

Michelangelo learned quickly, and soon after his arrival at the school took a chunk of marble and carved it to copy the head of an old faun from an ancient statue in the garden. Lorenzo happened by and saw the skill with which the head was made, but when he saw that Michelangelo had departed from his model and carved the mouth open and

nondescript door. What they're missing is an entire wall covered with the vibrant colors of Andrea del Castagno's masterful *Last Supper* (ca. 1450). Castagno used his paint to create the rich marble panels that checkerboard the *trompe l'oeil* walls and broke up the long white tablecloth with the dark figure of Judas the Betrayer, whose face is painted to resemble a satyr, an ancient symbol of evil.

Via XXVII Aprile 1. © 055-238-8607. Free admission. Daily 8:30am–1:50pm. Closed 1st, 3rd, and 5th Sun and 2nd and 4th Mon of each month. Bus: 1, 6, 7, 10, or 11.

Santissima Annunziata   In 1230, seven Florentine nobles had a spiritual crisis, gave away all their possessions, and retired to the forests to contemplate divinity. They returned to what were then the fields outside the city walls and founded a small oratory, proclaiming

laughing with teeth and a tongue, he commented only, "But you should have known that old people never have all their teeth and there are always some missing." The young artist reflected on this. When Lorenzo returned a while later, he found Michelangelo waiting anxiously, eager to show he had not only chipped out a few teeth but also gouged down into the gums of the statue to make the tooth loss look more realistic. Impressed, Lorenzo decided to take the boy under his wing and virtually adopted him into the Medici household.

After his success at age 19 with the *Pietà* sculpture in Rome, Michelangelo was given the opportunity by the city council to carve the enormous block of marble that became *David*. He worked on it behind shuttered scaffolding so few saw it until the unveiling. Legend has it that when Soderini, the head of the city council, came to see the finished work, he remarked the nose looked a tad too large. Michelangelo, knowing better but wanting to please Soderini, climbed up to the head (out of view), grabbed a handful of leftover plaster dust, and while tapping his hammer lightly against his chisel, let the dust sprinkle down gradually as if he were actually carving. "Much better," remarked Soderini when Michelangelo climbed down again and they stepped back to admire it. "Now you've really brought it to life."

they were Servants of Mary, or the Servite Order. The oratory was enlarged by Michelozzo (1444–81) and later redesigned in the baroque. Under the facade's **portico,** you enter the **Chiostro dei Voti (Votice Cloister),** designed by Michelozzo with Corinthian-capitaled columns and decorated with some of the city's finest Mannerist frescoes (1465–1515). Rosso Fiorentino provided an *Assumption* (1513) and Pontormo a *Visitation* (1515) just to the right of the door, but the main works are by their master, Andrea del Sarto, whose ***Birth of the Virgin*** ✸ (1513), in the far right corner, is one of his finest works. To the right of the door into the church is a damaged but still fascinating *Coming of the Magi* (1514) by del Sarto, who included a self-portrait at the far right, looking out at us from under his blue hat.

The **interior** is excessively baroque. Just to the left as you enter is a huge tabernacle hidden under a mountain of flowers and *ex votos* (votive offerings). It was designed by Michelozzo to house a small painting of the *Annunciation*. Legend holds that this painting was started by a friar who, vexed that he couldn't paint the Madonna's face as beautifully as it should be, gave up and took a nap instead. When he awoke, he found an angel had filled in the face for him. Newlywed brides in Florence don't toss their bouquets—they head here after the ceremony to leave their flowers at the shrine for good luck.

The large circular **tribune** was finished for Michelozzo by Leon Battista Alberti. You enter it from its left side via the left transept, but first pause to pay your respects to Andrea del Sarto, buried under a floor slab at the left-hand base of the great arch.

From the left transept, a door leads into the **Chiostro dei Morti (Cloister of the Dead;** track down a sacristan to open it), where over the entrance door is another of Andrea del Sarto's greatest frescoes, the **Madonna del Sacco** ✿, and a *Rest on the Flight into Egypt* scene that got its name from the sack Joseph is leaning against to do a little light reading. Also off this cloister is the **Cappella di San Luca (Chapel of St. Luke),** evangelist and patron saint of painters. It was decorated by late Renaissance and Mannerist painters, including Pontormo, Alessandro Allori, Santi di Tito, and Giorgio Vasari. On the **piazza** ✿✿ outside, flanked by elegant porticos (see Spedale degli Innocenti, below), is an equestrian statue of *Grand Duke Ferdinando I,* Giambologna's last work; it was cast in 1608 after his death by his student Pietro Tacca, who also did the two little fountains of fantastic mermonkey-monsters. The piazza's beauty is somewhat ruined by the car and bus traffic routed through both ends, but it's kept lively by students from the nearby university, who sit on the loggia steps for lunch and hang out here in the evenings.

Piazza Santissima Annunziata. ✆ 055-266-181. Free admission. Daily 7:30am–12:30pm and 4–6:30pm. Bus: 6, 31, or 32.

Spedale degli Innocenti Europe's oldest foundling hospital, opened in 1445, is still going strong as a convent orphanage, though times have changed a bit. The Lazy Susan set into the wall on the left end of the arcade—where once people left unwanted babies, swiveled it around, rang the bell, and ran—has since been blocked up. The colonnaded **portico** ✿ (built 1419–26) was designed by Filippo Brunelleschi when he was still an active goldsmith. It was his first great achievement as an architect and helped define the new Renaissance style he was developing. Its repetition by later artists in front of other buildings on the piazza makes it one of the most exquisite squares in all of Italy. The spandrels between the arches of Brunelleschi's portico are set with glazed **terra-cotta reliefs** of swaddled babes against rounded blue backgrounds—hands-down the masterpieces of Andrea della Robbia.

Piazza Santissima Annunziata 12. ℂ **055-249-1708**. www.istitutodeglinnocenti.it. Admission 2.60€ ($3.40). Thurs–Tues 8:30am–2pm. Bus: 6, 31, or 32.

Museo Opificio delle Pietre Dure

In the 16th century, Florentine craftsmen perfected the art of *pietre dure,* piecing together cut pieces of precious and semiprecious stones in an inlay process, and the Medici-founded institute devoted to the craft has been in this building since 1796.

Long ago misnamed a "Florentine mosaic" by the tourism industry, this is a highly refined craft in which skilled artisans (artists, really) create scenes and boldly colored intricate designs in everything from cameos and tabletops to never-fade stone "paintings." Masters are adept at selecting, slicing, and polishing stones so that the natural grain or color gradations in the cross sections will, once cut and laid in the design, become the contours, shading, and molding that give good *pietre dure* scenes their depth and illusion of three-dimensionality.

The collection in this museum is small, but the pieces are uniformly excellent. Souvenir shops all over town sell modern *pietre dure* items—much of it mass-produced junk, but some very nice. The best contemporary maestro is Ilio de Filippis, whose workshop is called Pitti Mosaici (p. 160).

Via degli Alfani 78. ℂ **055-265-1357**, or 055-294-883 for ticket reservations (not necessary). www.firenzemusei.it. Admission 2€ ($2.60), free for children under 6. Mon–Sat 8:15am–2pm (Thurs until 7pm). Bus: 6, 11, 17, 31, or 32.

Museo Archeologico (Archaeological Museum) 🟊🟊

This embarrassingly rich collection is often overlooked by visitors in full-throttle Renaissance mode. It conserves Egyptian artifacts, Roman remains, many Attic vases, and an important Etruscan collection. Parts of it have been undergoing restoration and rearrangement for years and are closed indefinitely, including the garden. The relics to be on the lookout for start in the first ground-floor room with an early-4th-century-B.C. bronze **Chimera** 🟊🟊, a mythical beast with a lion's body and head, a goat head sprouting from its back, and a serpent for a tail (the tail was incorrectly restored in 1785). The beast was found near Arezzo in 1553 and probably made in a Chiusi or an Orvieto workshop as a votive offering. The legend that claims Benvenuto Cellini recast the left paws is hogwash; the feet did have to be reattached, but they were the originals. Ground-floor room III contains a **silver amphora** studded with concave medallions, a work from Antioch (ca. A.D. 380).

In room III on the upper floor is an extraordinarily rare **Hittite wood-and-bone chariot** from the 14th century B.C. Room XIV upstairs has a cast bronze *Arringatore,* or orator, found near Perugia. It was made in the 1st century B.C. and helps illustrate how Roman society was having a great influence on the Etruscan world— not only in the workmanship of the statue but also in the fact that the Etruscan orator Aule Meteli is wearing a Roman toga. Room XIII contains the museum's most famous piece, the *Idolino* ✪. The history of this nude bronze lad with his outstretched hand is long, complicated, and in the end a bit mysterious. The current theory is that he's a Roman statue of the Augustan period (around the time of Christ), with the head modeled, perhaps, on a lost piece by the Greek master Polycleitus. The rub: *Idolino* was originally probably part of a lamp stand used at Roman banquets. The male torso displayed here was fished out of the sea near Livorno. It was made in Greece around 480 to 470 B.C.—the earliest known Greek bronze cast using the lost wax method. The horse's head also in this room once belonged to the Medici, as did much of this museum's collections, and tradition holds that it was a source of inspiration for Verrocchio and Donatello as they cast their own equestrian monuments. It was probably once part of a Hellenistic sculpture from the 2nd or 1st century B.C.

Via della Colonna 38. ✆ **055-23-575.** Admission 4€ ($5.20). Mon 2–7pm; Tues and Thurs 8:30am–7pm; Wed and Fri–Sun 8:30am–2pm. Closed 2nd and 4th Mon of month. Bus: 6, 31, or 32.

Cimitero degli Inglesi (Protestant Cemetery)

When this plot of green was nestled up against the city's medieval walls, it was indeed a quiet, shady, and reflective spot. When those walls were demolished in the late 19th century and the boulevard Viale put in their place, it became a traffic circle instead. We can only hope that frail and gentle Elizabeth Barrett Browning can block out the noise from her tomb off the left of the main path. The **sepulcher** was designed by her husband and fellow poet Robert Browning after her death in Florence in 1861.

Piazzale Donatello 38. ✆ **055-582-608.** www.florin.ms/cemetery.html. Free admission, donation suggested (ring at the gate). Easter–Oct Mon 9am–noon, Tues–Fri 3–6pm; Nov–Easter Mon 9am–noon, Tues–Sat 2–5pm. Bus: 6, 8, or 33.

6 Around Piazza Santa Croce

Piazza Santa Croce is pretty much like any in Florence—a nice bit of open space ringed with souvenir and leather shops and thronged with tourists. Its most unique feature (aside from the one time a year it's covered with dirt and violent Renaissance soccer is played on it) is the **Palazzo Antellisi** on the south side. This well-preserved, 16th-century patrician house is owned by a contessa who rents out a bunch of peachy apartments.

Santa Croce ☆☆   The center of the Florentine Franciscan universe was begun in 1294 by Gothic master Arnolfo di Cambio in order to rival the huge church of Santa Maria Novella being raised by the Dominicans across the city. The church wasn't completed and consecrated until 1442, and even then it remained faceless until the neo-Gothic **facade** was added in 1857 (and cleaned in 1998–99). The cloisters are home to Brunelleschi's Cappella de' Pazzi (see the Museo dell'Opera, below), the convent partially given over to a famous leather school (see chapter 6), and the church itself a shrine of 14th-century frescoes and a monument to notable Florentines, whose tombs and memorials litter the place like an Italian Westminster. The best artworks, such as the Giotto frescoes, are guarded by euro-gobbling light boxes; bring plenty of change.

The Gothic **interior**—for which they now charge a premium admission (it was free until recently)—is wide and gaping, with huge pointed stone arches creating the aisles and an echoing nave trussed with wood beams, in all feeling vaguely barnlike (an analogy the occasional fluttering pigeon only reinforces). The floor is paved with worn tombstones—because being buried in this hallowed sanctuary got you one step closer to Heaven, the richest families of the day paid big bucks to stake out small rectangles of the floor. On the right aisle is the first tomb of note, a mad Vasari contraption containing the bones of the most venerated of Renaissance masters, **Michelangelo Buonarroti,** who died of a fever in Rome in 1564 at the ripe age of 89. The pope wanted him buried in the Eternal City, but Florentines managed to sneak his body back to Florence. Past Michelangelo is a pompous 19th-century cenotaph to Florentine **Dante Alighieri,** one of history's greatest poets, whose manuscript *Divine Comedy* codified the Italian language. He died in 1321 in Ravenna after a long and bitter life in exile from his hometown (on trumped-up embezzlement charges), and that Adriatic city has never seen fit to return the bones to Florence, the city that would never readmit the poet when he was alive.

Against a nave pillar farther up is an elaborate **pulpit** (1472–76) carved by Benedetto di Maiano with scenes from the life of St. Francis. Next comes a wall monument to **Niccolò Machiavelli,** the 16th-century Florentine statesman and author whose famous book *The Prince* was the perfect practical manual for a powerful Renaissance ruler.

Past the next altar is an *Annunciation* (1433) carved in low relief of *pietra serena* and gilded by Donatello. Nearby is Antonio Rossellino's 1446 tomb of the great humanist scholar and city chancellor **Leonardo Bruni** (d. 1444). Beyond this architectural masterpiece of a tomb is a 19th-century knockoff honoring the remains of **Gioacchino Rossini** (1792–1868), composer of the *Barber of Seville* and the *William Tell Overture.*

Around in the right transept is the **Cappella Castellani** frescoed by Agnolo Gaddi and assistants, with a tabernacle by Mino da Fiesole and a *Crucifix* by Niccolò Gerini. Agnolo's father, Taddeo Gaddi, was one of Giotto's closest followers, and the senior Gaddi is the one who undertook painting the **Cappella Baroncelli** ✷ (1332–38) at the transept's end. The frescoes depict scenes from the *Life of the Virgin,* and to the left of the window is an *Angel Appearing to the Shepherds* that constitutes the first night scene in Italian fresco. The altarpiece *Coronation of the Virgin* is by Giotto. To the left of this chapel is a doorway, designed by Michelozzo, leading to the *sagrestia* (sacristy) past a huge *Deposition* (1560) by Alessandro Allori that had to be restored after it incurred massive water damage when the church was inundated during the 1966 flood. Past the gift shop is a leather school and store.

In the right transept, Giotto frescoed the two chapels to the right of the high altar. The frescoes were whitewashed over during the 17th century but uncovered from 1841 to 1852 and inexpertly restored. The **Cappella Peruzzi** ✷✷, on the right, is a late work and not in the best shape. The many references to antiquity in the styling and architecture of the frescoes reflect Giotto's trip to Rome and its ruins. His assistant Taddeo Gaddi did the altarpiece. Even more famous, if only as the setting for a scene in the film *A Room with a View,* is the **Cappella Bardi** ✷✷ immediately to the right of the high altar. The key panels here include the *Trial by Fire Before the Sultan of Egypt* on the right wall, full of telling subtlety in the expressions and poses of the figures. One of Giotto's most well-known works is the lower panel on the left wall, the *Death of St. Francis,* where the monks weep and wail with convincing pathos. Alas, big chunks of the scene are missing from when a tomb was stuck on top of it in the 18th century. Most people miss seeing *Francis Receiving the Stigmata*, which Giotto frescoed above the outside of the entrance arch to the chapel.

Agnolo Gaddi designed the stained-glass windows, painted the saints between them, and frescoed a *Legend of the True Cross* cycle on the walls of the rounded **sanctuary** behind the high altar. At the end of the left transept is another Cappella Bardi, this one housing a legendary ***Crucifix*** ⚓ by Donatello. According to Vasari, Donatello excitedly called his friend Filippo Brunelleschi up to his studio to see this *Crucifix* when he had finished carving it. The famed architect, whose tastes were aligned with the prevailing view of the time that refinement and grace were much more important than realism, criticized the work with the words, "Why Donatello, you've put a peasant on the cross!" Donatello sniffed, "If it was as easy to make something as it is to criticize, my Christ would really look to you like Christ. So you get some wood and try to make one yourself." Secretly, Brunelleschi did just that, and one day he invited Donatello to come over to his studio for lunch. Donatello arrived bearing the food gathered up in his apron. Shocked when he beheld Brunelleschi's elegant *Crucifix*, he let the lunch drop to the floor, smashing the eggs, and after a few moments turned to Brunelleschi and humbly offered, "Your job is making Christs and mine is making peasants." Tastes change, and to modern eyes this "peasant" stands as the stronger work. If you want to see how Brunelleschi fared with his Christ, visit it at Santa Maria Novella.

Past a door as you head back down the left aisle is a 16th-century ***Deposition*** by Bronzino. A bit farther along, against a pier, is the roped-off floor tomb of Lorenzo Ghiberti, sculptor of the baptistery doors. Against the wall is an altarpiece of the *Incredulity of St. Thomas* by Giorgio Vasari. The last tomb on the right is that of **Galileo Galilei** (1564–1642), the preeminent Pisan scientist who figured out everything from the action of pendulums and the famous law of bodies falling at the same rate (regardless of weight) to discovering the moons of Jupiter and asserting that Earth revolved around the sun. This last one got him in trouble with the church, which tried him in the Inquisition and—when he wouldn't recant—excommunicated him. At the urging of friends frightened his obstinacy would get him executed as a heretic, Galileo eventually kneeled in front of an altar and "admitted" he'd been wrong. He lived out the

rest of his days under house arrest near Florence and wasn't allowed
a Christian burial until 1737. Giulio Foggini designed this tomb for
him, complete with a relief of the solar system—the sun, you'll
notice, is at the center. The pope finally got around to lifting the
excommunication in 1992. Italians still bring him fresh flowers.

Piazza Santa Croce. ✆ **055-244-619**. Admission 4€ ($5.20). Mon–Sat 9:30am–
5:30pm; Sun 1–5:30pm. Bus: B, 13, 23, or 71.

Museo dell'Opera di Santa Croce ✹   Part of Santa Croce's convent has been set up as a museum, mainly to harbor artistic victims
of the 1966 Arno flood, which buried the church under tons of mud
and water. You enter through a door to the right of the church
facade, which spills into an open-air courtyard planted with cypress
and filled with birdsong.

At the end of the path is the **Cappella de' Pazzi** ✹, one of Filippo
Brunelleschi's architectural masterpieces (faithfully finished after his
death in 1446). Giuliano da Maiano probably designed the porch
that now precedes the chapel, set with glazed terra cottas by Luca
della Robbia. The rectangular chapel is one of Brunelleschi's signa-
ture pieces and a defining example of (and model for) early Renaissance architecture. Light gray *pietra serena* is used to accent the
architectural lines against smooth white plaster walls, and the only
decorations are della Robbia roundels of the *Apostles* (1442–52). The
chapel was barely finished by 1478, when the infamous Pazzi Conspiracy got the bulk of the family, who were funding this project,
either killed or exiled.

From back in the first cloister you can enter the museum proper
via the long hall of the **refectory.** On your right as you enter is the
painting that became emblematic of all the artworks damaged during
the 1966 flood, Cimabue's *Crucifix* ✹, one of the masterpieces of the
artist who began bridging the gap between Byzantine tradition and
Renaissance innovation, not the least by teaching Giotto to paint.

Piazza Santa Croce 16. ✆ **055-244-619**. Admission included with Santa Croce;
hours same. Bus: B, 13, 23, or 71.

Museo Horne   Of the city's several small once-private collections,
the one formed by Englishman Herbert Percy Horne and left to Florence in his will has perhaps the best individual pieces, though the
bulk of it consists of mediocre paintings by good artists. In a 15th-
century *palazzo* designed by Cronaca (not Sangallo, as had once been
believed), the collections are left, unlabeled, as Horne arranged them;
the reference numbers on the handout they give you correspond to

the stickers on the wall, not the numbers on the frames. The best works are a *St. Stephen* by Giotto and Sienese Mannerist Domenico Beccafumi's weirdly colored tondo of the *Holy Family.*

Via dei Benci 6. *©* **055-244-661.** Admission 5€ ($6.50). Mon–Sat 9am–1pm; in summer also Tues 8:30–11pm. Bus: B, 13, 23, or 71.

Casa Buonarroti Though Michelangelo Buonarroti never actually lived in this modest *palazzo,* he did own the property and left it to his nephew Lionardo. Lionardo named his own son after his famous uncle, and this younger Michelangelo became very devoted to the memory of his namesake, converting the house into a museum and hiring artists to fill the place with frescoes honoring the genius of his great uncle.

The good stuff is upstairs, starting with a display case regularly rotating pages from the museum's collection of original drawings. In the first room off the landing are Michelangelo's earliest sculptures: the *Madonna of the Steps,* carved before 1492 when he was a 15- or 16-year-old student in the Medici sculpture garden. A few months later, the child prodigy was already finished carving another marble, a confused tangle of bodies known as the *Battle of the Centaurs and Lapiths.* The sculptural ideals that were to mark his entire career are already evident here: a fascination with the male body to the point of ignoring the figures themselves in pursuit of muscular torsion and the use of rough "unfinished" marble to speak sculptural volumes.

Via Ghibellina 70. *©* **055-241-752.** www.casabuonarroti.it. Admission 6.50€ ($8.45). Wed–Mon 9:30am–2pm. Bus: A, 14, or 23.

Santa Maria Maddalena dei Pazzi The entrance to this church is an unassuming, unnumbered door on Borgo Pinti that opens onto a pretty cloister designed in 1492 by Giuliano da Sangallo, open to the sky and surrounded by large *pietra serena* columns topped with droopy-eared Ionic capitals. The interior of the 13th-century church was remodeled in the 17th and early 18th centuries and represents the high baroque at its restrained best. At the odd hours listed below, you can get into the chapter house to see the church's hidden main prize, a wall-filling fresco of the ***Crucifixion and Saints*** ✪ (1493–96) by Perugino, grand master of the Umbrian school. Typical of Perugino's style, the background is drawn as delicately in blues and greens as the posed figures were fleshed out in full-bodied volumes of bright colors.

Entrance next to Borgo Pinti 58. *©* **055-247-8420.** Free admission to church; Perugino *Crucifixion* 1€ ($1.30) "donation." Church daily 9am–noon; Mon–Fri

5–5:20pm and 6–6:50pm; Sat 5–6:20pm; Sun 5–6:50pm. Perugino *Crucifixion,* ring bell at no. 58 9–10am or enter through sacristy (knock at the last door on the right inside the church) at 5pm or 6:15pm. Bus: A, 6, 14, 23, 31, 32, or 71.

Sinagoga (Synagogue) and Jewish Museum The center of the 1,000-strong Jewish community in Florence is this imposing Moorish-Byzantine synagogue, built in the 1870s. In an effort to create a neo-Byzantine building, the architects ended up making it look rather like a church, complete with a dome, an apse, a pulpit, and a pipe organ. The intricate polychrome arabesque designs, though, lend it a distinctly Eastern flavor, and the rows of prayer benches facing each other, and the separate areas for women, hint at its Orthodox Jewish nature. Though the synagogue is technically Sephardic, the members of the Florentine Jewish community are Italian Jews, a Hebrew culture that has adapted to its Italian surroundings since the 1st century B.C. when Jewish slaves were first brought to Rome. (The Florentine community dates from the 14th c.)

Via Farina 4. ✆ **055-234-6654.** www.firenzebraica.net. Admission 4€ ($5.20) adults, 3€ ($3.90) students. June–Aug Sun–Thurs 10am–6pm; Apr–May and Sept–Oct Sun–Thurs 10am–5pm; Nov–Mar Sun–Thurs 10am–3pm.; obligatory 45-min. guided tours every 25 min. Bus: C, 6, 31, or 32.

7 In the Oltrarno

Santa Felícita The 2nd-century Greek sailors who lived in this neighborhood brought Christianity to Florence with them, and this little church was probably the second to be established in the city, the first edition of it rising in the late 4th century. The current version was built in the 1730s. The star works are in the first chapel on your right, paintings by Mannerist master Pontormo (1525–27). *The Deposition* and frescoed *Annunciation* are rife with his garish color palette of oranges, pinks, golds, lime greens, and sky blues. The four round paintings of the *Evangelists* surrounding the dome are also by Pontormo, except for the *St. Mark* (with the angel), which was probably painted by his pupil Bronzino.

Piazza Santa Felícita (2nd left off Via Guicciardini across the Ponte Vecchio). ✆ **055-213-018.** Free admission. Daily 8am–noon and 3:30–6:30pm. Bus: B or D.

Palazzo Pitti & Giardino Boboli (Pitti Palace & Boboli Gardens) 𝕽𝕽𝕽 Though the original, much smaller Pitti Palace was a Renaissance affair probably designed by Filippo Brunelleschi, that *palazzo* is completely hidden by the enormous Mannerist mass we see today. Inside is Florence's most extensive set of museums, including the Galleria Palatina, a huge painting gallery second in town only to the Uffizi, with famous works by Raphael, Andrea del Sarto, Titian, and Rubens. When Luca Pitti died in 1472, Cosimo de' Medici's wife, Eleonora of Toledo, bought this property and unfinished palace to convert into the new Medici home—she hated the dark, cramped spaces of the family apartments in the Palazzo Vecchio. They hired Bartolomeo Ammannati to enlarge the *palazzo,* which he did, starting in 1560, by creating the courtyard out back, extending the wings on each side, and incorporating a Michelangelo architectural invention, "kneeling windows," on the ground floor of the facade. (Rather than being visually centered between the line of the floor and that of the ceiling, kneeling windows' bases extend lower to be level with the ground or, in the case of upper stories, with whatever architectural element delineates the baseline of that story's first level.) Later architects finished the building off by the 19th century, probably to Ammannati's original plans, in the end producing the oversize rustication of its outer walls and overall ground plan that make it one of the masterpieces of Florentine Mannerist architecture.

The ticket office for the painting gallery—the main, and for many visitors, most interesting of the Pitti museums—is off Ammannati's excellent **interior courtyard** ✫ of gold-tinged rusticated rock grafted onto the three classical orders.

GALLERIA PALATINA ✫✫✫   If the Uffizi represents mainly the earlier masterpieces collected by the Medici, the Pitti Palace's painting gallery continues the story with the High Renaissance and later eras, a collection gathered by the Medici, and later the Grand Dukes of Lorraine. The works are still displayed in the old-world fashion, which hung paintings according to aesthetics—how well, say, the Raphael matched the drapes—rather than that boring academic chronological order. In the first long **Galleria delle Statue (Hall of Statues)** are Peter Paul Rubens's *Risen Christ,* Caravaggio's ***Toothpuller*** ✫, and a 19th-century tabletop inlaid in *pietre dure*—an exquisite example of the famous Florentine mosaic craft. The next five rooms made up the Medici's main apartments, frescoed by Pietro da Cortona in the 17th-century baroque style—they're home to the bulk of the paintings.

The **Sala di Venere (Venus Room)** is named after the neoclassical *Venus,* which Napoleon had Canova sculpt in 1810 to replace the *Medici Venus* the emperor had appropriated for his Paris digs. Four masterpieces by the famed early-16th-century Venetian painter Titian hang on the walls. Art historians still argue whether ***The Concert*** ✫ was painted entirely by Titian in his early 20s or by Giorgione, in whose circle he moved. However, most now attribute at most the fop on the left to Giorgione and give the rest of the canvas to Titian. There are no such doubts about Titian's *Portrait of Julius II,* a copy of the physiologically penetrating work by Raphael in London's National Gallery (the version in the Uffizi is a copy Raphael himself made), or the *Portrait of a Lady (La Bella).* Titian painted the *Portrait of Pietro Aretino* for the writer/thinker himself, but Aretino didn't understand the innovative styling and accused Titian of not having completed the work. The painter, in a huff, gave it to Cosimo I as a gift. The room also contains Rubens's *Return from the Hayfields,* famous for its classically harmonious landscape.

The **Sala di Apollo (Apollo Room)** has another masterful early *Portrait of an Unknown Gentleman* by Titian as well as his sensual, luminously gold ***Mary Magdalene*** ⚘, the first in a number of takes on the subject the painter was to make throughout his career. There are several works by Andrea del Sarto, whose late *Holy Family* and especially *Deposition* display the daring chromatic experiments and highly refined spatial compositions that were to influence his students Pontormo and Rosso Fiorentino as they went about mastering Mannerism.

The **Sala di Marte (Mars Room)** is dominated by Rubens, including the enormous ***Consequences of War*** ⚘⚘, which an aged Rubens painted for his friend Sustermans at a time when both were worried that their Dutch homeland was on the brink of battle. Rubens's ***The Four Philosophers*** ⚘ is a much more lighthearted work, in which he painted himself at the far left, next to his seated brother Filippo.

The star of the **Sala di Giove (Jupiter Room)** is Raphael's ***La Velata*** ⚘⚘, one of the crowning achievements of his short career and a summation of what he had learned about color, light, naturalism, and mood. It's probably a portrait of his Roman mistress called La Fornarina, a baker's daughter who sat for many of his Madonnas.

Raphael is the focus of the **Sala di Saturno (Saturn Room)** ⚘⚘, where the transparent colors of his *Madonna*s and probing portraits show the strong influence of both Leonardo da Vinci (the *Portrait of Maddalena Strozzi Doni* owes much to the *Mona Lisa*) and Raphael's old master Perugino, whose *Deposition* and *Mary Magdalene* also hang here. The **Sala dell'Iliade (Illiad Room)** has another Raphael portrait, this time of a ***Pregnant Woman*** ⚘, along with some more Titian masterpieces. Don't miss *Mary Magdalene* and ***Judith*** ⚘, two paintings by one of the only female artists of the late Renaissance era,

Artemisia Gentileschi, who often turned to themes of strong biblical women.

From here, you enter a series of smaller rooms with smaller paintings. The **Sala dell'Educazione di Giove (Room of Jupiter's Education)** has two famous works: one a 1608 *Sleeping Cupid* ✫✫ that Caravaggio painted while living in exile from Rome (avoiding murder charges) on the island of Malta; and the other Cristofano Allori's *Judith with the Head of Holofernes* ✫, a Freudian field day where the artist depicted himself in the severed head, his lover as Judith holding it, and her mother as the maid looking on.

APARTAMENTI REALI ✫   The other wing of the *piano nobile* is taken up with the Medici's private apartments, which were reopened in 1993 after being restored to their late-19th-century appearance when the kings of the House of Savoy, rulers of the Unified Italy, used the suites as their Florentine home. The over-the-top sumptuous fabrics, decorative arts furnishings, stuccoes, and frescoes reflect the neobaroque and Victorian tastes of the Savoy kings. Amid the general interior-decorator flamboyance are some thoroughly appropriate baroque canvases, plus some earlier works by Andrea del Sarto and Caravaggio's *Portrait of a Knight of Malta* ✫. January through May, you can visit the apartments only by guided tour Tuesday and Saturday (and sometimes Thurs) hourly from 9 to 11am and 3 to 5pm (reserve ahead at ✆ **055-238-8614;** inquire about admission fees).

GALLERIA D'ARTE MODERNA ✫   Modern art isn't what draws most people to the capital of the Renaissance, but the Pitti's collection includes some important works by the 19th-century Tuscan school of art known as the Macchiaioli, who painted a kind of Tuscan Impressionism, concerned with the *macchie* (marks of color on the canvas and the play of light on the eye). Most of the scenes are of the countryside or peasants working, along with the requisite lot of portraits. Some of the movement's greatest talents are here, including Silvestro Lega, Telemaco Signorini, and Giovanni Fattori, the genius of the group. Don't miss his two white oxen pulling a cart in *The Tuscan Maremma* ✫.

GALLERIA DEL COSTUME & MUSEO DEGLI ARGENTI
These aren't the most popular of the Pitti's museums, and the **Museo degli Argenti** has what seems like miles of the most extravagant and often hideous objets d'art and housewares the Medici and Lorraines could put their hands on. If the collections prove anything, it's that as the Medici became richer and more powerful, their taste declined

proportionally. Just be thankful their **carriage collection** has been closed for years. The **Costume Gallery** is more interesting. The collections concentrate on the 18th to 20th centuries but also display outfits from back to the 16th century. The dress in which Eleonora of Toledo was buried, made famous by Bronzino's intricate depiction of its velvety embroidered silk and in-sewn pearls on his portrait of her in the Uffizi, is usually on display.

Giardino Boboli (Boboli Gardens) 👫👫 The statue-filled park behind the Pitti Palace is one of the earliest and finest Renaissance gardens, laid out mostly between 1549 and 1656 with box hedges in geometric patterns, groves of ilex, dozens of statues, and rows of cypress. In 1766, it was opened to the Florentine public, who still come here with their families for Sunday-morning strolls. Just above the entrance through the courtyard of the Palazzo Pitti is an oblong **amphitheater** modeled on Roman circuses. Today, we see in the middle a **granite basin** from Rome's Baths of Caracalla and an **Egyptian obelisk** of Ramses II, but in 1589 this was the setting for the wedding reception of Ferdinando de' Medici's marriage to Christine of Lorraine. For the occasion, the Medici commissioned entertainment from Jacopo Peri and Ottavio Rinuccini, who decided to set a classical story entirely to music and called it *Dafne*—the world's first opera. (Later, they wrote a follow-up hit *Erudice,* performed here in 1600; it's the first opera whose score has survived.)

Around the park, don't miss the rococo **Kaffehaus,** with bar service in summer, and, near the top of the park, the **Giardino del Cavaliere,** the Boboli's prettiest hidden corner—a tiny walled garden of box hedges with private views over the wooded hills of Florence's outskirts. At the north end of the park, down around the end of the Pitti Palace, are some fake caverns filled with statuary, attempting to invoke some vaguely classical sacred grotto. The most famous, the **Grotta Grande,** was designed by Giorgio Vasari, Bartolomeo Ammannati, and Bernardo Buontalenti between 1557 and 1593, dripping with phony stalactites and set with replicas of Michelangelo's unfinished *Slave* statues. (The originals were once placed here before being moved to the Accademia.) All the grottoes are being restored, but you can visit them by appointment by calling ✆ **055-218-741.** Near the exit to the park is a Florentine postcard fave, the *Fontana di Bacco* (**Bacchus Fountain;** 1560), a pudgy dwarf sitting atop a tortoise. It's actually a portrait of Pietro Barbino, Cosimo I's potbellied dwarf court jester.

Piazza Pitti. **Galleria Palatina:** ⓒ 055-238-8614; reserve tickets at ⓒ 055-294-883 or www.firenzemusei.it. Admission 8.50€ ($11) adults, 18 and under free. Tues–Sun 8:15am–5:50pm; last admission 45 min. before close. **Galleria d'Arte Moderna:** ⓒ 055-238-8601. Admission 8.50€ ($11) adults, under 18 free. Daily 8:15am–6:50pm. Closed 1st, 3rd, and 5th Mon and 2nd and 4th Sun of each month. **Museo degli Argenti:** ⓒ 055-238-8709. Admission 6€ ($7.80) adults, under 18 free. Nov–Feb daily 8:15am–4:30pm; Mar daily 8:15am–5:30pm; Apr–May and Oct daily 8:15am–6:30pm; June–Sept daily 8:15am–7:30pm. **Giardino Boboli:** ⓒ 055-265-1816. Admission 2€ ($2.60) adults, under 18 free. Nov–Feb daily 8:15am–4:30pm; Mar daily 8:15am–5:30pm; Apr–May and Oct daily 8:15am–6:30pm; June–Sept daily 8:15am–7:30pm. Cumulative tickets for the Gelleria Palatina, Museo degli Argenti, Galleria d'Arte Moderna and Giardino Boboli 12€ ($15) adults. Bus: D, 11, 36, 37, or 68.

Santo Spirito ⌖   One of Filippo Brunelleschi's masterpieces of architecture, this 15th-century church doesn't look like much from the outside (no true facade was ever built), but the **interior** ⌖ is a marvelous High Renaissance space—an expansive landscape of proportion and mathematics worked out in classic Brunelleschi style, with coffered vaulting, tall columns, and the stacked perspective of arched arcading. Good late-Renaissance and baroque paintings are scattered throughout, but the best stuff lies up in the transepts and in the east end, surrounding the extravagant **baroque altar** with a ciborium inlaid in *pietre dure* around 1607.

The **right transept** begins with a *Crucifixion* by Francesco Curradi. Against the back wall of the transept, the first chapel holds an early-15th-century *Madonna del Soccorso* of uncertain authorship. Two chapels down is one of Filippino Lippi's best works, a *Madonna and Child with Saints and Donors.* The background seen through the classical arches was painted with an almost Flemish exacting detail. In the east end of the church, the center two chapels against the back wall contain Alessandro Allori altarpieces: *The Martyred Saints* (1574), on the right, has a predella view of what the Palazzo Pitti looked like before its enlargement; and the *Christ and the Adulteress,* on the left, is extremely advanced in style, already almost a work of the late baroque. In the **left transept,** the first chapel on the right side is a late-15th-century *Madonna Enthroned with Child and Saints.* Next to this is the highly skilled *St. Monica and Augustinian Nuns,* an almost monochrome work of black and pale yellow, faintly disturbing in its eerie monotony and perfection of composition. It's now usually attributed to the enigmatic Andrea del Verrocchio, one-time master of Leonardo da Vinci.

The famed **piazza** outside is one of the focal points of the Oltrarno, shaded by trees and lined with trendy cafes that see some bar action in the evenings. It's not quite the pleasant hangout it once was, however—especially since the heroin set moved in a few years ago, making it a less than desirable place to be after midnight (though early evening is still fine). Stop by Bar Ricci, at no. 9r, where more than 300 facade designs for faceless Santo Spirito line the walls, the product of a fun-loving contest the bar held in 1980.

Piazza Santo Spirito. ℂ **055-210-030.** Free admission. Daily 8am–noon; Thurs–Tues 4–6pm. Bus: D, 6, 11, 36, 37, or 68.

Cenacolo di Santo Spirito Museum   The dark and haphazard museum in the church's old refectory (entrance to the left of Santo Spirito's facade) has a gathering of Romanesque and paleo-Christian stone sculptures and reliefs. The main reason to drop by is the end wall frescoed by Andrea Orcagna and his brother Nardo di Cione in 1360 with a *Last Supper* (of which only one apostle and a half, and a halo are left) and above it a beautiful *Crucifixion,* one of 14th-century Florence's masterpieces.

Piazza Santo Spirito 29. ℂ **055-287-043.** Admission 2.20€ ($2.85). Tues–Sat 10:30am–1:30pm (until 2pm Apr–Nov). Bus: D, 6, 11, 36, 37, or 68.

Santa Maria della Carmine 𝕮𝕮𝕮   Following a 1771 fire that destroyed everything but the transept chapels and sacristy, this Carmelite church was almost entirely reconstructed and decorated in high baroque style. Ever since a long and expensive restoration of the famous frescoes of the **Cappella Brancacci** in the right transept, they've blocked off just that chapel and you have to enter through the cloisters (doorway to the right of the church facade) and pay admission. The frescoes were commissioned by an enemy of the Medici, Felice Brancacci, who in 1424 hired Masolino and his student Masaccio to decorate it with a cycle on the life of St. Peter. Masolino probably worked out the cycle's scheme and painted a few scenes along with his pupil before taking off for 3 years to serve as court painter in Budapest, during which time Masaccio kept painting, quietly creating one of his masterpieces and some of the early Renaissance's greatest frescoes. Masaccio left for Rome in 1428, where he died at age 27. The cycle was completed between 1480 and 1485 by Filippino Lippi, who faithfully imitated Masaccio's technique.

Even before Lippi's intervention, though, the frescoes had been an instant hit. People flocked from all over the city to admire them, and almost every Italian artist of the day came to sketch and study

Masaccio's mastery of perspective, bold light and colors, and unheard-of touches of realism. Even later masters like Leonardo da Vinci and Michelangelo came to learn what they could from the young artist's genius. A 1980s restoration cleaned off the dirt and dark mold that had grown in the egg-based pigments used to "touch up" the frescoes in the 18th century and removed additions like the prudish ivy leaves trailing across Adam and Eve's privates.

Masolino was responsible for the *St. Peter Preaching,* the upper panel to the left of the altar, and the two top scenes on the right wall, which shows his fastidiously decorative style in a long panel of *St. Peter Healing the Cripple* and *Raising Tabitha,* and his *Adam and Eve.* Contrast this first man and woman, about to take the bait offered by the snake, with the ***Expulsion from the Garden*** &&, across from it, painted by Masaccio. Masolino's figures are highly posed models, expressionless and oblivious to the temptation being offered. Masaccio's Adam and Eve, on the other hand, burst with intense emotion and forceful movement. The top scene on the left wall is also by Masaccio, and it showcases both his classical influences and another of his innovations, perfect linear perspective. On the end wall, Masaccio painted the lower scene to the left of the altar of *St. Peter Healing the Sick with His Shadow,* unique at the time for its realistic portrayal of street beggars and crippled bodies. The two scenes to the right of the altar are Masaccio's as well, with the *Baptism of the Neophytes* taking its place among his masterpieces. Most of the rest of the frescoes were painted by Filippino Lippi. The left transept chapel, which isn't blocked off, is one of Florence's most harmonious examples of the baroque (1675–83), with a ceiling painted by Luca Giordano.

Piazza della Carmine. ✆ **055-238-2195.** Free admission to church; Brancacci chapel 4€ ($5.20), cumulative ticket with Palazzo Vecchio available. Mon–Sat 10am–5pm; Sun 1–5pm. Bus: D, 6, 11, 36, 37, or 68.

Museo Zoologico La Specola   Italy has very few zoos, but this is the largest zoological collection, with rooms full of insects, crustaceans, and stuffed birds and mammals—everything from ostriches and apes to a rhinoceros. The museum was founded here in 1775, and the collections are still displayed in the style of an old-fashioned natural sciences museum, with specimens crowded into beautiful old wood-and-glass cases. The last 10 rooms contain an important collection of human anatomical wax models crafted between 1775 and 1814 by Clemente Susini for medical students. The life-size figures are flayed, dissected, and disemboweled to varying degrees and are truly disgusting, but fascinating.

Via Romana 17. ℭ **055-228-8251.** www.msn.unifi.it. Admission 4€ ($5.20) adults, 2€ ($2.60) children 6–18, free for children under 6. Thurs–Tues 9am–1pm. Bus: C, D, 11, 36, or 37.

San Felice   This tiny Gothic church just south of the Pitti Palace sports a High Renaissance facade by Michelozzo (1457) and a *Crucifixion* over the high altar recently attributed to Giotto. Also peek at the remnants of Niccolò Gerini's early-15th-century *Pietà* fresco over the first altar on the right.

At no. 8 on the piazza is the entrance to the **Casa Guidi,** where from 1846 English poet Elizabeth Barrett Browning lived with her husband, Robert, moving in just after their secret marriage. When the unification of Italy became official in Florence, Elizabeth recorded the momentous event in a famous poem, "Casa Guidi Windows": "I heard last night a little child go singing / 'Neath Casa Guidi windows, by the church, / O bella libertà, O bella!" Mrs. Browning died in this house on June 18, 1861.

Piazza di San Felice. No phone. Free admission. Bus: D, 11, 36, 37, or 68.

8 In the Hills

Piazzale Michelangiolo ⊛   This panoramic piazza is a required stop for every tour bus. The balustraded terrace was laid out in 1885 to give a sweeping vista of the entire city, spread out in the valley below and backed by the green hills of Fiesole beyond. The monument to Michelangelo in the center of the piazza is made up of bronze replicas of *David* and his Medici chapel sculptures.

Viale Michelangelo. Bus: 12 or 13.

San Miniato al Monte ⊛⊛   High atop a hill, its gleaming white-and-green facade visible from the valley below, San Miniato is one of the few ancient churches of Florence to survive the centuries virtually intact. San Miniato was an eastern Christian who settled in Florence and was martyred during Emperor Decius's persecutions in A.D. 250. The legend goes that the decapitated saint picked up his head, walked across the river, climbed up the hillside, and didn't lie down to die until he reached this spot. He and other Christians were buried here, and a shrine was raised on the site as early as the 4th century.

The current building began to take shape in 1013, under the auspices of the powerful Arte di Calimala guild, whose symbol, a bronze eagle clutching a bale of wool, perches atop the **facade** ⊛⊛. The Romanesque facade is a particularly gorgeous bit of white Carrara- and green Prato-marble inlay. Above the central window is a 13th-century mosaic of *Christ Between the Madonna and St. Miniato* (a theme repeated in a slightly later mosaic filling the apse inside).

The **interior** has a few Renaissance additions, but they blend in well with the overall medieval aspect—an airy, stony space with a raised choir at one end, painted wooden trusses on the ceiling, and tombs interspersed with inlaid marble symbols of the zodiac paving the floor.

Below the choir is an 11th-century **crypt** with small frescoes by Taddeo Gaddi. Off to the right of the raised choir is the **sacristy,** which Spinello Aretino covered in 1387 with cartoonish yet elegant frescoes depicting the *Life of St. Benedict* ✺. Off the left aisle of the nave is 15th-century **Cappella del Cardinale del Portogallo** ✺✺, a brilliant collaborative effort by Renaissance artists built to honor young Portuguese humanist Cardinal Jacopo di Lusitania, who was sent to study in Perugia but died an untimely death at 25 in Florence. Brunelleschi's student Antonio Manetti started the chapel in 1460 but soon died, and Antonio Rossellino finished the architecture and carving by 1466. Luca della Robbia provided the glazed terra-cotta dome, a cubic landscape set with tondi of the four *Virtues* surrounding the *Holy Spirit* to symbolize the young scholar's devotion to the church and to humanist philosophy. It stands as one of della Robbia's masterpieces of color and classical ideals. The unfinished **bell tower** seen from the outside was designed by Baccio d'Agnolo. In 1530 the combined troops of Charles V and Medici Pope Clement VII, who had recently reconciled with each other, lay siege to the newly declared Republic of Florence in an attempt to reinstate the Medici dukes. San Miniato al Monte was one of the prime fortifications, and an artilleryman named Lapo was stationed up in the tower with two small cannons—he was basically bait, stuck there to draw the fire of the enemy where it would do little harm. The man in charge of the defenses was Michelangelo, who, the authorities figured, was so good at everything else, why not military fortifications? After throwing up dirt ramparts and cobbling together defensible walls out of oak timbers, Michelangelo helped poor Lapo out by devising an ingenious way to protect the tower: He hung mattresses down the sides to absorb the shock of the cannonballs fired at it and left the tower (and, more important, Lapo) still standing.

The siege was eventually successful, however, and the Florentine Republic fell, but while it lasted, Michelangelo spent his day up here and referred to the church of **San Salvatore al Monte** just below as "my pretty country maid." It's a simple 1400 church built by

Catching *Calcio* Fever

To Italians, *calcio* (soccer) is something akin to a second religion. You don't know what a fan is until you've attended a soccer match in a country such as Italy, and an afternoon at the football stadium can offer you as much insight (if not more) into Italian culture as a day in the Uffizi. Catch the local team, the Fiorentina, Sundays September through May at the Stadio Comunale, Via Manfredi Fanti 4 (© **055-262-5537** or 055-50-721). Tickets go on sale at the stadium box office 3 hours before each game.

Cronaca, with a Giovanni della Robbia *Deposition* and a Neri di Bicci *Pietà* inside.

Via del Monte alle Croci/Viale Galileo Galilei (behind Piazzale Michelangiolo). © **055-234-2731**. Free admission. Easter–early Oct daily 8am–7:30pm; winter Mon–Sat 8am–1pm and 2:30–6pm, Sun 8am–6pm. Bus: 12 or 13.

Museo Stibbert   Half Scotsman, half Italian, Frederick Stibbert was nothing if not eccentric. A sometime artist, intrepid traveler, voracious accumulator, and even hero in Garibaldi's army, he inherited a vast fortune and this villa from his Italian mother. He connected the house to a nearby villa to create an eclectic museum housing his extraordinary collections, including baroque canvases, fine porcelain, Flemish tapestries, Tuscan crucifixes, and Etruscan artifacts. The museum was partially rearranged in past decades to try and make some sense out of 57 rooms stuffed with over 50,000 items. More recently, however, the city has come to appreciate this rare example of a private 19th-century museum and is busily setting it all back the way Stibbert originally intended.

Stibbert's greatest interest and most fascinating assemblage is of **armor** 𝒜—Etruscan, Lombard, Asian, Roman, 17th-century Florentine, and 15th-century Turkish. The museum has the largest display of Japanese arms and armor in Europe and a new exhibit of porcelain. The high point of the house is a remarkable grand hall filled with an entire cavalcade of mannequins in 16th-century armor (mostly European, but with half a dozen samurai foot soldiers thrown in for good measure). Stibbert even managed to get some seriously historic Florentine armor, that in which Medici warrior Giovanni delle Bande Nere was buried.

Via Stibbert 26. © **055-475-520**. www.museostibbert.it. Admission 5€ ($6.50) adults, 2€ ($2.60) children. Mon–Wed 10am–2pm; Fri–Sun 10am–6pm. Bus: 4.

PARKS & GARDENS

Florence's best park is the Medici grand dukes' old backyard to the
Pitti Palace, the **Giardino Boboli** (p. 148). Less scenic, but free and
more jogger-friendly, is the **Parco della Cascine** along the Arno at
the west end of the historic center. Originally a wild delta of land
where the Arno and Mugnone rivers met, the area later became a
Medici hunting reserve and eventually a pasture for the grand duke's
milk cows. Today, the Cascine is home to tennis courts, pools, a
horse racetrack, and some odd late-18th- and early-19th-century features like an incongruous pyramid and funky neoclassical fountains.
There's a flea market here every Tuesday morning. Though perfectly
safe in the daylight, this park becomes a den of thieves and a hangout for heroin addicts after dark, as do most sections of the Arno's
banks, so steer clear.

6

Shopping

The cream of the crop of Florentine shopping lines both sides of the elegant **Via de' Tornabuoni,** with an extension along **Via della Vigna Nuova** and other surrounding streets. Here you'll find such big names as Gucci, Armani, Ferragamo, and Mila Schön ensconced in old palaces or modern minimalist boutiques.

On the other end of the shopping spectrum is the haggling and general fun of the colorful and noisy **San Lorenzo street market.** Antiques gather dust by the truckload along **Via Maggio** and other Oltrarno streets. Another main corridor of stores somewhat less glitzy than those on the Via de' Tornabuoni begins at **Via Cerretani** and runs down **Via Roma** through the Piazza della Repubblica area; it keeps going down **Via Por Santa Maria,** across the **Ponte Vecchio** with its gold jewelry, and up **Via Guicciardini** on the other side. Store-laden side tributaries off this main stretch include **Via della Terme, Borgo Santissimi Apostoli,** and **Borgo San Jacopo.**

Generally, Florentine **shopping hours** are daily from 9:30am to noon or 1pm and 3 or 3:30 to 7:30pm, though increasingly, many shops are staying open through that midafternoon *riposo* (especially the larger stores and those around tourist sights).

1 Shopping A to Z

Here's **what to buy in Florence:** leather, high fashion, shoes, marbleized paper, hand-embroidered linens, lace, lingerie, Tuscan wines, gold jewelry, *pietre dure* (known also as Florentine mosaic, inlaid semiprecious stones), and Renaissance leftovers and other antiques.

ART & ANTIQUES

The antiques business is clustered where the artisans have always lived and worked: the Oltrarno. Dealers' shops line Via Maggio, but the entire district is packed with venerable chunks of the past. On "this side" of the river, Borgo Ognissanti has the highest concentration of aging furniture and art collectibles.

The large showrooms of **Gallori-Turchi,** Via Maggio 14r (© **055-282-279**), specialize in furnishings, paintings, and weaponry (swords, lances, and pistols) from the 16th to 18th centuries. They also offer majolica and ceramic pieces and scads of excellent desks and writing tables of hand-carved and inlaid wood. Nearby you'll find **Guido Bartolozzi Antichità,** Via Maggio 18r (© **055-215-602**), under family management since 1887. This old-fashioned store concentrates on the 16th to 19th centuries. They might be offering a 17th-century Gobelin tapestry, an inlaid stone tabletop, or wood intarsia dressers from the 1700s. The quality is impeccable: The owner has been president of Italy's antiques association and secretary of Florence's biannual antiques fair. There's another showroom at Via Maggio 11.

For the serious collector who wants his or her own piece of Florence's cultural heritage, the refined showroom at **Gianfranco Luzzetti,** Borgo San Jacopo 28A (© **055-211-232**), offers artwork and furniture from the 1400s to 1600s. They have a gorgeous collection of 16th-century Deruta ceramics and majolica, canvases by the likes of Vignale and Bilivert, and even a glazed terra-cotta altarpiece from the hand of Andrea della Robbia. Bring sacks of money.

BOOKS

Even the smaller bookshops in Florence these days have at least a few shelves devoted to English-language books. **Feltrinelli International,** Via Cavour 12–20 (© **055-219-524;** www.lafeltrinelli.it), is one of the few of any size.

For English-only shops, hit **Paperback Exchange,** Via Fiesolana 31r (© **055-247-8154;** www.papex.it); it's not the most central, but it is the best for books in English, specializing in titles relating in some way to Florence and Italy. Much of their stock is used, and you can't beat the prices anywhere in Italy—dog-eared volumes and all Penguin books go for just a few euros. You can also trade in that novel you've already finished for another. **BM Bookshop,** Borgo Ognissanti 4r (© **055-294-575**), is a bit smaller but more central and carries only new volumes. They also have a slightly more well-rounded selection—from novels and art books to cookbooks and travel guides. A special section is devoted to Italian- and Tuscany-oriented volumes.

G. Vitello, Via dei Servi 94–96r (© **055-292-445**), sells coffee table–worthy books on art and all things Italian at up to half off the price you'd pay in a regular bookstore. Other branches are at Via

Verdi 40r (© **055-234-6894**) and Via Pietrapiana 1r (© **055-241-063**). **Libreria Il Viaggio,** Borgo degli Albizi 41r (© **055-240-489**), is a cozy niche specializing in specialty travel guides, related literature, and maps, with a sizable selection in English.

DEPARTMENT STORES

Florence's central branch of the national chain **Coin,** Via Calzaiuoli 56r (© **055-280-531;** www.coin.it), is a stylish multifloored display case for upper-middle-class fashions—a chic Macy's. **La Rinascente,** Piazza della Repubblica 2 (© **055-219-113;** www.rinascente.it), is another of Italy's finer department stores. This six-floor store serves as an outlet for top designers (Versace, Zegna, Ferré, and so on). It also has areas set up to sell traditional Tuscan goods (terra cotta, alabaster, olive oils, and wrought iron).

DESIGN, HOUSEWARES & CERAMICS

Viceversa ⨍, Via dello Stell 3 (© **055-696-392;** www.viceversa shop.com), offers one of the largest selections of the latest Robert Graves–designed teakettle or any other whimsical Alessi kitchen product. The friendly staff will also point out the Pavoni espresso machines, Carl Merkins' totemic bar set, the Princess motorized gadgets, and shelf after shelf of the best of Italian kitchen and houseware designs.

Tiny **La Botteghina,** Via Guelfa 5r (© **055-287-367**), is about the best and most reasonably priced city outlet for true artisan ceramics I've found in all Italy. Daniele Viegi del Fiume deals in gorgeous hand-painted ceramics from the best traditional artisans working in nearby Montelupo, the famed Umbrian ceramics centers of Deruta and Gubbio, and Castelli, high in the Abruzzi mountains.

If you can't make it to the workshops in the hill towns themselves, La Botteghina is the next best thing. If you like the sample of pieces by **Giuseppe Rampini** you see here (or in his Chianti workshop) and want to invest in a full table setting, visit Rampini's classy showroom at Borgo Ognissanti 32–34 (right at Piazza Ognissanti; © **055-219-720**).

For big-name production-line china and tablewares, visit **Richard Ginori,** Via Giulio Cesare 21 (© **055-420-491;** www.richardginori 1735.com). Colorful rims and whimsical designs fill this warehouse-like salesroom of the firm that has sold Florence's finest china since 1735. Other houseware bigwigs are represented as well—Alessi coffeepots, Nason and Meretti Murano glass, and Christofle flatware.

FASHION & CLOTHING

Although Italian fashion reached its pinnacle in the 1950s and 1960s, the country has remained at the forefront of both high (Armani, Gucci, Pucci, Ferragamo, just to name a few) and popular (evidenced by the spectacular success of Benetton in the 1980s) fashion. Florence plays second fiddle to Milan in today's Italian fashion scene, but the city has its own cadre of well-respected names, plus, of course, outlet shops of all the hot designers. Also see "Leather, Accessories & Shoes," below.

FOR MEN & WOMEN   Cinzia, Borgo San Jacopo 22r (© 055-298-078), is a grab bag of hand-knit, usually bulky wool sweaters offered by an elderly couple who've been sending their creations around the world for more than 30 years. **Luisa Via Roma,** Via Roma 19–21r (© 055-217-826; www.luisaviaroma.com), is a famed gathering place for all the top names in avant-garde fashion, including Jean Paul Gaultier, Dolce & Gabbana, and Issey Miyake. Men can hand over their wallets upstairs, and women can empty their purses on the ground floor. Service can be chilly.

The address may be a hint that this isn't your average fashion shop: **Emilio Pucci,** Palazzo Pucci, Via de' Pucci 6 (© 055-283-061; www.pucci.com). Marchese Emilio Pucci's ancestors have been a powerful banking and mercantile family since the Renaissance; and, in 1950, Marchese suddenly turned designer and shocked the fashion world with his flowing silks in outlandish colors. His women's silk clothing remained the rage into the early 1970s and had a renaissance of its own in the 1990s club scene. The design team is now headed by daughter Laudomia Pucci. If you don't wish to visit the showroom in the ancient family palace, drop by the shop at Via dei Tornabuoni 20–22r (© 055-265-8082).

Then there's **Giorgio Armani,** Via Tornabuoni 48r (© 055-219-041; www.giorgioarmani.com), Florence's outlet for Italy's top fashion guru. The service and store are surprisingly not stratospherically chilly (the Official Armani Attitude at the moment is studied, casual indifference). The **Emporio Armani** branch at Piazza Strozzi 16r (© 055-284-315; www.emporioarmani.com) is the outlet for the more affordable designs. The merchandise is slightly inferior in workmanship and quality and greatly inferior in price.

But the biggest name to walk out of Florence onto the international catwalk has to be **Gucci,** with the world flagship store at Via de' Tornabuoni 73r (© 055-264-011; www.gucci.com). This is where this Florentine fashion empire was started by saddlemaker

Guccio Gucci in 1904, now run by a gaggle of grandsons. You enter through a phalanx of their trademark purses and bags. Forget the cheesy knockoffs sold on street corners around the world; the stock here is elegant.

Nearby is another homegrown fashion label, **Enrico Coveri,** Via Tornabuoni 81r (✆ **055-211-263;** www.coveri.com). Enrico started off in the nearby textile town of Prato and has a similar penchant for bright colors as contemporary Emilio Pucci. The major difference is that Enrico Coveri's firm produces downscale fashion that fits the bods and wallets of normal folk—not just leggy models. Some of the men's suits are particularly fine, but the children's collection may be best left alone. There's another tiny branch at Via Tornabuoni 81r.

FOR WOMEN   Loretta Caponi, Piazza Antinori 4r (✆ **055-213-668**), is world famous for her high-quality intimates and embroidered linens made the old-fashioned way. Under Belle Epoque ceilings are nightgowns of all types, bed and bath linens of the highest caliber, curtains, and feminine unmentionables. There's also a large section for the little ones in the back. Peek through the pebble-glassed doors to see the workshop.

STOCK HOUSES   ** To get your high fashion at bargain-basement prices, head to one of the branches of **Guardaroba/Stock House Grandi Firme. The store at Borgo degli Albizi 78r (✆ **055-234-0271**) carries mainly the past season's models, while the Via dei Castellani 26r branch (✆ **055-294-853**) carries spring/summer remaindered collections, and the Via Verdi 28r (✆ **055-247-8250**) and Via Nazionale 38r (✆ **055-215-482**) stores have outfits from the past winter. **Stock House Il Giglio,** Via Borgo Ognissanti 86 (no phone), also carries big-name labels at 50% to 60% off.

GIFTS & CRAFTS

Florentine traditional "mosaics" are actually works of inlaid stone called *pietre dure*. The creations of young Ilio de Filippis and his army of apprentices at **Pitti Mosaici,** Piazza Pitti 16r and 23–24r (✆ **055-282-127;** www.pittimosaici.it), reflect traditional techniques and artistry. Ilio's father was a *pietre dure* artist, and his grandfather was a sculptor. (The family workshop was founded in 1900.) Besides the pieces on display down the road toward the Arno at Via Guicciardini 80r and across the river at Lungarno Vespucci 36r, the firm will custom make works to your specifications.

Professore Agostino Dessi presides over the traditional Venetian Carnevale–style maskmaking at **Alice Atelier,** Via Faenza 72r (✆ **055-287-370**). All masks are made according to 17th-century techniques, using papier-mâché, leather, and ceramics, and are hand-painted with tempera, touched up with gold and silver leaf, and polished with French lacquer.

JEWELRY

If you've got the financial solvency of a small country, the place to buy your baubles is the Ponte Vecchio, famous for its gold- and sil-versmiths since the 16th century. The craftsmanship at the stalls is usually of a very high quality, and so they seem to compete instead over who can charge the highest prices. A more moderately priced boutique is Milan-based **Mario Buccellati,** Via della Vigna Nuova 71r (© **055-239-6579**), which since 1919 has been making thick, heavy, high-quality jewelry.

Florence is also a good place to root around for interesting cos-tume jewelry. The audacious bijoux at **Angela Caputi,** Borgo San Jacopo 82r (© **055-212-972;** www.angelacaputi.com), aren't for the timid. Much of Angela's costume jewelry—from earrings and neck-laces to brooches and now even a small clothing line—is at least oversize and bold and often pushes the flamboyance envelope.

LEATHER, ACCESSORIES & SHOES

It has always been a buyers' market for leather in Florence, but these days it's tough to sort out the jackets mass-produced for tourists from the high-quality artisan work. The most fun you'll have leather shopping, without a doubt, is at the outdoor stalls of the **San Lorenzo** market, even if the market is rife with mediocre goods (see "Markets," below). Never accept the first price they throw at you; sometimes you can bargain them down to almost half the original asking price. The shops below should guarantee you at least quality merchandise, but not the bargaining joys of the market. (See also "Fashion & Clothing," above.)

Anna, Piazza Pitti 38–41r (© **055-283-787**), is a fine store for handcrafted leather coats and clothing set in the remains of a 14th-century tower. You can also pick up discounted Versace purses and funky colorful Missoni sweaters. For the best of the leather, head down the stairs in the back, where you'll find fur-collared coats, suede jackets, and supple pigskin vests. They'll do alterations and even full tailoring in 24 hours. **John F.,** Lungarno Corsini 2 (© **055-239-8985;** www.johnflorence.it), is a purveyor of high-quality leather goods as well as Missoni sweaters, Krizia purses, and Bettina bags.

More fun, but no less expensive, is to watch the artisans at work at the **Scuola del Cuoio (Leather School) of Santa Croce.** You enter through Santa Croce church (right transept), Piazza Santa

Croce 16, or on Via San Giuseppe 5r on Sunday morning (© **055-244-533** or 055-244-534; www.leatherschool.it). The very-fine-quality soft-leather merchandise isn't cheap.

In the imposing 13th-century Palazzo Spini-Feroni, lording over Piazza Santa Trínita, are the flagship store, museum, and home of **Ferragamo,** Via de' Tornabuoni 4–14r (© **055-292-123;** www.ferragamo.it). Salvatore Ferragamo was the man who shod Hollywood in its most glamorous age and raised footwear to an art form. View some of Ferragamo's funkier shoes in the second-floor museum (call ahead at © **055-336-0456**) or slip on a pair yourself in the showrooms downstairs—if you think your wallet can take the shock.

If you prefer to buy right from the cobbler, head across the Arno to **Calzature Francesco da Firenze,** Via Santo Spirito 62r (© **055-212-428**), where handmade shoes run 80€ to 165€ ($104–$215), and you can hear them tap-tapping away on soles in the back room.

For more made-in-Florence accessorizing, head to **Madova Gloves,** Via Guicciardini 1r (© **055-239-6526;** www.madova.com). Gloves are all they make in this tiny shop, and they do them well. The grandchildren of the workshop's founders do a brisk business in brightly colored, supple leather gloves lined with cashmere and silk. Although they display a bit of everything at **Beltrami,** Via della Vigna Nuova 70r (© **055-287-779**), their forte is still beautiful well-built footwear, bags, briefcases, and luggage. Beltrami is based in Florence, so prices are as low here as you're going to find.

MARKETS

Haggling is accepted, and even expected, at most outdoor markets (but don't try it in stores). The queen of Florentine markets is the **San Lorenzo street market,** filling Piazza San Lorenzo, Via del Canto de' Nelli, Via dell'Ariento, and other side streets. It's a wildly chaotic and colorful array of hundreds of stands hawking T-shirts, silk scarves, marbleized paper, Gucci knockoffs, and lots and lots of leather. Many of the stalls are merely outlets for full-fledged stores hidden behind them. Haggling is tradition here, and though you'll find plenty of leather lemons, there are also great deals on truly high-quality leather and other goods—you just have to commit to half a day of picking through it all and fending off sales pitches. March through October, most stalls are open daily about 8am to 8pm (it varies with how business is doing); November through February, the market is closed Sundays and Mondays, except for the 2 weeks or so around Christmas, when it remains open daily.

Somewhere in the center of this capitalist whirlwind hides the indoor **Mercato Centrale food market** (between Via dell'Ariento and Piazza del Mercato Centrale). Downstairs you'll find meat, cheese, and dry goods. There's one stall devoted to tripe aficionados, a second piled high with *baccalà* (dried salt cod), and a good cheap eatery called **Nerbone** (p. 79). The upstairs is devoted to fruits and veggies—a cornucopia of fat eggplants, long yellow peppers, stacks of artichokes, and pepperoncini bunched into brilliant red bursts. In all, you couldn't ask for better picnic pickings. The market is open Monday through Saturday from 7am to 2pm and Saturday also 4 to 7:30pm.

As if two names weren't enough, the **Mercato Nuovo (Straw Market)** is also known as Mercato del Porcellino or Mercato del Cinghiale because of the bronze wild boar statue at one end, cast by Pietro Tacca in the 17th century after an antique original now in the Uffizi. Pet the well-polished *porcellino*'s snout to ensure a return trip to Florence. Most of the straw stalls disappeared by the 1960s. These days, the loggia hawks mainly poor-quality leather purses, mediocre bijoux, souvenirs, and other tourist trinkets. *Note:* Beware of pickpockets. In summer, it's open daily around 9am to 8pm; but, in winter, it's closed at 5pm and all day Sunday and Monday.

MUSIC
Although restrictions are ever tightening, Italy still remains one of the best places in western Europe to get bootlegs. Quality, obviously, can vary drastically (most places will let you listen before you buy). Some of the more "reputable" pirate labels include Pluto, Great Dane, Bugsy, On Stage, Teddy Bear, Beech Marten, and Red Line. **Data Records,** Via dei Neri 15r (© 055-287-592), is a hip place with a sassy funk attitude, knowledgeable staff, plenty of cutting-edge music (Italian and international), and scads of good bootlegs. They also run a more mainstream outlet, **Super Records** (© 055-234-9526; www.superecords.com), in the pedestrian passage leading from Santa Maria Novella train station, with some of the best prices in town on first-run presses from major labels. Both are closed in August.

PAPER & JOURNALS
Giulio Giannini and Figlio, Piazza Pitti 36–37r (© 055-212-621; www.giuliogiannini.it), offers an expensive but quality selection of leather-bound notebooks, fine stationery, and, the shop's specialty, objects garbed in decorative papers. This was one of the first stores to paste marbleized sheets onto desktop items, but its real trademark is objects sheathed in genuine 17th- to 19th-century manuscript and

choir-book sheets. **Il Papiro,** Via dei Tavolini 13r (© **055-213-823;** www.madeinfirenze.it/papiro_e.htm), is now a modest Tuscan chain of jewel box–size shops specializing in marbled and patterned paper, as plain gift-wrap sheets or as a covering for everything from pens and journals to letter openers or full desk sets. There are several branches, including the head office at Via Cavour 55r (no phone) and shops at Piazza del Duomo 24r (no phone), Lungarno Acciaiuoli 42r (© **055-215-262**), and Piazza Rucellai 8r (© **055-211-652**).

Scriptorium, Via dei Servi 5–7r (© **055-211-804**), is my own journal supplier, a small shop that's one of the few fine stationery stores in Florence with very little marbleized paper. Come here for hand-sewn notebooks, journals, and photo albums made of thick paper—all bound in soft leather covers. With classical music or Gregorian chant playing in the background, you can also shop for calligraphy and signet wax sealing tools. There's a new branch in the Oltrarno at Piazza de' Pitti 6 (© **055-238-2272;** www.scriptorium firenze.com).

PRINTS

Little Bottega delle Stampe, Borgo San Jacopo 56r (© **055-295-396**), carries prints, historic maps, and engravings from the 1500s through the Liberty-style and Art Deco prints of the 1930s. You can dig out some Dürers here, as well as original Piranesis and plates from Diderot's 1700 Encyclopedia. There are Florence views from the 16th to 19th centuries, plus a fine collection of 18th-century French engravings.

TOYS

Since 1977, Florence's owner-operated branch of national chain **La Città del Sole,** Borgo Ognissanti 37r (© **055-219-345;** www.citta delsole.it), has sold old-fashioned wooden brain teasers, construction kits, hand puppets, 3-D puzzles, science kits, and books. There's nary a video game in sight.

WINE & LIQUORS

The front room of the **Enoteca Alessi,** Via dell'Oche 27–31r (© **055-214-966;** www.enotecaalessi.it), sells boxed chocolates and other sweets; but, in the back and in the large cellars, you can find everything from prime vintages to a simple-quality table wine. This large store, 2 blocks from the Duomo, also offers tastings. The **Enoteca Gambi Romano,** Borgo SS. Apostoli 21–23r (© **055-292-646**), is another central outlet for olive oil, vin santo, grappa, and (upstairs) lots of wine.

7

Florence After Dark

Florence doesn't have the musical cachet or grand opera houses of Milan, Venice, or Rome, but there are two symphony orchestras and a fine music school in Fiesole. The city's public theaters are certainly respectable, and most major touring companies stop in town on their way through Italy. Get tickets to all cultural and musical events at the city's main clearinghouse, **Box Office,** Via Alamanni 39 (© **055-210-804;** www.boxol.it). In addition to tickets for year-round events of all genres, they handle the summertime Calcio in Costume folkloric festival and the Maggio Musicale.

1 The Performing Arts

Many concerts and recitals staged in major halls and private spaces across town are sponsored by the **Amici della Musica** (© **055-607-440** or 055-608-420; www.amicimusica.fi.it), so contact them to see what "hidden" concert might be on while you're in town. When Florentines really want a fine night out at the theater, they skip town and head to nearby Prato for the **Teatro Metastasio,** one of Italy's finest.

CHURCH CONCERTS

Many Florentine churches fill the autumn with organ, choir, and chamber orchestra concerts, mainly of classical music. The tiny **Santa Maria de' Ricci** (© **055-215-044**) on Via del Corso seems always to have music wafting out of it; slipping inside to occupy a pew is occasionally free, but sometimes there's a small charge. Around the corner at Santa Margherita 7, the **Chiesa di Dante** (© **055-289-367**) puts on quality concerts of music for, and often played by, youths and children (tickets required). **The Florentine Chamber Orchestra,** Via E. Poggi 6 (© **055-783-374**), also runs an autumn season in the Orsanmichele; tickets are available at Box Office (see above) or at the door an hour before the 9pm shows.

CONCERT HALLS & OPERA

One of Italy's busiest stages, Florence's contemporary **Teatro Comunale,** Corso Italia 12 (© **055-213-535** or 055-211-158; www.maggio fiorentino.com), offers everything from symphonies to ballet to plays, opera, and concerts. The large main theater seats 2,000, with orchestra rows topped by horseshoe-shaped first and second galleries. Its smaller Piccolo Teatro, seating 500, is rectangular, offering good sightlines from most any seat. The Teatro Comunale is the seat of the annual prestigious Maggio Musicale.

The Teatro Verdi, Via Ghibellina 99–101 (© **055-212-320** or 055-263-877; www.teatroverdifirenze.it), is Florence's opera and ballet house, with the nice ritual of staging Sunday-afternoon shows during the January-through-April season. **The Orchestra della Toscana** (© **055-280-670;** www.orchestradellatoscana.it) plays classical concerts here December through May. Like the Teatro Comunale, they do a bit of theater, but it's not of the caliber of La Pergola (see below).

THEATER

The biggest national and international touring companies stop in Florence's major playhouse, the **Teatro della Pergola,** Via della Pergola 12 (© **055-226-4335;** www.pergola.firenze.it). La Pergola is the city's chief purveyor of classical and classic plays from the Greeks and Shakespeare through Pirandello, Samuel Beckett, and Italian modern playwrights. Performances are professional and of high quality, if not always terribly innovative. (Of course, all are in Italian.)

2 The Club & Music Scenes

Italian clubs are rather cliquey—people usually go in groups to hang out and dance only with one another. There's plenty of flesh showing, but no meat market. Singles hoping to find random dance partners will often be disappointed.

LIVE MUSIC

For live bands you can dance to in the center, head to **Dolce Zucchero,** Via dei Pandolfini 36–38r (© **055-247-7894**). "Sweet Sugar" is one of the better recent efforts to spice up Florence's nightlife and is popular with all ages. Under high ceilings are a long bar and a small dance floor with a stage for the nightly live musicians, usually a fairly talented cover act cranking out American and Italian dance songs for the packed crowd.

Cafe Culture

Florence no longer has a glitterati or intellectuals' cafe scene, and when it did—from the late-19th-century Italian *Risorgimento* era through the *dolce vita* of the 1950s—it was basically copying the idea from Paris. Although they're often overpriced tourist spots today, Florence's high-toned cafes are fine if you want designer pastries and hot cappuccino served to you while you sit on a piazza and people-watch.

At the refined, wood-paneled, stucco-ceilinged, and very expensive 1733 cafe **Gilli**, Piazza della Repubblica 36–39r/Via Roma 1r (© **055-213-896**), tourists gather to sit with the ghosts of Italy's *Risorgimento*, when the cafe became an important meeting place of the heroes and thinkers of the unification movement from the 1850s to the 1870s. The red-jacketed waiters at **Giubbe Rosse**, Piazza della Repubblica 13–14r (© **055-212-280**), must have been popular during the 19th-century glory days of Garibaldi's red-shirt soldiers. This was once a meeting place of the Florentine futurists, but aside from organized literary encounters on Wednesdays, today it too is mainly a tourists' cafe with ridiculous prices.

Once full of history and now mainly full of tourists, **Rivoire**, Piazza della Signoria/Via Vacchereccia 5r (© **055-214-412**), has a chunk of prime real estate on Piazza della Signoria. Smartly dressed waiters serve smartly priced sandwiches to cappuccino-sipping patrons. **Giacosa**, Via de' Tornabuoni 83r (© **055-239-6226**), was a 19th-century hangout for literati and intellectual clutches as elegant as any of the others, but today it's really more of a high-class bar, with no outside tables. It makes a good shopping break, though, with panini, pastries, cold salads, and hot pasta dishes.

DANCE CLUBS & NIGHTCLUBS

Florence's clubs have a "minimum consumption" charge of 10€ to 16€ ($13–$21). **Universale,** Via Pisana 77r (© **055-221-122;** www.universalefirenze.it), is still the biggest thing in town for the under-22 set, housed in a converted 1940s cinema. From 8pm it's a popular restaurant in the balcony and a pizzeria on the main floor. Around 11pm a live band takes the main-floor stage for an hour or so, after which a DJ comes on board to conduct the disco until 3am.

In the city center near Santa Croce, **Full-Up,** Via della Vigna Vecchia 25r (℃ **055-293-006**), is a long-enduring disco/piano bar that's one of the top (and more restrained) dance spaces in Florence for the postcollegiate set. There are plenty of theme evenings (revival, samba, punk), so call to find out what's on.

Not exactly cutting edge, but the most centrally located is **Yab,** Via Sassetti 5r (℃ **055-215-160**), just behind the main post office on Piazza della Repubblica. This dance club for 20-somethings is a perennial favorite, a relic of a 1980s disco complete with velvet rope and surly bouncers.

A balanced combination of visitors and Italians—teenagers, students, and an under-30 crowd—fill the two-floor **Space Electronic,** Via Palazzuolo 37 (℃ **055-293-082**). On the first floor are a video karaoke bar, a pub, an American-style bar, and a conversation area. Head upstairs for the dance floor.

3 Pubs, Bars & Wine Bars
PUBS & BARS

There's an unsurprising degree of similarity among Florence's half-dozen **Irish-style pubs'** dark, woody interiors usually with several back rooms and plenty of smoke; and a crowd (stuffed to the gills on weekends) of students and 20- and 30-something Americans and Brits along with their Italian counterparts. The better ones are the Florence branch of the successful Italian chain **Fiddler's Elbow,** Piazza Santa Maria Novella 7r (℃ **055-215-056**); **The Old Stove,** Via Pellicceria 4r (℃ **055-284-640**), just down from Piazza della Repubblica; and, under the same management, **The Lion's Fountain,** Borgo Albizi 34r (℃ **055-234-4412**), on the tiny but lively Piazza San Pier Maggiore near Santa Croce. You'll find plenty of others around town—they pop up like mushrooms these days, but often disappear just as quickly.

Red Garter, Via de' Benci 33r (℃ **055-234-4904**), is a speak-easy attracting a 20s-to-30s crowd of Italians and some Americans, Australians, and English. There's a small bi-level theater room in the back with live music some nights, karaoke others, nearly always with a one-man band with a guitar playing American and Italian rock hits with some blues mixed in.

For a swanky cocktail with a panoramic view of the city, check out the rooftop terrace of the **Hotel Continentale,** Vicolo dell'Oro 6r (next to the entrance of the Ponte Vecchio; ✆ **055-272-62** www. lungarnohotels.com). The music is New Age lounge with a tropical feel. Sunset is the best time to visit. The million-dollar view is amortized by the steep price of a Martini.

WINE BARS

The most traditional wine bars are called *fiaschetterie,* after the word for a flask of chianti. They tend to be hole-in-the-wall joints serving sandwiches or simple food along with glasses filled to the brim—usually with a house wine, though finer vintages are often available. The best are listed in chapter 4 under "Where to Dine," including **I Fratellini,** Via dei Cimatori 38r (✆ **055-239-6096**); **Antico Noè,** off Piazza S. Pier Maggiore (✆ **055-234-0838**); and **La Mescita,** Via degli Alfani 70r (✆ **347-795-1604**). There's also a traditional wine shop in the Oltrarno called simply **La Fiaschetteria,** Via de' Serragli 47r (✆ **055-287-420**), which, like many, doubles as a small locals' wine bar.

A more high-toned spot is the **Cantinetta Antinori,** Piazza Antinori 3 (✆ **055-292-234**), also reviewed in chapter 4; see p. 80. It's housed in the palace headquarters of the Antinori wine empire at the top of Florence's main fashion drag, Via Tornabuoni. For a trendier wine bar focusing on handpicked labels offered with plates of cheese and other snacks, head to the Oltrarno and a real oenophile's hangout, **Il Volpe e L'Uva,** Piazza de' Rossi, behind Piazza Santa Felícita off Via Guicciardini (✆ **055-239-8132**). The Avuris, who run the Hotel Torre Guelfa (p. 57), have recently opened a great little wine bar right across from the Pitti Palace called **Pitti Gola e Cantina,** Piazza Pitti 16 (✆ **055-212-704**), with glasses of wine from 4€ to 9€ ($5.20–$12) to help unwind from a day of museums. They also have light dishes, meat and cheese platters, and cakes for 7€ to 15€ ($9.10–$20).

4 The Gay & Lesbian Scene

The gay nightlife scene in Florence isn't much, and for lesbians it's pretty much just the Thursday through Saturday nights mixed gay-and-lesbian party at the **Flamingo Bar,** Via Pandolfini 26r (✆ **055-243-356**), whereas the rest of the week it's men only. The main bar is downstairs, where an international gay crowd shows up in everything from jeans and T-shirts to full leather. Upstairs are a lounge and a theater showing videos and the occasional show. September through June, the ground floor becomes a dance floor Friday and Saturday nights pumping out commercial pop and lots of disco. The bar is open Sunday through Thursday from 10pm to 4am (until 6am Fri–Sat).

Florence's dark room is the **Crisco Bar,** Via Sant'Egidio 43r, east of the Duomo (© 055-248-0580), for men only. Its 18th-century building contains a bar and a dance floor open Wednesday through Monday from 9pm to 3am (until 5am weekends). They also have male strippers and drag shows some weekends.

The only real gay dance floor of note is at the **Tabasco Bar,** Piazza Santa Cecilia 3r (© **055-213-000**). Italy's first gay disco attracts crowds of men (mostly in their 20s and 30s) from all over the country. The music is techno, disco, and retro rock, but entertainment offerings also include cabaret, art shows, and the occasional transvestite comedy. In summer, foreigners arrive in droves. It's open Sunday through Thursday from 10pm to 3 or 4am (until 6am Fri–Sat). Tuesday, Friday, and Saturday it's all disco; Wednesday is leather night. They've also recently opened up a gay cruising bar called **Silver Stud,** Via della Fornace 9 (© **055-688-466**).

Cover charges vary, but it's generally 10€ ($13) or less and often includes the first drink.

Index

See also Accommodations and Restaurant indexes below.

Find the right words fast with a *Frommer's PhraseFinder & Dictionary*. Put one in your pocket or purse for quick access to more than 5,000 words and phrases. Real-world situations and expressions. A two-way dictionary with pronunciation guide. Phrases listed by topic *and* dictionary entry. Basic grammar. Sample dialogues. And much more.

Real language for real travelers—new from the most trusted name in travel guides.

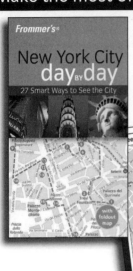

FROMMER'S® COMPLETE TRAVEL GUIDES

Alaska
Amalfi Coast
American Southwest
Amsterdam
Argentina
Arizona
Atlanta
Australia
Austria
Bahamas
Barcelona
Beijing
Belgium, Holland & Luxembourg
Belize
Bermuda
Boston
Brazil
British Columbia & the Canadian
  Rockies
Brussels & Bruges
Budapest & the Best of Hungary
Buenos Aires
Calgary
California
Canada
Cancún, Cozumel & the Yucatán
Cape Cod, Nantucket & Martha's
  Vineyard
Caribbean
Caribbean Ports of Call
Carolinas & Georgia
Chicago
Chile & Easter Island
China
Colorado
Costa Rica
Croatia
Cuba
Denmark
Denver, Boulder & Colorado Springs
Eastern Europe
Ecuador & the Galapagos Islands
Edinburgh & Glasgow
England
Europe
Europe by Rail

Florence, Tuscany & Umbria
Florida
France
Germany
Greece
Greek Islands
Guatemala
Hawaii
Hong Kong
Honolulu, Waikiki & Oahu
India
Ireland
Israel
Italy
Jamaica
Japan
Kauai
Las Vegas
London
Los Angeles
Los Cabos & Baja
Madrid
Maine Coast
Maryland & Delaware
Maui
Mexico
Montana & Wyoming
Montréal & Québec City
Morocco
Moscow & St. Petersburg
Munich & the Bavarian Alps
Nashville & Memphis
New England
Newfoundland & Labrador
New Mexico
New Orleans
New York City
New York State
New Zealand
Northern Italy
Norway
Nova Scotia, New Brunswick &
  Prince Edward Island
Oregon
Paris
Peru

Philadelphia & the Amish Country
Portugal
Prague & the Best of the Czech
  Republic
Provence & the Riviera
Puerto Rico
Rome
San Antonio & Austin
San Diego
San Francisco
Santa Fe, Taos & Albuquerque
Scandinavia
Scotland
Seattle
Seville, Granada & the Best of
  Andalusia
Shanghai
Sicily
Singapore & Malaysia
South Africa
South America
South Florida
South Korea
South Pacific
Southeast Asia
Spain
Sweden
Switzerland
Tahiti & French Polynesia
Texas
Thailand
Tokyo
Toronto
Turkey
USA
Utah
Vancouver & Victoria
Vermont, New Hampshire & Maine
Vienna & the Danube Valley
Vietnam
Virgin Islands
Virginia
Walt Disney World® & Orlando
Washington, D.C.
Washington State

FROMMER'S® DAY BY DAY GUIDES

Amsterdam
Barcelona
Beijing
Boston
Cancun & the Yucatan
Chicago
Florence & Tuscany

Hong Kong
Honolulu & Oahu
London
Maui
Montréal
Napa & Sonoma
New York City

Paris
Provence & the Riviera
Rome
San Francisco
Venice
Washington D.C.

PAULINE FROMMER'S GUIDES: SEE MORE. SPEND LESS.

Alaska
Hawaii
Italy

Las Vegas
London
New York City

Paris
Walt Disney World®
Washington D.C.

FROMMER'S® PORTABLE GUIDES

Acapulco, Ixtapa & Zihuatanejo	Florence	Rio de Janeiro
Amsterdam	Las Vegas	San Diego
Aruba, Bonaire & Curacao	Las Vegas for Non-Gamblers	San Francisco
Australia's Great Barrier Reef	London	Savannah
Bahamas	Maui	St. Martin, Sint Maarten, Anguila &
Big Island of Hawaii	Nantucket & Martha's Vineyard	St. Bart's
Boston	New Orleans	Turks & Caicos
California Wine Country	New York City	Vancouver
Cancún	Paris	Venice
Cayman Islands	Portland	Virgin Islands
Charleston	Puerto Rico	Washington, D.C.
Chicago	Puerto Vallarta, Manzanillo &	Whistler
Dominican Republic	Guadalajara	

FROMMER'S® CRUISE GUIDES

Alaska Cruises & Ports of Call	Cruises & Ports of Call	European Cruises & Ports of Call

FROMMER'S® NATIONAL PARK GUIDES

Algonquin Provincial Park	National Parks of the American West	Yosemite and Sequoia & Kings
Banff & Jasper	Rocky Mountain	Canyon
Grand Canyon	Yellowstone & Grand Teton	Zion & Bryce Canyon

FROMMER'S® WITH KIDS GUIDES

Chicago	National Parks	Toronto
Hawaii	New York City	Walt Disney World® & Orlando
Las Vegas	San Francisco	Washington, D.C.
London		

FROMMER'S® PHRASEFINDER DICTIONARY GUIDES

Chinese	German	Japanese
French	Italian	Spanish

SUZY GERSHMAN'S BORN TO SHOP GUIDES

France	London	San Francisco
Hong Kong, Shanghai & Beijing	New York	Where to Buy the Best of Everything.
Italy	Paris	

FROMMER'S® BEST-LOVED DRIVING TOURS

Britain	Ireland	Scotland
California	Italy	Spain
France	New England	Tuscany & Umbria
Germany	Northern Italy	

THE UNOFFICIAL GUIDES®

Adventure Travel in Alaska	Ireland	San Francisco
Beyond Disney	Las Vegas	South Florida including Miami &
California with Kids	London	the Keys
Central Italy	Maui	Walt Disney World®
Chicago	Mexico's Best Beach Resorts	Walt Disney World® for
Cruises	Mini Mickey	Grown-ups
Disneyland®	New Orleans	Walt Disney World® with Kids
England	New York City	Washington, D.C.
Hawaii	Paris	

SPECIAL-INTEREST TITLES

Athens Past & Present	Frommer's Exploring America by RV
Best Places to Raise Your Family	Frommer's NYC Free & Dirt Cheap
Cities Ranked & Rated	Frommer's Road Atlas Europe
500 Places to Take Your Kids Before They Grow Up	Frommer's Road Atlas Ireland
Frommer's Best Day Trips from London	Retirement Places Rated
Frommer's Best RV & Tent Campgrounds in the U.S.A.	